YOUR BODY
SPEAKS
YOUR MIND

DEB SHAPIRO

YOUR BODY SPEAKS YOUR MIND

Understanding how Your Emotions and Thoughts
Affect You Physically

PIATKUS

Although anyone may find the practices, disciplines, and exercises in this book to be useful, it is sold with the understanding that neither the author nor the publisher are engaged in presenting specific medical, psychological, or emotional advice. Nor is anything in this book intended to be a diagnosis, prescription, or cure for any specific kind of medical, psychological, or emotional problem. Each person has unique needs, and this book cannot take these individual differences into account. Any person suffering from severe stress, anxiety, or depression should consult with a medical doctor or licensed therapist before practising the methods described in this book.

Copyright © 1996, 2006 by Deb Shapiro

First edition published in 1996 by Piatkus Books Ltd
5 Windmill Street, London W1T 2JA

Reprinted 11 times

This revised and updated edition first published in the USA in 2006 by Sounds True, Boulder, CO 80306, USA

This edition published in Great Britain in 2007 by Piatkus Books Ltd
5 Windmill Street, London W1T 2JA

Reprinted 2007

The moral right of the author has been asserted

A catalogue record for this book is available from the British Library

ISBN 978 0 7499 2783 7

This book has been printed on paper manufactured with respect for the environment using wood from managed sustainable resources

Data manipulation by Phoenix Photosetting, Chatham, Kent
www.phoenixphotosetting.co.uk

Printed and bound in Great Britain by
MPG Books, Bodmin, Cornwall

To my husband and life partner, Ed,
and to all my teachers,
both past and present.
May all beings be free from suffering.

CONTENTS

ACKNOWLEDGEMENTS

A great big thank you to the crew at Sounds True—especially to Tami Simon and Alice Feinstein for their inspiration and support, and to Nancy Smith for her clear ear and technical expertise.

I would like to thank the many people who contributed their stories: Christine Evans, Padma O'Gara, Jenny Britton, Leela, Steve Hennessy, Karuna King, John Taylor, Cheryl, and Sheila, and the many others whose stories there was no room for. I deeply appreciate your honesty and openness. And a very special thank you to my old friend and deeply caring acupuncturist James MacRitchie.

I also thank my husband, Ed Shapiro, for his unbelievable patience, generosity, and enduring love. His contribution to this book is incalculable.

INTRODUCTION

J enny was sixty-five when we met. She had broken her hip three times in her life, always in the same place and always because of an accident. The first time she fell off a horse, the second time was in a car crash, and the third time she fell down a flight of stairs. The accidents were many years apart.

The first time Jenny broke her hip was two weeks after her fiancé had died, when she was twenty-one. She never married after this, but went to live with her parents. When she was forty-five, her mother died; a few weeks later Jenny had a car crash and broke her hip again. When she was fifty-seven, her father died, and a few weeks later she fell down the stairs and broke her hip yet again. Each time she broke her hip, the person upon whom she was most emotionally dependent had died.

With each death she transferred her dependency to the next person in line—from fiancé to mother to father. When Jenny, who was now having to use a walking stick to get around, realized this pattern and the emotional relationship to her accidents, she vowed to take herself off on a solitary retreat to: "Find out who I am so I can walk by myself for once."

It is people like Jenny who have made me so grateful to be doing this work, to witness their courage, strength, and ability to look within themselves for the answers to their dilemmas. But to be able to do this work has also meant that I've had to go on my own journey of personal work, for I have always believed that we cannot help anyone else any further than we have gone ourselves.

I was introduced to meditation when I was only fifteen. We lived in London, and it was during the school holidays. My mother wanted to go on a meditation retreat for three days. She did not trust leaving me on my own as I was a fairly wild teenager and my older siblings were all busy elsewhere. As I had already met some of the people who would be at the retreat, I reluctantly agreed to go with her—I reckoned I could survive three days. However, the outcome was that she stayed three days and I stayed ten. I don't remember any of the teachings, but I do remember the meditation, the merging into the quiet, the stillness. And I loved it.

By the time I was twenty-one I was teaching meditation. It had become my way of life, my focus, and my healer. I had had a difficult childhood, with an emotionally abusive father. My parents were divorced when I was six, and I was in boarding school from age eight. Consequently, I was carrying a lot of old, repressed anger. Through meditation I came face to face with those lost feelings. I also connected with a sense of myself that was deeper than the anger. Eventually, I was able to observe my feelings without identifying with them. This enabled me to heal an enormous amount of the pain and confusion.

Meditation also led me in different directions. For three years I immersed myself in Jungian psychology by joining a Jungian dream-therapy group, studying and encountering the archetypes and unconscious. It awoke a deep awareness of the human experience. I went on to study rebirthing, massage, reflexology, and bioenergetics. This was the late 1970s in London, an exciting time of exploration and personal development, and I did it all.

Eventually I came to the Metamorphic Technique, a treatment that had evolved out of reflexology but approached the reflex points from a very different perspective. Metamorphosis suggests that the spinal reflexes mapped on the foot are not only the reflexes for the spine but also reflect the nine-month time period of gestation from conception to birth. By working with this understanding on these reflexes, a level of change in our inherent patterns of health and behaviour can be affected. The creator of this work, the late Robert St. John, also explored other relationships between the physical and the non-physical, and here I discovered a way of looking at the body that expanded my thinking and awoke my intuition.

In 1982 I wrote *The Metamorphic Technique* with Gaston Saint Pierre, the founder of the Metamorphic Association. As that book was finished I knew that one chapter within it was going to take me even farther. It was the Principle of Correspondences, the relationship between mind, emotion, and spirit, and the cells within the physical body, based on the work of the 18th-century philosopher Emanuel Swedenborg.

Meditation was and still is my sounding board, so I used my quiet times to contemplate this extraordinary bodymind relationship that was unfolding in front of me the deeper I delved. I found that when I was really quiet I could intuitively *feel* what the body was feeling, that I could enter into the body and *hear* what symptoms or illnesses were saying. As I included ancient Chinese acupuncture and the Eastern chakra teachings with personal experiences and those of my clients, my understanding became clearer. I began to see that the mind is reflected in every part of the human body, that through the body we can get in touch with the issues that we have been repressing, denying, or ignoring in the mind.

In 1990 I was ready to put together all the ideas and insights I had accumulated into my first book on this subject, *The Bodymind Workbook*. Within a few years I wanted to go further—to enable the readers to enter into an understanding of their own bodymind, to awaken their own intuition, to learn how to listen to their own bodies. In 1996 I published *Your Body Speaks Your Mind* in the UK, and it continues to be a bestseller. Ten years later this updated version brings together an even greater awareness of this remarkable body-mind in which we live. However, most of the Western world is not exactly in agreement with me.

Human beings are extremely good at inventing unbelievably complicated pieces of technology and stunningly beautiful designs, at understanding detailed scientific theories, or producing majestic musical compositions. As a race we have developed, and continue to develop, our mental and creative capacities beyond every limitation. But there is one area where our understanding falters. This is in relation to ourselves and in particular to our own bodies. Although we can tour outer space and surmise how the universe began, we are unable to agree on how the body works. A great number of different approaches to understanding the body have developed over the last few thousand years, each totally valid on its own yet differing vastly from the others.

In the West most people believe that the body is a thing: a machine that needs to be fueled (with food and water) and exercised in the hope that this will stop it from going wrong. We greatly enjoy the pleasure the body gives and work hard to keep it looking good. If something in this machine goes wrong then it can usually be mechanically repaired. Difficulties are cured with surgery, radiation, or drugs—the offending part is cut out or eliminated with chemicals—and life goes on as before. In this context, modern Western medicine has worked wonders. It is extraordinary when we consider the breakthroughs that have occurred: the development of antibiotics and vaccinations, laser surgery, and organ transplants, to name but a few. Medical science has saved millions of lives and dramatically reduced suffering. Modern understanding of the body machine and the ways in which it can go wrong is undeniably impressive.

However, this approach does not always work. Sometimes the side effects of drugs cause worse complications. Other difficulties may emerge even if the original cause is cured. Or the problem might go beyond the bounds of medicine; there may simply be no available cure. For instance, illnesses related to stress are numerous, and their incidence is rapidly rising. Maladies directly caused by stress include migraine headaches, irritable bowel syndrome, muscle tension, and chronic fatigue, to name but a few. Modern medicine does not have a cure for stress, and, as it does not acknowledge the influence of a patient's mental or emotional state on their physical well-being, no medical cures are available. Yet up to 70 percent of patient visits to the doctor are for stress-related illnesses.

In Hippocrates' day a physician took into account not just the physical symptoms but also the climate, race, sex, living conditions, and social and political environment of the patient. However, in the seventeenth century, René Descartes posited that the mind and body operate separately with no interconnection, thus rendering the body to the status of a machine, something that could be fixed by mechanical means. Western medicine was developed on the basis of this idea. But such a mechanistic approach left us with a void in our relationship with our bodies. As much as we may be able to apply corrective procedures to repair many of the things that go wrong, it is without a sense of living inside this machine or of any connection to the energy that makes it work.

In the East, particularly in China and Japan, we find a very different approach. Far from seeing the body as a machine, people view it as an energy system. This understanding is far older than the Western model—it dates back at least 5,000 years—and has proved to be extremely effective in curing illness and disease. Eastern medicine is based on detailed maps of energy, the *meridians*, that flow through the body. These maps chart the type of energy flow as well as where and how to access it. Each patient is also diagnosed according to the elements: earth, water, wood, metal, and air. Each element is seen as relating to specific functions in the body and when out of balance can manifest as symptoms. Illness is recognized as an imbalance or blockage in the flow of energy caused by poor habits, stress, or negative emotions. Balance is therefore sought through adjusting the energy flow.

While Western medicine sees the patient as a machine, acupuncture (and related healing methods) sees the patient as an energy system that is alive and constantly changing. Rather than pointing the finger at outside *causes* when something goes wrong, they look to outside *influences* and the circumstances of the patient's life, mind-set, and feelings, and at how it all interacts. In *The Web That Has No Weaver*, Ted Kaptchuk highlights this difference when he explains that a Western doctor will ask, "What X is *causing* Y?" while the acupuncturist will ask, "What is the *relationship* between X and Y?"

There are also cultural and religious factors that help to explain the development of the Western approach to medicine. In early Christianity the body was seen as something that threatened one's moral virtue. Lust and desire were unacceptable and to be repressed. There are wonderful descriptions of the early missionaries who went to persuade the "wild and sinful" people of Hawaii that they needed to be saved. In the blistering heat of the tropics the missionaries preferred to stay dressed in layers of dark wool clothing rather than expose their bodies to the sun and run the risk of exciting their lust. Surrounded by the brown and laughing Hawaiians, happily naked or barely clothed, many of these missionaries died from the heat and bacteria generated beneath their garments.

For hundreds of years the Church was believed to own man's soul, while doctors simply looked after the body. This differs from the traditional Native American culture, where there is no separation of mind and form, and a doctor is seen as a doctor of the soul as well as of the physical body. Although he or she may have no formal medical training, the shaman or witchdoctor learns how to interpret everyday events as well as the "other world" in order to understand the specific causes of illnesses.

In other cultures the body is revered as the vehicle through which we are able to develop beyond our personal limitations. In both Buddhism and Hinduism great value is placed on the preciousness of human life in the belief that it is only in a human form that we can achieve true spiritual fulfillment. Sickness is seen as being both of the mind and of the body, for ultimately both mind and body are limited, impermanent, and temporary. The medicine the Buddha offered, therefore, is that which leads to complete freedom, beyond the bounds of the physical.

Into this picture of the body—as just a machine or as a vehicle for enlightenment—comes another dimension. The last few years have seen a growing recognition of the direct relationship between the mind and the body with the emergence of a field now known as psychoneuroimmunology. This new understanding does not deny the organic causes of illness—such as germs, bacteria, or microorganisms—or that some illnesses are genetically inherited. At the same time, we all know that not everyone in the office falls sick when "the flu is doing the rounds," and that a disease does not have the same effect on every afflicted person.

It appears that our emotional and psychological states do greatly influence the onset and passage of illness, as well as our ability to heal. "Medicine is beginning to see that the origin of disease cannot be spoken of without including lifestyle, diet, social milieu, the environment, and, perhaps most interestingly, consciousness and the emotions," writes Marc Ian Barasch in *The Healing Path*.

Back in the 1970s and 1980s it felt like I was discovering all these different pieces of a jigsaw puzzle that, when put together, created an extraordinary map of the physical body, with this other underlying map of the psyche and emotions. Since that time there has been an explosion of understanding of the bodymind relationship. No longer are people like myself regarded as oddities; even conventional medicine is beginning to concur that the mind plays an important role in the health of the whole. Perhaps the greatest contribution has been made by the scientific and medical community, through such people as Dr. Candace Pert and Dr. Andrew Weil. Dr. Pert first discovered and scientifically proved the role of neuropeptides, which has transformed our understanding of how the mind directly affects the body. And Dr. Andrew Weil has made integrative medicine—which takes into account the whole person, not just the symptoms—completely mainstream through his books and medical practise.

Because of these changes in our understanding, it felt appropriate and timely to update this book. My aim is to enable you to read this map—your own bodymind—for yourself. Sounds True have produced a CD that contains two different visualization practices to help you with the process. The two practices—"Talking with Your Body" and "Bodymind Appreciation"—enable you to develop a deeper relationship with yourself, so that your body is no longer a stranger but becomes a treasured and trusted friend. The CD is available from www.SoundsTrue.com.

I sincerely hope you discover the same excitement that I have found as you explore your bodymind. In understanding the interconnectedness of the many aspects of your own being, the interconnectedness between all beings—between all life—becomes clearer. Our world is built upon this interconnection, relationship, and communication. May this understanding bring you health and happiness!

—DEB SHAPIRO
Boulder, Colorado
2005

PART ONE
FINDING MEANING IN THE MIDST OF CHAOS

ONE

MIND & MATTER UNITE

want to make something very clear. Illness is real. Accidents happen. Medicine can help. I am not writing this book in order to convince you that the sole reason for your illness is in your mind and that you must have done something wrong or are to blame for being ill. And I am not saying that simply by understanding how the mind and body work together you will be able to miraculously cure yourself of whatever ails you.

What I am saying is that the role of the mind and emotions in your state of health is a vital one. It is only a part of the overall picture, but it is the part that is invariably overlooked. By understanding this relationship you can understand yourself more deeply and can claim a greater role in your own well-being. I remember having an upset stomach when I was a child and my grandmother asking me if I was having a problem at school. What she knew instinctively we are at last beginning to prove scientifically: that there is an intimate and dynamic relationship between what is going on in your life, with your feelings and thoughts, and what happens in your body. Recently, a *Time* magazine special showed that happiness, hopefulness, optimism, and contentment "appear to reduce the risk or limit the severity of cardiovascular disease, pulmonary disease, diabetes, hypertension, colds, and upper-respiratory infections." At the same time, according to this article, "depression—the extreme opposite of happiness—can worsen heart disease, diabetes, and a host of other illnesses."

If we separate an organism into its component parts it cannot function. Each piece has a role to play, even if it is a very small role, so if only one part is malfunctioning it will affect the whole. Recently our car broke down. When we went to pick it up after it was fixed, we were told that it had been just one small wire that had caused the problem, yet the engine could not function properly without it. In the same way, if you ignore the role that your feelings and thoughts play, you are ignoring one of the most important component parts that make up your whole being. And it may be the one that needs to get fixed.

AS YOU THINK SO YOU BECOME

Generally speaking, most of us tend to think of our bodies and minds as separate systems and believe they function, for the most part, independently. We feed and water the body, take it for walks, or give it exercise, and enjoy its sensory capabilities. Likewise, we feed the mind with ideas and intellectual pursuits and amuse it with various sorts of entertainment, while also experiencing all sorts of emotions that we usually attribute to the way we treat ourselves or how other people treat us: making us feel either good or bad. When anything goes wrong in any of these systems we go to someone to sort it out, such as a doctor to treat the body or a psychotherapist to treat the mind.

Yet instinctively we know that is not the whole story. For instance, can you remember the last time you had an interview for a job? Or went on a first date with someone you really wanted to impress? In either case, no doubt you wanted to appear calm and collected but at the same time you were feeling quite self-conscious and nervous. Can you recall how your body felt? Self-consciousness will tighten your buttock muscles (so you are literally sitting on your tension), you will sweat more than usual, may feel slightly nauseous, and you will probably fluff your words, just when you want to appear suave and confident. In other words, your psycho-emotional state affects you physically. This much is easy to understand, but when it comes to more complex emotions or illnesses, few of us consider this relationship to be relevant. As there are obvious physical causes for illness, such as viruses or accidents, how can states of mind have anything to do with it? Emotions may influence the nerves, but how can that have any relevance when we're faced with a disease? As Geoffrey Cowley said in *Newsweek* magazine: "People may not be surprised that they blush when they are embarrassed, that a frightening thought can set their hearts racing, or a sudden piece of bad news can throw all their systems temporarily out of whack. Yet they find it hard to believe that mental abstractions like loneliness or sadness can also, somehow, have an impact on their bodies."

In this book I want to show you how the mind and body are not two but one—a single bodymind—and how every part of the body is the mind expressing itself through that part. When something goes wrong it is usually a *combination* of both physical and psycho-emotional causes. I am not saying that by understanding the bodymind relationship you will be able to cure all your physical difficulties. What I am saying is that such an understanding adds an essential, and invariably overlooked, component to your healing process.

By learning the bodymind language of symptoms and illness you can learn what is being repressed or ignored in your psyche and emotions and the effect this is having on your physical body. From this vantage point you will soon discover that there is an extraordinarily intimate two-way communication going on that affects both your physical state and your mental and emotional health.

THE EFFECT OF THOUGHTS REVIEW

This is a simple exercise that shows the effect that thinking has on the physical body. You need to do this with a partner.

Stand at right angles to your partner.
Hold your right arm (or left arm if you are left-handed) straight out in front of you at shoulder height. Your partner then puts his or her hand on your outstretched wrist. Now try to hold your arm steady while your partner tries to gently but firmly push your arm down (not too forcibly!). The aim is to find your natural level of resistance. Relax.

Now close your eyes.
For a few moments, think of something that makes you feel upset, sad, or depressed. When you get the feeling, stick your arm out and resist your partner trying to push your arm down. Then relax.

Now think of something positive.
Put your mind on something that makes you feel joyful and happy, that puts a smile on your face. When you have that feeling of happiness, stick your arm out and once more try to resist as your partner tries to push your arm down. Then relax.

Switch roles.
If you want, you can now change places and repeat this with your partner.

Most people notice an immediate difference between the two arm tests. They find that when they have upsetting or sad thoughts and feelings there is no ability to resist, as if all the energy has been sapped out of their arm. Yet when they focus on joyful thoughts and feelings the arm becomes strong and resists easily. In particular, notice how immediately your thoughts and feelings are translated into a physical response.

CHEMICAL SOUP

The truth is that you are little more than a chemistry set. All your thoughts and feelings get translated into chemicals that fire off throughout your body, altering the chemical composition and behaviour of your cells. Hence a sad feeling will influence the cells of your tear ducts and make them produce tears, or a scary feeling will give you goose bumps or make your hair stand on end.

During the past ten years there has been a growing body of research showing how the mind and body respond to each other, clearly demonstrating how emotional and psychological states translate into altered responses in the chemical balance of the body. This in turn affects the immune, neural, endocrine, digestive, and circulatory systems.

But how does all this happen? How do your thoughts and feelings affect you physically? The answer, in a word, is neuropeptides. Secreted by the brain, the immune system, and the nerve cells, neuropeptides are chemical messengers that carry information from the mind to the body—and back again—through the body fluids. Every cell in the body is covered with thousands of receptor cells. Each receptor cell has a specific pattern that locks into specific neuropeptides. Once in position, the neuropeptides transmit information through the receptor cell into the cell itself, influencing the behaviour of that cell. For instance, one of the neuropeptides is beta endorphin, which is responsible for that blissful feeling that every runner knows as the "runner's high." As endorphin receptor cells are found everywhere, that blissful state is experienced both in the brain and throughout the physical body.

Neuroscientists have known for some time that the limbic system is the emotional centre of the brain. The limbic system includes the hypothalamus, a small gland that transforms emotions into physical responses. It also controls appetite, blood-sugar levels, body temperature, and the automatic functioning of the heart, lungs, and digestive and circulatory systems. It is like a pharmacy, releasing the neuropeptides necessary to maintain a balanced system.

In the limbic system sits the amygdala, a brain structure that is connected to fear and pleasure, and the pineal gland, which monitors the hormone system and releases powerful endorphins that not only act as painkillers but also as anti-depressants. This indicates the intimate relationship between the mind, the endocrine system, and the nervous system—the connection between how you feel and how you behave, between your emotions and your physical state.

Clusters of neuropeptides are found throughout the limbic system, the heart, the sexual organs, and the gut or stomach area, accounting for those moments when you have a "gut feeling" about something. Neuropeptides provide the link between perception, feelings, and thought, on the one hand, and the brain, hormonal secretions, and every cell of the body, including those of the immune system, on the other, thereby creating a single, whole-body communications system. In other words, each part or system of your body is listening and responding to your mental chatter, your every thought and feeling.

"We can no longer think of the emotions as having less validity than physical or material substance," writes Candace Pert in *Molecules of Emotion*, "but instead must see them as cellular signals that are involved in the process of translating information into physical reality, literally transforming mind into matter."

There is no major section of the physical system that is not influenced by your thoughts and feelings that in turn become neuropeptides or information messengers. "A basic emotion such as fear can be described as an abstract feeling or as a tangible molecule of the hormone adrenaline," writes Deepak Chopra in *Ageless Body, Timeless Mind*. "Without the feeling there is no hormone; without the hormone there is no feeling. The revolution we call mind-body medicine was based on this simple discovery: wherever thought goes, a chemical goes with it."

So can we honestly say there is any real difference between one part of our being and another? Is the only difference the means of expression? H_2O exists as water, steam, rain, sea, cloud, or ice, yet is still H_2O. In the same way, your feelings are expressed through your behaviour and actions, your voice, or through different chemicals and physical systems within your body. As Dianne Connelly writes in *Traditional Acupuncture: The Law of the Five Elements:* "The skin is not separate from the emotions, or the emotions separate from the back, or the back separate from the kidneys, or the kidneys separate from will and ambition, or will and ambition separate from the spleen, or the spleen separate from sexual confidence."

This complex unity of body and mind is reflected in our state of physical health or illness. Each state is a means the bodymind has of giving us an indication of what is going on beneath the surface. If damage to one part of your being is repressed or ignored, then it can manifest as damage in another part. Having been rejected by your lover you walk out and hit the door, bruising your arm. Is the pain in your arm not expressing your feelings of anger or confusion at being pushed away? To say "I have hurt my arm" is the same as saying that "a hurt inside me is manifesting in my arm." What the arm is expressing is simply a repressed form of the verbal expressions of anger or hurt. In his film *Manhattan*, Woody Allen brilliantly captures this bodymind relationship. When his girlfriend, played by Diane Keaton, announces that she is leaving him for another man, Allen does not respond. Keaton wants to know why he isn't angry. "I don't get angry," Allen replies, "I grow a tumour instead."

In the words of the great Indian Yogi Paramahansa Yogananda, "There is an innate connection between the mind and the body … All diseases have their origins in the mind. The pains that affect the physical body are secondary diseases." To isolate the effect (the illness) as being unconnected from anything else is to deny the cause. In which case the cause (underlying feelings and attitudes) will make another effect known at some other time: another area of disease or discomfort will arise in an attempt to show you where you are out of balance.

Thoughts have energy; emotions have energy. They make you do and say things, and act in certain ways. They make you jump up and down or lie prone in bed. They determine what you eat and who you love. The energy behind what you think and feel does not just disappear if it is held back or repressed. When you cannot, or do not, express what is happening on an emotional or psychological level, that feeling becomes embodied (you take it deeper within yourself) until it manifests through the physical body. The emotion most often repressed is rage, as that is often the most inappropriate or difficult to express. It may be rage from childhood issues, from current relationship or work issues, or from too many life changes.

Invariably, this rage is connected to a loss of control, which is also the most prevalent problem in stress-producing circumstances.

THE STRESS FACTOR

Imagine you are trying to squeeze some toothpaste out of a tube but you have forgotten to take the top off (or to flip the lid!). What happens? The toothpaste has to find some other way out. This usually means that it will come out of the bottom of the tube or perhaps force a hole in the side—whatever or wherever is the weakest point.

Now imagine that the tube of toothpaste is you. You are under pressure and beginning to experience psychological or emotional stress. But you do not take your lid off, as it were, by recognizing what is happening and taking time to relax or deal with your inner conflicts. So what happens to the mental or emotional pressure building up inside you? Eventually it has to find a way out, and if it can't come out through the top (by being expressed and resolved), it will come out somewhere else. It will find the weakest point—whether through your digestive system, your nerves, your immune system, or your sleep patterns. Pushed down it becomes illness, depression, addiction, or anxiety; projected outward it becomes hostility, aggression, prejudice, or fear.

The clearest way to see how the mind directly affects the body is through stress. The cerebral cortex in the brain sounds the alarm whenever there is a form of perceived life-threatening or stressful activity. This affects the limbic and hypothalamus organization, which in turn affect hormone secretion, the immune system, and the nervous system. This fight-or-flight response enables you to respond to danger if, for instance, you are on the front line of a battle or face-to-face with a large bear. However, seemingly unimportant events can also cause a stress reaction because the brain is unable to tell the difference between real and imagined threats. When you focus on your fear about what *might* happen, it plays as much havoc with your hormones and chemical balance as when you confront a dangerous situation in real life. For instance, try remembering a gruesome scene from a horror movie, and you will feel the muscles in your back, shoulders, or stomach contract. The images are just in your mind, yet they trigger an instant response in your body.

Being pushed or knocked during rush hour, coping with an ill child, dealing with a dispute with the neighbours—your response to all these situations has to be contained, for society does not normally permit you to react by screaming or throwing a tantrum. Suppressing the normal fight-or-flight response in this way means that the chemicals coursing through your body have nowhere to go. How are they to dissipate? How are they to find expression?

More importantly, the fight-or-flight response built into your body was only intended to be temporary. Once the danger has passed, the body is meant to come back to normal functioning. When there is consistent psychological and emotional pressure, the higher levels of adrenaline and cortisol that the stress response releases are sustained, leading to a compromised immune system and more likelihood of physical sickness.

Some of the physical symptoms that result from excessive stress are headaches, high blood pressure, heart palpitations, muscle tension, heavy breathing, disturbed sleep, loss of appetite, nausea, dry mouth, gastritis, ulcers, irritable bowel syndrome, backache, excessive sweating, rashes, acne, and hives. The immune system becomes compromised, so it is much easier to catch a cold or other infectious illness. Alongside these, there may be psychological changes such as depression, anger, rapid mood changes, and anxiety. You may also experience impaired concentration, memory loss, an inability to make decisions, confusion, irrational fears, self-consciousness, or marital and sexual problems. Behavioural changes may include sloppy dressing, fidgeting, sudden outbreaks of tears, over-indulgence in habits such as smoking or drinking, phobias, and impaired sexual performance. This is quite a list, and many of these symptoms can easily lead to more serious states of ill health.

The link between psychological stress and physical problems is perhaps best illustrated by research, cited by Dr. Larry Dossey in *Healing Breakthroughs*, which shows that more heart attacks occur on a Monday than on any other day of the week—and not only on a Monday, but most often at 9 o'clock in the morning. No other animal dies more frequently on a particular day or time of the week. What causes so many heart attacks to take place just as the first work day of the week is about to begin? Obviously, job dissatisfaction does not always result in death! But the relationship between job stress and physical problems cannot be underestimated—millions of working days are lost each year due to the effects of such stress. A study carried out by Dr. Norman Beale found that redundancy (or the threat of it) led to a 20 percent increase in visits to doctors and a 60 percent rise in hospital visits.

Padma O'Gara's story shows how badly one's health can be affected by the stress of being in the wrong job:

"I had suffered from low-back pain for many years with pains down my legs. Doctors told me it was wear and tear. I managed to contain it through practising yoga and was even able to teach yoga on a part-time basis, my main job being in the management sector of the Careers Service. Then in 1990 I started to have trouble with my eyes. I kept losing vision, and it was quite painful. I lost my vision for three weeks and was told it was glaucoma. Leading up to all this was a feeling that I was wasting my time in my job, that I should be teaching yoga more, rather than attending endless meetings at work. In the process of having two operations on my eyes I thought that I should finally resign, but I did not trust that I would manage financially. On returning to work, my back flared up very badly, and I was in considerable pain.

"A few months later I was given a proverbial push up the backside. I was driving on the motorway when a car hit me very hard from behind. I never saw what it was, but it knocked my car out of control, and my foot seemed to jam on the accelerator. I was going faster and faster. I was sure I was going to die. I found myself promising that if I lived I would give up my job and be true to my heart by teaching more. Immediately, I felt the accelerator lift and the car come under control.

"The next week I gave in my notice. Since then I have built a teaching practise and have thankfully not noticed the financial change. What I have noticed is that my back problem is now non-existent and my eyes are fine. Finally, I feel that I can see where I am going, and it is in the right direction!"

Stress can arise at many times and in many different ways. In particular there is the emotional stress caused by major life changes such as moving house, getting married, or losing a loved one. At these times you may experience tremendous uncertainty and fear, nervous excitement, or overwhelming sadness. Emotions contract the muscles and blood vessels, heighten the release of hormones such as adrenaline, affect digestion and breathing, and weaken the immune system.

When I was eight years old, I was sent to boarding school, an experience I was not too thrilled about. Within a few weeks I had developed tonsillitis. In those days having your tonsils removed meant staying in the hospital for a week. After that I had a week at home, eating nothing but mashed potatoes and ice cream—good comfort foods! What those two weeks really did was reconnect me with home, security, and a sense of belonging. I then returned to school without further mishap. I can now see that the nature of the illness—inflamed glands and a sore throat—indicated that I was having a very hard time swallowing my reality of being at boarding school.

However, that was not the end of the bodymind relationship. I was given gas (ether) to put me to sleep for the operation, but as I was going under I thought I was dying. For many years afterward, just as I was going to sleep, I would see coffins spinning around my room. In my twenties, when I was training in massage therapy, I was asked to be the model when it came to demonstrating massage on the neck. The other students all stood around me on the massage table. When the demonstration was over, I opened my eyes and my immediate thought was, "Why are all those people staring at a corpse?" It was only many years later that deep tissue massage was able to release the perceived memory of death from my neck and jaw.

Trauma does not necessarily equal illness, but unexpressed fears and anxieties surrounding trauma can lead to physical problems. Obviously, you cannot avoid crisis. What you can do is become more conscious of your feelings, acknowledging and releasing them as they arise or as soon as possible afterward, rather than repressing or denying them. Steve Hennessy changed almost every aspect of his life and subsequently became ill, partly because he hadn't expressed his real feelings about those changes:

"The illness started with severe colic pains. I was incapacitated with exhaustion and energy loss. It was eventually diagnosed as irritable bowel syndrome. During the acute phase, which lasted three months, I ate very little and lost thirty pounds.

"On reflection, the illness made complete sense. Prior to moving I had spent my time looking after others (in the Social Services), always putting others first. My move was to allow myself something good for myself. I actually found it difficult to digest this change, difficult to allow myself the good things. Superficially, I had moved to a happier life, but on a deeper level I was still struggling to resolve all the restrictions I had lived with for so many years. The illness provided me with a chance to see what was going on, to really look at those deeper levels."

As we have seen, excessive stress has a direct effect on the immune system, as it lowers the ability to destroy invading viruses and bacteria through the production of adrenaline and cortisol. For instance, the stress of exams can depress the immune response, which in turn increases the likelihood of catching a cold or flu. "Has it ever struck you as unfair that glandular fever likes to attack young people at examination time?" asked Dr. Trisha Greenhalgh in *The Times*. "In the past three weeks, I have seen half a dozen of the brightest and best take reluctantly to their beds with burning tonsils, swollen glands, and an overwhelming, miserable lethargy. They were all within a month of their exams."

You may have noticed something like this yourself, perhaps when you were experiencing a difficulty in a relationship that was affecting your ability to sleep properly and making you want to eat more comfort food. Then you went to work on a crowded train. A few hours later you felt the onset of a cold. Did so many infectious agents surrounding you on the train cause the cold? Was it the lack of sleep or poor diet? Or was it an accumulation of emotional stress resulting in a weakened physical state and specifically a weakened immune system?

When there is a flu bug going around not everyone gets it. Some remain healthy, while others are confined to bed. What other factors are present in those who succumb? Is it overwork, problems at home, loneliness, or a depressed state of mind? If you have been ill can you see what was weakening your immune system from the inside, reducing its ability to resist infection? Have you been feeling emotionally or psychologically weakened?

SELF-PERCEPTION

In itself, stress is neither good nor bad. Rather, it is how we respond or react to stress-creating factors that makes the difference. Some people will respond to pressure or crisis with an increased sense of purpose. Others will respond with panic, denial, or fear. Faced with a deadline, one may find it spurs him or her on to greater creativity, while another becomes frozen into inactivity.

The difference is in our perception of our coping abilities. If you perceive a situation as one that you can deal with, one that excites your creativity and makes you feel empowered, then you will not have a negative stress response. But if you perceive yourself as being unable to cope, fearful of what is going to happen, and get yourself worked up into a sweat, then soon you will be displaying a variety of stress symptoms. This perception of yourself is based on your personal emotional history. It may be due to past childhood influences and conditioning, beliefs, religion, or your social environment, but it is your perception of your inability to cope that causes the stress response in your body, rather than any external factors. That perception results in shutting down the digestive system, speeding up the heart rate, and flooding your body with hormones, without any direct physical cause. (For more on stress, see chapter 9.)

However, the bodymind relationship obviously goes deeper than just how you perceive yourself in relation to stress-creating situations. What we find is that any emotion that is repressed, denied, or ignored will get stuck in the body. As Candace Pert defines it, *"Your body is your subconscious mind."* And as Caroline Myss says, *"Your biology is your biography."* In other words, the thoughts and emotions you are not acknowledging, dealing with, resolving, or healing will simply make themselves known elsewhere.

"If a woman smokes to relieve the stress of an intolerable marriage, what is the 'cause' of her lung cancer? Is it a genetic predisposition? The histology of oat-cell carcinoma? The smoking itself? Her relationship?" asks Marc Ian Barasch in *The Healing Path*. "How thorough is her cure if she has a lung removed but does not change her marital circumstances, let alone inquire into the personality patterns that permitted her to cling to her longtime unhappiness?"

Such self-examination is not easy. You may prefer to believe that any illness you experience is entirely due to something external, rather than having anything to do with your own thoughts, feelings, or behaviour. You may prefer to believe that it is inherited or due to a foreign substance such as a virus, bacteria, or pollution. Getting ill invariably feels like something over which you have no control, that you are simply the helpless victim. Despite living inside your body for so many years, when something goes wrong it can feel as if you are living inside a complete stranger. Illness can make you feel disconnected, unable to understand how this stranger works or why it has stopped working. However, the more deeply you look into the causal chain of illness, the further you go beyond the more obvious, physical reasons, to ever more subtle layers of non-physical, psycho/emotional connections. To help you start this process within yourself, try doing the "Body Awareness Review" below.

BODY AWARENESS REVIEW

Over the next week, practise watching the physical effects in your body of different situations, thoughts, or feelings. You may want to note these physical changes in a diary.

Be aware of times when you are irritated or frustrated.
Take note of where you are experiencing those feelings in your body. If you are stuck in a traffic jam, a client is late for an appointment, or

the children keep interrupting your conversation, what happens to your breathing, shoulders, back, or stomach?

Observe anxiety reactions.
What happens in your body when you are worried or anxious about something (perhaps a child is late coming home, you have to give a presentation, or you are about to receive the results of your partner's blood test?) Where do you hold the anxiety? What physical effect does it have? Do fears about the future create a pain in your stomach? Or in your legs?

Watch your reactions.
If your boss or your partner shouts at you, what happens to your heart, your head, your insides? Is your headache because you were shouted at, or because you feel insecure or angry? What do you do with angry feelings? Do you express them, or is there somewhere you put them? Do you swallow hard, clench your muscles, or get constipated?

Observe the effects of memories.
What happens if you recall past events? Do you feel warm and relaxed, or do you break out in a sweat and feel nervous? Pay particular attention to what happens when you recall unhappy memories, perhaps when a parent hit you or you were bullied at school. As you follow these memories, watch where in your body there is a reaction.

Analyze illness and injuries.
Think back to past illnesses or times when you were hurt. Note the parts of your body that were involved. Have you always held your stomach muscles in tight? Have you always had recurring headaches? Have you always hurt on the same side of your body?

Observe yourself, your reactions, and your body. As you do this, you will begin to see how closely all the different parts of your being, both physical and psycho/emotional, are interwoven.

WHO CREATES YOUR REALITY?

There is one catch in all this: the more you understand the bodymind relationship, the easier it is to think that you must be responsible for everything that happens to you, that you are to blame for being ill, that you have brought this state upon yourself, even that you have "caused" your own illness. There is a popular belief that you create your own reality and that you are 100 percent responsible for everything that happens in your life, that every thought you have determines your future, both good and bad. This idea can be helpful, as it enables you to see where, often without being aware of it, you may be causing extra difficulties for yourself. It can teach you to stop blaming other people or external events for your problems and instead to take responsibility for your actions. It also shows you that you cannot really change other people or the world, but you can work with your attitudes toward them.

However, the moment you start thinking you are responsible for your own reality *in its entirety* you develop an inflated sense of self, a belief that you are all-powerful. This generates egocentricity and self-centredness, both of which set the stage for guilt, shame, and failure. Blaming yourself for getting ill, you then blame yourself for not getting well. Feeling guilty for repressing your anger and subsequently developing an ulcer or a tumour, you then believe you must be a hopeless example of humankind. Saying you are totally responsible for creating your reality means you are equating physical health with spiritual or psychic development, so if you become ill it implies you are a spiritual failure. Yet the many spiritual teachers who have died of cancer or other illnesses have disproved such an equation over and over again.

Believing that you create your own reality—both cause and outcome—implies that "I" am in complete control. But the individual can never be in complete control; there are always other factors present. You are not alone on this earth. Rather, each one of us is an essential component of an interwoven, interrelated whole that is constantly changing and moving. Reality is co-created through our mutual dependency. It is this intimate relationship with all other things that gives life its depth and beauty.

As Treya Wilber, quoted in Ken Wilber's book *Grace and Grit*, says,

> *While we can control how we respond to what happens to us, we can't control everything that happens to us. We are all too interconnected, both with each other and our environment—life is too wonderfully complex—for a statement like 'you create your own reality' to be simply true. A belief that I control or create my own reality actually attempts to rip out of me the rich, complex, mysterious, and supportive context of my life ... to deny the web of relationships that nurtures me and each of us daily.*

You are in charge of your own attitudes and feelings, of the way you treat yourself and your world, but you cannot determine the outcome of every circumstance, just as you do not make the sun rise or set, keep the earth in orbit, or make the rain fall. You do not create your own reality so much as you are responsible *to* your reality. *You cannot direct the wind, but you can adjust your sails.* You are responsible for developing peace of mind, but you may still need to have chemotherapy. The resolution and healing of your inner being is within your control, and this may also bring a cure to the physical body. But if it does not, it is vital to remember that you are not guilty and you are not a failure.

In *Healing into Life and Death*, Stephen Levine recalls a woman with terminal cancer who believed she had created her own illness. But she was unable to create the cure. As a result she was rapidly losing faith in herself. "I'm not the person I thought I was. No wonder I'm sick," she says. Levine asks her if she was the sole creator of her reality. In response, he writes, "Her mouth hung agape with confusion and helplessness, and then gradually a smile came across her face. She said, 'No, I guess not after all. But I sure am a major contributor.'"

Through illness your body is giving you a message, telling you that something is out of balance. This is not a punishment for bad behaviour; rather it is nature's way of creating equilibrium. Your body is actually a source of great wisdom. By listening and paying attention to it you have a chance to contribute to your own health, to participate with your body in coming back to a state of wholeness and balance. So, rather than blaming yourself by saying "Why did I choose to have this illness?" you can ask, "How am I choosing to grow with this illness?" You can use whatever difficulties you have in order to learn and grow, to release old patterns of negativity, to deepen compassion, forgiveness, and insight.

Your difficulties can then become stepping-stones along the way rather than stumbling blocks. Instead of becoming overwhelmed by a sense of hopelessness and guilt that you are responsible for everything that is happening to you (which simply adds to the negativity), you can see illness as an invitation and opportunity for awakening. In this way, illness is seen as a great gift and your body as a wonderful source of information. It is there to help you, not to hinder you.

TWO

THE LANGUAGE OF
THOUGHTS AND EMOTIONS

A s you think so you become: your thoughts and words are like seeds that germinate and grow. Your state of health shows how you have been thinking: the seeds take root and begin to influence and shape the cell structures of your physical body. When you think of illness—or life—as being out of your control, or as an obstacle that you cannot overcome, then none of your physical energy will be directed toward healing, as no "living" message will be sent to your body. When illness—or living—is seen as a learning experience, an opportunity to deepen your relationship with yourself, then healing is possible. As the late Native American Sun Bear wrote in *Healers on Healing*:

"The most common blocks are the negative attitudes that a lot of people carry around all the time ... In order to become healed, a person has to throw out hatred, envy, jealousy, and other destructive attitudes and feelings. Although such factors start within the mind, they quickly manifest in the body, becoming a stiff shoulder, a sluggish liver, cancer, or other illnesses. I believe that all genuine healing addresses the problem of unblocking negativities in one way or another."

Before we explore the psychological and emotional causes—and benefits—of illness, let us first look at the external causes, those which are to some extent beyond our control, for they are just as important. It is invariably a *combination* of both external and internal causes that creates illness, rather than just one cause on its own. This is important to remember, as healing almost always comes through the combination of both physical and psycho/emotional therapeutic work.

ENVIRONMENTAL FACTORS

Wherever you are and whatever you do, you are surrounded by viruses, bacteria, and other contagious substances; there is basically no escaping them. And such substances can certainly be one of the causes of illness, although under normal circumstances the immune system is well equipped to deal with foreign entities. Illness is actually an essential part of health; the immune system needs antigens to stimulate a response and build greater immunity. Hence, we have childhood diseases such as chicken pox and measles, all of which serve to increase our overall strength.

Without such immunity acquired in childhood, simple viruses can kill, as when the missionaries first arrived on the shores of Hawaii. They brought with them the measles virus that began to kill the native Hawaiians, as the external antigen was completely foreign to its new host. However, as we have seen and will return to, emotional-stress levels, emotional repression, and lifestyle preferences also have an effect on the health of the immune system, so that, when confronted with an external factor such as a virus, there may be little or no resistance.

Meanwhile, chemical pollution is rising at an alarming rate, whether in our external environment or in our foodstuffs, and is creating long-term difficulties, such as chemical intolerance, for which we have few solutions. The acute rise in asthma, especially childhood asthma, is one example of a health problem that has been exacerbated by increased air pollution, as in car exhaust. Now, childhood cancers are also being linked to car exhaust, as research shows increased numbers of cancer cases in high-pollution areas such as bus stations and transport hubs.

Environmental issues should be considered in every case of illness or disease, especially if you are living in a city, and more research on the relationship between pollution and ill health is urgently needed. We cannot treat our crops, animals, and air with chemicals, continue to pour chemical waste into the ecosystem, or ingest it through adulterated foodstuffs, without it affecting our health.

However, you can introduce some limits on the amount of toxins you consume, through the foods you eat and your lifestyle. More importantly, you need to be aware of those attitudes within yourself that stop you from caring for yourself and the environment (i.e., feeling helpless, that there's nothing you can do that will make any difference, believing that it is already too late, so why bother). You have to want to make a difference, and the best place you can start is in your own home.

GENETIC INFLUENCES

Inherited or genetic factors are another undisputed cause of illness: physical difficulties are passed between generations, so you can be born with a higher-than-normal chance of developing the same illnesses as your parents or other relatives. However, genes alone do not determine destiny. Other factors also contribute to how genetic influences might manifest, such as diet, exercise, and lifestyle, all of which in turn create strength, resilience, and good health, counterbalancing the effects of genetic predisposition.

Attitude is also vital. The more you fear or expect something to happen, the more that fear will influence your mind. Saying to yourself, "I know I will get this illness because my mother had it and so did my grandmother," encourages a sense of fatalism and hopelessness, which depletes your physical resistance. The body hears and responds to your thoughts and words. Developing a loving relationship with yourself that supports an acceptance of life, no matter what happens, encourages greater resilience.

PSYCHO/EMOTIONAL FACTORS

Emotional pain is just as real as physical pain and can be far more invasive. Long-held resentments, anger, bitterness, hurt, fear, guilt, and shame, all play their role in debilitating your energy. You may feel shame or guilt for something you did or didn't do, or long-held resentment or anger for something that was done to you. You may feel unworthy or lacking in confidence, overcome by fear or panic, helpless, depressed, or full of grief. You may spend many years building a wall around your heart in order to protect it from being hurt, but in so doing you also wall off your own feelings of love and passion. Eventually, you become isolated, locked into separation, unable to love for fear of being hurt, unable to forgive due to past resentment, unable to achieve success for dread of failure. All these feelings have their effect in the body: on your immune system, your blood circulation, your digestion, and so on.

Dr. Ashley Montague, author of *Touching*, has shown that children who do not receive enough love—who are not touched or communicated with on a regular basis—can actually stop growing. X-rays provide evidence of periods of slow or minimal bone growth corresponding to times of isolation or loneliness in the child's life. Without the reassurance of love and emotional security the body begins to shut down. "I have come to see that emotional experiences, psychological choices, and personal attitudes and images not only affect the functioning of the human organism," writes Ken Dytchwald in *Bodymind*, "but also strongly influence the way it is shaped and structured."

The love and support of others not only enhance your growth, but they help you develop the ability to cope, as well as a sense of self-appreciation and self-worth. Humans are social animals. We need each other. We need to be touched. We need to be loved and wanted and cared for, just as we need to love and care for others. And we need this not just to feel better but for our actual survival. In a study on the effect of diet on heart disease, rabbits at Ohio University were fed high-cholesterol diets. This led to an increase in clogged arteries, except for one group of rabbits that unexpectedly displayed 60 percent fewer symptoms. It was found that the keeper of this particular group was very fond of rabbits and was holding and stroking each one before he fed them.

However, few people grow up in an environment that is so supportive, kind, and loving, or that encourages free expression of feelings. Instead, most of us learn how to repress our feelings so as to conform to a certain norm. But those feelings don't just disappear. Karuna King's suppression of her feelings almost destroyed her:

"My mother had four children, of which I was the eldest. There was always a sibling who needed more attention than me, and my enduring impression is of neglect of my emotional needs. I became more and more introverted and disconnected. When I was eighteen I joined a convent, following a desire to do something spiritual but utterly confused as to how to go about it.

"In the convent I began to lose touch with my own inner reality. I felt hopeless and guilty and absolutely alone. Food appeared as something I could have control over. I think deep down I was in such despair that I even wanted to die, as it seemed like a way out. I became anorexic. This created continual friction between the nuns and myself, but I was so disconnected by this time that I became locked in a dismal, colourless world. No one, throughout my childhood or at the convent, had ever said 'I love you.' I felt like I had not been hugged or touched for years. In rejecting food I was confirming the rejection I was feeling inside.

"By the time I was persuaded to leave the convent I was desperately thin and emotionally so repressed that I no longer knew what my feelings really were. The two psychiatrists I saw simply made me clam up even more. The turning point came when I read about a young woman who had starved herself to death, and I knew that I too could die. Finally something inside me began to stir.

"Getting better was excruciating. I had to want to eat for my own sake, as no one else seemed to care. Falling in love eventually proved to be my healer. It brought up all my fears and anxieties, but my partner was unfazed by anything I threw at him. Slowly I learned how to open my heart, and it unleashed in me a tremendous desire to live."

Margaret Bird's story further illustrates this strong link between love and health:

"It began by coughing up blood. I decided it was probably just from coughing too violently. Then two days later I began coughing up blood in earnest, and I was diagnosed with a partially collapsed lung.

"The previous year had been a very sad and difficult one for me. There had been a growing alienation from my younger son, and conflict with my ex, who was dying. I had been made redundant and had no means of livelihood. A dear friend had moved away; a new priest at my church was making changes I found difficult to accept. My victim mentality was flourishing!

"Being cared for in hospital made me realize how much I needed human love, how alone and unloved I was feeling. It was as if I had emotionally collapsed. Having a collapsed lung confronted me with questions about being alive—did I want to go on, to keep breathing? As I thought and prayed, the answer came as 'Yes!' Slowly I began the process of healing, of loving myself, and developing a deeper trust in life."

REPRESSED, IGNORED, AND DENIED

As we have seen, love is our most basic human need. If it is lacking, then it will affect every part of our being. Therefore, every emotion that is repressed is invariably due to our experience of love—either being hurt and rejected by those we love or simply not being loved at all. In the 1990s, research done in San Diego documented the relationship between adverse childhood experiences (ACEs) and adult health. This study revealed a powerful relationship between emotional experiences as children and detrimental adult emotional health, physical health, and major causes of mortality in the United States. It also showed a far higher incidence in those who had experienced an ACE having negative habits such as drinking, smoking, overeating, or sexual promiscuity, behaviour that can be a way of self-medicating unresolved emotional pain.

Emotions that are repressed, ignored, or denied, that never find expression, or were never fully acknowledged, are the ones that go deepest and need your greatest attention. Repression may arise because you have been taught to put other people's feelings first and feel you must make them happy, you feel unworthy of love, you feel you must appear perfect, or you have learned how to do this from your parents, perhaps watching your mother withdraw or repress her own emotions at times of conflict. Can you find patterns of repression in your family? Are there unresolved family problems or hidden secrets?

Many different emotions get repressed, such as hurt, anger, and betrayal, to name but a few. Every time you "swallow" your feelings you are potentially dooming them to repression or denial. Rage is the most obvious of the emotions to be repressed, whether arising from childhood trauma, from the way you have been treated, from the way your mother dealt with her rage, from the losses you have incurred, or the difficulties with which you have had to deal.

Rage is repressed because it is rarely appropriate to release it at the time, and after a while you are hardly even aware it is there, buried in the unconscious. With rage comes denial that anything was ever wrong, or self-blame because surely you must have been the one at fault. Repressed rage also gives rise to irrational fear, hate, and bitterness, all of which detrimentally influence your health. For your body does know that the rage is there, hidden in your cells.

Rage is about how *you* feel, not about anyone else. Making peace with your rage is about taking responsibility for it and being willing to look at it and let it go, rather than repress it or blame the world for it. "To take responsibility for our anger means to relate to it instead of from it," writes Stephen Levine. This is especially true for rage that is buried in the unconscious.

RAGE REVIEW

Find a quiet place to be.
Lie down and close your eyes. Follow your breath as you relax.

Slowly begin to scan your body.
Ask where your rage is stored. See if you can find those places where you keep your rage.

Watch as rage arises.
Observe the effects on your body, your mind, your heart. Can you hear what it is saying? Rage often acts as a mask. Beneath it you may find tender feelings of loss or abuse, of insecurity or fear, of intense grief or shame.

Find these feelings.
Give them a voice, accept them as a reclaimed part of you, and see what happens to the rage.

Release.
When you are ready, take a deep breath and let it go.

Grief is also repressed: grief at what has been lost or at what might have been but never will be. Few of us know how to fully grieve, thinking that we have to "pull ourselves together" or "get back to work," without taking time to acknowledge the inner pain. That pain is real, and when repressed it can lead to heart or immune issues, or a change in eating patterns. Shame, hurt, shock, horror, abuse: they all get repressed, buried inside where no one can see them and where we can delude ourselves into thinking they are gone.

Emotions that are denied can disappear for a very long time, as denial is like a large and heavy blanket. Denial enables you to convince yourself that everything is fine and no problem, when beneath the surface, if you dare look, you will find a mass of feelings and traumas. "Not only does the mind have strategies for walling off psychological conflict," writes Marilyn Ferguson in *The Aquarian Conspiracy*, "it can also deny the illnesses from the first round of denial."

Denied emotions can erupt. They can spill out through other emotions or strange behaviour. They can cause physical difficulties, sexual problems, relationship problems, or addiction. It is not always easy to find them, to get beneath the blanket, for they are often carefully locked away. The event itself may have gone, but the emotional impact can stay with us for many years, affecting us on the cellular level. As Stephen Belgin says, "Whatever we don't bring to consciousness comes back to haunt us."

Elizabeth was forty-six years old and suffering from a large amount of excess weight extending from her waist to her knees. We determined that this had started twenty-three years earlier. I asked her what had happened at that time, but she could not recall anything of real significance. Unable to control herself, Elizabeth's mother butted in, explaining that something certainly *had* happened then. Apparently, that was when Elizabeth found out that her husband of only six months, the first (and only) man she had ever loved, was gay. What had this meant to her? Even though her husband loved her as a person, it meant a complete rejection of her as a woman, and especially of her sexuality. Elizabeth had completely buried this memory. That act of denial contributed directly to her excess weight, which was acting as padding around her sexual organs, enabling her to continue avoiding the feelings locked inside.

Ignored emotions can be equally as detrimental. Ask yourself how you feel when someone is ignoring you, and you will get an idea of how your feelings feel when they are being ignored. They have to find some way to express themselves, so it may be through your body or through your behaviour.

However, discovering the hidden emotional states that have caused your current predicament does not mean that you can simply shrug your shoulders and blame it all on what happened in the past. The reason you are experiencing difficulties now is because the impact of those past events, circumstances, or experiences is still affecting you. Your body is constantly changing. Seven million red blood cells die and are reformed every second. Every seven years your body is completely rebuilt. So why are your cells reformed in the same pattern if that pattern is an unhealthy one? It is because the inner programming has not changed. To work with that inner programming in order to affect a lasting change means entering into a dialogue of communication and healing with yourself. You may not know what the issue is, and in many ways you do not need to know what it is. It is enough to acknowledge that there is something the body is trying to say, and to open yourself to hearing it.

LISTENING TO YOUR BODY: A QUIZ

Below is a list of questions you can ask yourself to begin to determine the psycho/emotional causes of your illness. Be as honest as you can in answering these questions; they are for your benefit.

If you answer yes to one or more of the questions, then use that question to go deeper within yourself, whether through quiet reflection, talking, counseling, writing, or creative expression (see Chapter 4). If you have a recurring illness, then see if you can relate the same questions to when you were previously ill, so as to find the issues that have not yet been resolved.

- In the past few weeks/months have you experienced more emotional stress than usual, such as conflicts with your spouse, parents, or children, or financial or job insecurity?
- In the past two years have you experienced anything traumatic or profoundly upsetting? For instance, have you been separated or divorced, had children move away, lost a close relative or friend, lost a job, or moved house?
- Have you been grieving or feeling particularly sad about something?
- Have you been feeling like a failure, unworthy, or invalid?
- Do you feel guilty or shameful? Are you beating yourself up for a past mistake?
- Is there anyone you want to get revenge on or make feel guilty for what they have done?
- Do you feel you are being punished for bad behaviour?
- Have you had this sort of illness before? Were you experiencing similar emotions at that time? (Try writing a brief synopsis of your life, noting any physical difficulties and illnesses you have had and any traumas or emotions that occurred around the same time.)

- What does the illness stop your being able to do? Does it stop your being able to make love, deal with conflicts, make decisions, or go to a family gathering?
- What does your illness enable you to do? Does it mean you can have time to yourself, avoid personal problems, or avoid unpleasant issues? Is the illness actually hiding a fear of failure or a lack of self-esteem?
- Have you been doing too much—or feeling unsupported—and not asking for help? Are you able to express your feelings, to say what your needs are?
- Does your illness mean you get extra attention? Is it keeping your partner there when he/she might have already left if you were well?
- Has your partner gone through a recent crisis or change? If so, have you acknowledged how you feel about this or how it affects your life?
- Do you like yourself? Do you care for yourself? Do you have time for yourself? Do you acknowledge that you too have needs?

FRINGE BENEFITS

As well as observing the history and background of your symptoms, you can also explore the possible benefits the illness might be offering you. This must sound crazy—surely nobody wants to be sick or can benefit from being ill? You do not purposefully beat yourself up or plan to have an accident. Nonetheless, illness is not always an entirely negative experience, and unconsciously you may be participating more than you realize.

Illness is very distracting. It blots out all other issues and centres your energy firmly on yourself. On the one hand this can be very beneficial, for it gives you a chance to let go of those things that are really trivial and unnecessary. No longer do you take everything for granted; life becomes very precious because it has become so fragile and impermanent. If you can fully enter into this state then illness will open your heart, connecting you with what is really important, with your true priorities.

But more often you are focused on the "poor me" aspect of illness. The word *invalid* means both someone who is unwell and a state of not being valid—of being void or unsound. But which comes first: the sick person in bed who feels helpless, useless, and unimportant, or the person who feels unacknowledged, dismissed as incompetent, and who then becomes sick?

Illness can give you permission to avoid a difficult situation or to offload responsibilities. Does your condition distract you from dealing with other situations? Does it provide a way of avoiding your feelings? What activities are you prevented from doing? A migraine headache can get you out of having to read aloud in class or visit the in-laws, a broken leg can postpone a wedding or a holiday, while a herpes outbreak keeps intimacy at a distance. How is your illness or difficulty changing your circumstances? Are there benefits to this?

Children and even the elderly can unconsciously use sickness to get attention. How often has your child suddenly run a high fever just as you were leaving for the theatre? When a child is unwell his or her mother will usually be more attentive and loving than at any other time. Is it any different for adults? Is your illness an unconscious cry for that love, a longing to be looked after and nourished? Can you tell people that you need to be cared for? Are you struggling on your own, trying to cope so as not to be a nuisance to anyone? Or are you expecting them to know what you need without having to be told?

Illness gives you something to occupy your days and is a constant conversation piece. Ask someone how they are and a long list of complaints, visits to the doctor, tests, medications, and a detailed prognosis will follow. We all love to talk about our illnesses, and although this is a very natural way of finding comfort, it can also make you dependent on the illness in order to get the companionship you need. Does having something wrong make you feel more important, even more lovable? Would your friends and relatives still care about you if you had nothing wrong with you? Do you fear the changes that being well might cause in your relationships?

Are you holding on to your loved ones through your illness? Or are you stopping others from getting too close?

Being ill also has a profound effect on your primary relationships, often shifting the roles and creating a new dynamic. This can have very beneficial results, such as enabling a male partner to connect with his more nurturing qualities, or teenagers to start participating more. When you can no longer do the things you always did, whether at home or at work, others have to step in, while you have to learn how to let go and to share those responsibilities.

Relationships of real honesty are not easy to maintain. Too often we pull back into our separate selves and get involved in a silent battle of wills. Was your relationship threatening to break up before or at the time you got ill? Were you afraid of losing someone? Are you playing games of guilt and blame? Do you feel a slight sense of satisfaction if a previously wayward partner has to stay at home to care for you? Or has your illness given you both a chance to get closer and to be more loving?

Illness can arise out of self-dislike and shame. Do you have underlying feelings of shame that are eating away at you? Have you done something that feels overwhelmingly bad or shameful? Have you told anyone about it? Or are you holding it inside where you think no one can see it? Does being ill feel like some kind of retribution for this bad deed? Does it feel impossible for you to be well because you are somehow too dirty, too bad, and illness is all that you merit?

Life can sometimes seem far too stressful to deal with. Illness can give you a respectable way out of having to meet your own high expectations or the demands of others. If illness is due to stress, then why are you pushing yourself so hard? Are you trying to prove something to someone? To your parents? Is success worth it if you are not well enough to enjoy it? Or do you actually want to get away, to avoid something? Is the illness hiding a fear of failure?

Exploring your own hidden agenda is not easy for the simple reason that it is hidden. It means being very honest about how you feel being ill and the way it is affecting your life. One way to do this is to imagine someone coming to you right now with an instant cure. You could be completely well with no more doctors or problems, today, right now! How does this make you feel? What effect would it have on you, your life, or your relationships?

I once did a survey in a bodymind workshop. Some of the participants responded with statements such as: "If I get well I will lose my friends," "Without my illness I have nothing special about me," and, "If I get well life will become lonely and meaningless again." It may appear that without the illness you would have nothing that makes you special, nothing to talk about. Recognizing this is a way of understanding your hidden fears more deeply.

When you are ill you surrender control of the future, and it has to look after itself for a while. There is a pause, a time to breathe and reconnect, a time to remember who you really are. Illness allows you to do things you would otherwise have denied yourself, such as painting or writing. It provides space to reflect, to reassess, in a way that may not have been possible previously. It gives you the chance to get to know yourself. These are tremendous benefits.

FRINGE BENEFITS REVIEW

While being ill is unpleasant and frequently painful, at the same time there are often hidden benefits to illness. The positive things that we get from being ill can often serve as clues to the cause of illnesses. Ask yourself these questions:

- Make a list of all the things that you can no longer do as a result of being ill. Are you glad to no longer be doing those things?
- Write a list of all the things that you can now do. Are you happy or sad about this?
- Write down all the ways your illness has affected the lives of the people closest to you. How have your relationships changed?
- What would happen if you were now well? Does that feel comfortable, or not?

THREE
THE LANGUAGE OF THE BODY

The body speaks to us through symptoms. Symptoms tell us something is going on, whether through the nature of the symptom, the effect it has, or the changes it demands. The word "symptom" derives from the Greek *syn,* meaning "together," and *piptein,* meaning "to fall." In other words, disturbances, difficulties, or conflicting issues may have been present for days, months, or even years before finally "falling together" and creating a symptom.

A woman who is abused as a child later becomes an alcoholic as an unconscious way of obliterating her deeper feelings of shame and anger. After drinking regularly for some years she develops a chronic liver complaint. The factors that came together and formed the weak liver had therefore begun to gather many years before they became apparent physically, yet if we were to diagnose the cause of the chronic liver disease it would be easy to say it was due to too much alcohol.

From this you can see that your history is vital to your understanding of yourself. The events of your life have shaped and coloured your behaviour, feelings, attitudes, and health: *Your biology is your biography*. By paying attention to both the history of the symptom as well as its effect, you can begin to discover deeper and ever more subtle causes, ones which invariably hold the key to healing.

As a physical symptom is usually the first indication that something is out of balance, the relationship to psychological or emotional issues is not always obvious. In fact, it often seems that the physical problem is causing a psycho/emotional response, as it may do, for this is a two-way communication. When we investigate more deeply, the interwoven relationships become clearer. "I wondered which came first, the thought 'I lost my nerve' or the loss of the physical nerve energy that resulted from the tumour. At first I believed that my physical disabilities led to my fearful outlook. My physical condition was literally and symbolically an unnerving experience," writes Barbara Hoberman Levine in *Your Body Believes Every Word You Say*, in which she shares her story of being diagnosed with a brain tumour. "Today, I can see that my physical condition encouraged me to feel the unconscious emotions and fears already within me. It enabled me to realize how fearful I had always been."

A symptom is never an isolated event. It is connected to the past because it has arisen out of previous events and conditions. It is connected to the present in the way it affects you now. And it has a tangible effect on the future, given its prognosis. It is a gathering of disturbances, difficulties, or conflicting issues that may have been present for days, months, or even years. No matter how far down you may push a feeling it does not go away. Your body is like an airplane's black box that records your every experience and response.

Symptoms help you get in touch with your buried feelings. They are like messengers from the unconscious. Recognizing trauma that was present prior to the onset of symptoms alerts you to what you might have sensed but never fully acknowledged—deep feelings of fear, rage, guilt, or grief kept locked inside. You may find you are experiencing recurring symptoms, perhaps every few months or years. The symptoms may move around the body, such as nerve pains appearing in different places yet of a similar nature.

When you look back over the past few months or years you may find that the issue actually goes back much farther, such as into your childhood, but something in the more immediate past may have brought those childhood memories to the surface. Children will easily bury confusing, frightening, or unhappy feelings in their unconscious so as not to have to deal with the pain. The symptom leads you to the feelings. And getting in touch with your feelings opens the door to healing. This is what happened to Cheryl:

"I was abused as a child. Constantly. My father raped me at least once a week. After I got away from him I got into drinking. I was a happy alcoholic—as soon as anything got too much to bear I just had another drink and all the pain went away. I was doing fine, the years ticking by, until I got a letter from my father asking me to meet with him. This really upset me. I went on a bender and ended up in hospital after crashing my car. I was paralyzed from the waist down, told I would probably never walk again.

"Being in hospital made me get sober. That was the hardest part. No place to hide my feelings. After that I began to think that I'd been given a second chance. I realized that my body was telling me that I wasn't going anywhere in the old direction, that it was time to start again. And somewhere inside I knew my pelvis was numb because I didn't want to feel all the feelings that were locked in there, all the sexual memories. And I knew that if I was to walk again I was going to have to get those memories out, and I was going to have to forgive my father. So that's what I did—day by day, week by week. Eventually, I walked out of the hospital. Now I teach dancing."

ACCUMULATED HISTORY

"It is certainly quite often the case that the physical aspects of disease, i.e., the pathology, can be influenced in some way by the scientific approach," writes Dr. John Ball in *Understanding Disease*, "but in most cases the physical manifestation is only the final expression of a process that has been continuing for a long time."

Sometimes the body reflects the repressed feelings quite quickly but usually, as the body tends to change more slowly than the mind, it may take a few years before anything physical becomes manifest. A central factor in your understanding of your bodymind language is, therefore, to be found in exploring what was happening emotionally and psychologically in the years immediately prior to the onset of symptoms.

Generally speaking, it is the previous two years that are the most crucial, as it can take this long for the body to change, although this two-year time period is a guideline only. "At the Albert Einstein College of Medicine in the Bronx, it was found that children with cancer had suffered twice as many recent crises as other children ... thirty-one out of thirty-three children with leukaemia had experienced a traumatic loss or more within the two years preceding the diagnosis," writes Louis Proto in *Self-Healing*. Obviously not all children who experience trauma will develop leukaemia. This research was simply looking at those who did, but I also found this to be true with a 10-year-old boy I met who had leukaemia. His parents had divorced two years previously, his father had remarried and had a new baby, while his mother had been barely able to cope with her own emotions, let alone her son's.

This two-year period occurs frequently in reference to the onset of symptoms. What you are looking for are the psycho/emotional symptoms that began before the physical ones: the places where emotions got repressed, ignored, or denied, the unresolved issues that are undermining your normal sense of vitality and aliveness.

Due to the nature of denial it is often hard to be honest about what you felt then and may still feel now. It is more likely that you will have rationalized any difficulties. This is a normal defence mechanism to protect yourself from the pain of your feelings. So take some time to think about what you have been through and to what extent you have really accepted or dealt with your inner responses. It is not just a matter of seeing the event and giving it the label "cause of illness." You need to focus on how you feel inside, not what society says you should feel.

It is possible to spend years denying your feelings and convincing yourself, as well as everyone else, that you are fine. To then begin to dig up those feelings can seem impossible. You may even have blanked out your memory of the event. In this case, it may be helpful to ask a family member or close friend to talk it through with you to see if there are events that affected you that you have since pushed into your unconscious. Giving voice to hidden feelings is an important step on the healing journey. You can cure a problem, but to find your healing takes courage and honesty. It means looking objectively and clearly, not just at the outer events but also at what you felt then. What feelings were ignored, denied, thought of as silly or unimportant? What had you no time for? What were all the different pieces that eventually came together to form a symptom?

HISTORY REVIEW

- Take some time to explore your medical history.
- See where psychological or emotional difficulties may be related to physical illnesses, difficulties, or accidents.
- Look back at least two years before the symptoms began or farther if necessary.
- Apply the same preview to any accidents you have had.

DECODING THE LANGUAGE

There are many ways to explore the language of the body. Only when they are all put together will you start to get the bigger picture.

An important clue in investigating symptoms is the specific *function* of the part that is not well, for the underlying psychological or emotional issues usually relate to the purpose or function of the part affected. Try exploring the part of the body you are concerned about and all the different uses it has. What does that part of your body do? What role does it play in the functioning of the whole? How does its purpose relate to what is happening in your life? In particular, what does that function mean in psycho/emotional terms? (Refer to specific parts of your body in Part Two.)

For instance, the neck is normally thought of as just being the link between the head and the rest of the body, and this is correct. But it is also much more than that. The neck enables you to turn your head so that you can see in all directions. If it becomes stiff then there may be a conflict in knowing which way to turn, a resistance to seeing another's point of view, or a prejudice that means you can only see what is right in front of you, as if you are wearing blinders.

A stiff neck is a sign of emotional stiffness and inner rigidity. This is also where someone is described as being a "pain in the neck," implying that they are trying to get your attention but you would prefer to ignore them, perhaps because they are reminding you of something you would rather forget. The neck also enables you to move your head in response, such as nodding yes or shaking no. A stiff neck may indicate you have been keeping your head lowered for too long in submission or fear.

A drooping head is a sign of an inner hopelessness, an inability to face whatever lies ahead. As much as the neck is the link between the head and the shoulders, it is more than just a physical link. It is symbolic of the energy flow between the head or more cerebral and mental part of your being, and your heart or feeling centre. A stiff or painful neck can therefore indicate a blocking of the energy flow, perhaps because of a resistance to or fear of expressing feelings, such as anger or love.

Another example is the hands. It is here that you handle your world—through giving and receiving—so their function is to represent your creative, outward-doing activity. How you feel about what you are doing as well as the way you are being treated will be shown here, as your hands represent how you feel about how others are handling you. Hands are used to express your feelings, extending from your heart through your arms, when movement is added to words. Here you caress and touch to show your love. Here you can form a fist to show your anger.

The more you go into the particular function of a body part, the more you will also see how it interconnects with all the other parts. For instance, the hands are the outward expression of the energy from your heart coming up and out through your arms and expressing itself in what you do or who you hug. In the same way, the feet are the most outward expression of the movement that begins in your pelvis and comes down your legs, taking you in a certain direction. Your feet are also the part you stand on; they give you stability and uprightness.

FUNCTIONING REVIEW

From these examples of hands and feet you can see how each part of the body has a myriad of functions. Examining those functions can supply clues to the hidden causes of illness.

Choose any part of your body.
Choose any part of your body and begin to unravel what it does.

Begin your exploration.
View the part from as many angles as you can: physically, emotionally, psychologically.

Place it in context.
Remember to include the relationship of that particular part to the whole, such as the neck in relationship to the head, body, and heart, or the hands in relationship to the arms and the expression of feelings. Now see how the function of that part relates to you, your behaviour, and your feelings.

NATURE OF DIFFICULTY

As well as the function, you need to explore the nature of the illness or difficulty. Is it a muscle strain or bone break, an infection or an irritation, a nerve problem, a digestive issue or a blood disorder? Each one of these has a different implication. For instance, an infection means that something from outside (such as a bacteria or virus) has affected you, causing a fever or cold, septicaemia, or inflammation. This means that something (or somebody) has found its way inside you and is causing a disturbance. In response you become red, hot, inflamed—all symbols of rage or unexpressed emotion building up inside.

The nature of an infection is different from breaking out in an itchy rash. Is something or someone annoying you so much that they have literally gotten under your skin? Or are you itching to do or say something? If you have cold feet, this is to do with circulation and the withdrawal of blood/ love. Are you emotionally fearful of moving forward, or are you pulling back from the direction in which you have been going?

From these examples, you can begin to explore the nature of the difficulty and its psycho/emotional relevance. You can also explore the type of tissue involved.

Tissue: Hard, Soft, and Fluid

According to the work of Emanuel Swedenborg, a Swedish philosopher of the 18th century, "Every physical state is in relationship to a non-physical state." Robert St. John further expanded the idea in his work, known as Metamorphosis Therapy. Applying this understanding to the body we can say, figuratively speaking, that there are three types of physical structure in the human body: hard tissue, found in the bones and teeth; soft tissue, as in the flesh, fat, skin, organs, muscles, ligaments, and nerves; and fluid, as in the blood, urine, water, and lymph. We can also say these correspond to three non-physical states of being: soul or spirit, thought, and feeling.

The hard tissue corresponds to your core being. Just as rock forms the core of the earth, so the skeleton forms the supportive inner framework of the body. And just as bones are fundamental to the health of the whole, so your soul-level beliefs give meaning to every aspect of your life. The skeleton enables your muscles to move, to communicate, for your thoughts and feelings to find expression. This is your primary form, the inner basis of your being. If there is to be life, it must have a form, and the bones provide that form. And just as there cannot be life without the bones, so you are not truly alive unless you are in touch with your deepest core or soul energy. A break or difficulty here, therefore, implies a conflict at this deepest level within yourself, a conflict that hinders if not stops your movement forward.

The soft tissue is like the earth. It corresponds to your psychological attitudes and thinking patterns. Your thoughts and experiences directly affect the state of your nerves and are visible in the condition of your muscles, skin, and flesh, reflecting the continual movement of change within you. *As we think, so we become; as we have become, so we can see how we have been thinking.* Or, as the Sufi teacher Reshad Field says in *Here to Heal*, "What we put out in thought will always come back and land in the same area where we tightened at that moment."

Deep within your flesh are memories of your past, unexpressed traumas, shocks, and sadness. Layers of fat are built to protect painful memories, or the events and thoughts that have formed your fears and prejudices. Your innermost beliefs find expression through the soft tissue, through your shape and ability to move. Issues to do with the soft tissue correspond to where your thinking is self-negating, angry, bitter, hurt, self-destructive, or self-limiting.

As you read this try holding your stomach and buttock muscles tight and watch how your thoughts change. If tense or strained muscles are an issue for you, see how this condition is being perpetuated by tense or stressful thinking patterns. Where are you holding so tightly? What will happen if you let go? Rigid tendons reflect rigid tendencies, just as tight muscles reflect an inner tightness, such as fear or anger. When these attitudes are maintained over a long period of time the muscles form what is known as "body armour," a rigidity that stops the free expression of feeling.

The **fluids** correspond to your emotions and feelings—you boil with anger or overflow with love—and to the distribution of those feelings throughout your being. The fluids in the body circulate life-giving nourishment through the blood and release emotion through tears and through urine. You are made of 94 percent water, and these fluids are constantly moving, shifting, and flowing, like an ocean flowing with your desires and feelings.

To move is to emote, to express and demonstrate, to give direction and purpose. Just as the blood circulates out from your heart to every cell in your being, so your love circulates from your heart both within you and from you to others. And just as your face will flush with embarrassment, so you go red with anger or white with rage. Fluid issues are tenderness issues, to do with love and hurt, grief and passion, reflecting where your feelings are being repressed and locked away or are overflowing and out of control.

Where the muscles and soft tissue give movement to your bones, so the fluids give power and expression to that movement. In the same way, your thoughts and feelings give expression and direction to your deepest beliefs.

LEFT AND RIGHT SIDES OF THE BODY

The brain is split into two hemispheres, left and right, and these have quite different influences. Left-brained people tend to be logical, rational, verbal, rapid-fire thinkers. They process information sequentially, looking first at the pieces then putting them together to get the whole picture. Right-brained people tend to be visual thinkers who process information in an intuitive and visionary way, looking first at the whole picture and then at the details. They are also more introverted and sensitive, especially to light, sound, and criticism.

Our educational system is set up for left-brained children, as they think in a linear way that is easy to teach. Right-brained children are not accommodated so easily as they are more visual and need imagery to grasp concepts. Because of this, those who are right-brained are often diagnosed as being unable to pay attention and as having ADHD. Such children simply learn in a different way, and when that is accommodated they actually have no problem learning at all.

As the brain stem enters the spine at the top of the neck the nerves emanating from these two sides cross over. So the right side of your body relates to the rational and logical part of your being and the left side to the more creative and feeling qualities. However, the logic does not follow through to which hand—left or right—is most dominant. Apparently it makes little difference: there are a higher proportion of artists who are left-handed, but there are also a higher proportion of left-handed tennis players!

In many of the Eastern traditions this right/left split is described as the masculine/feminine split. This is not about gender but the masculine and feminine qualities that we all possess. When we apply these principles to understanding the bodymind language, we invariably find a connection between physical problems occurring on only one side of the body and an inner conflict with some aspect of the relevant principle.

The **right** side of the body represents the masculine principle in both men and women. It has to do with the ability to give and to be dominant or assertive. It is the authoritative and intellectual part of your being. It is about the external world of work, business, competition, your function in society, about politics and power. In both men and women the right side of the body reflects their relationship to the masculine principle within themselves.

In a man this could mean conflict with expressing his masculinity, having to be responsible for a family, difficulties in having to compete at work, a lack of self-esteem, or confusion over sexual orientation. In a woman the right side may reflect her conflict with having to be a mother while also having a career, or a difficulty in being assertive and confident in the workplace, which is largely dominated by men. Single mothers have to develop their masculine side more, becoming both the decision maker and the nurturer, and this can easily lead to an inner conflict.

The right side also reflects your relationships to the males in your life, such as your father, brother, lover, son; and any conflicts there might be in those relationships.

An example of this was Ellie, who came to see me complaining that she had experienced a slight numbness in the whole of her right side since she was a teenager. She had been a happy tomboy all her childhood. As we talked she realized that the numbness had developed shortly after her father imposed his desire on her that she become a proper "young lady" and train as a secretary, when all she really wanted to do was to become a fighter pilot. In response she had cut off her more assertive tendencies, or rather she withdrew feeling from that part of her, thereby creating a rejected or numb feeling in her right side. For Ellie, her healing involved forgiving her father for imposing his wishes on her, developing the confidence to do what she really wanted to, and bringing this repressed and unacknowledged part of her being back to life. Last time I saw her she was off to start training as a pilot—although not a fighting one!

The **left** side of the body represents the feminine principle in both men and women. It indicates the ability to ask for help, to receive and to surrender, to nurture and care for others, to be creative and artistic, to listen to and trust your own wisdom. It is about the home and the inner world of reflection and intuition.

Issues on the left side in a man reflect his difficulty in being nurturing and sensitive, to crying or showing his feelings, to being in touch with his creativity, intuition, and inner wisdom. Boys get told that brave men don't cry, and so many men are not in touch with this more sensitive part of themselves. For a woman, the left side reflects issues to do with expressing her femininity and vulnerability, conflicts with mothering and nurturing, and how to be both receptive and responsive.

The left side also reflects your relationships to females—your mother, sister, lover, wife, daughter—and any conflicts there may be in those relationships.

"David came for a massage complaining of a pain in his lower back, on the left side," describes massage therapist Jenny Britton. "As I started massaging his back, he began to tell me how he had just cancelled his wedding, scheduled for two months ahead. The church had already been booked, the dress made, and he and his fiancée had even bought a house together. He said he was happy to continue living with her, but she wanted the wedding or nothing. David was taking a step forward for himself and it wasn't easy. His back—lower left, the area of emotional support/ standing up for yourself/ relationship with the feminine—was constricted and tense. He told me that he had moved straight from living with his mother to living with his fiancée and now realized how badly he needed to stand for himself on his own feet."

Finding a Balance

Our roles as men and women have changed dramatically in the last fifty years, and many of us are still struggling to find a balance. Men are being challenged to move away from the image of "Marlboro man," who is stoic and strong, holding his emotions in place while single-handedly providing for his family, to that of a man who can change a nappy, say "I love you" to his children, is willing to explore his creativity, and who can share decision making and leadership. A woman has a different predicament. She has moved from being a full-time homemaker concerned only with children and home affairs to now being both a homemaker and a working professional. Her challenge is in being able to develop her confidence and assertiveness in being able to speak out for herself and feel her equal place in the world.

In a sense the challenge for both men and women is the same— to balance the differing energies of masculine and feminine, to be nurturing and assertive, to appreciate beauty and, practise practicality, and to honor the needs of others while also listening to one's own inner voice.

BALANCING REVIEW

Paying attention to whether your illness or injury affects the right or left side of your body can provide significant clues about its cause. Here are some points to focus on:

Notice which side of your body is most dominant.
Does one side get hurt more than the other? Is one side stronger or more well-developed?

Think back to past accidents or illnesses.
Was one side most often affected?

Consider gender issues.
Which part of your personality is more developed—the feminine or masculine qualities?

Focus on balance.

Are there conflicts with either the feminine or masculine energies in your life? In your relationships? What is needed to bring greater balance? What changes could you make in order to express both sides of your nature?

ENERGY CENTRES: THE CHAKRA SYSTEM

Here we move into a different arena—energetic rather than physical—but one that is just as important. According to the Eastern teachings there are seven major energy centres in the body, located at specific areas in the spinal column. These are known as *chakras*. If you have not worked with this aspect of your body before, it may sound pretty far out or esoteric, but these chakras have been proven to be very relevant in bodymind understanding.

The chakras are levels of consciousness that influence your perception of reality. They are not physical but they connect the physical with the non-physical, and in this way influence the health of the whole body. Chakras are like energy gateways within your being that process information and through which you can gain access to greater states of perception or consciousness. Although each chakra is described separately, they work together vibrationally, the energy flowing between each one.

If you are familiar with chakras, you may have seen them represented as wheels or mandalas, by specific colours or sounds, or even by many-petalled lotus flowers. These are symbolic representations. The lotus arises from the mud, through the water, to emerge pristine in the light. As such it symbolizes your growth from the realms of darkness and ignorance to the awakened state of enlightenment. Beginning below the base of the spine and moving upward to the top of the head, the chakras reflect this movement from more instinctive, self-centreed behaviour, through the exertion of the ego, to higher states of compassion and wisdom.

However, the energy in your body does not necessarily travel in this upward movement. At different times a specific chakra may exert more influence or need more attention than at other times. For instance, when stress levels are rising and you are facing a flight-or-fight situation, the first and second chakras will assert dominance, shutting down the higher chakra energy in preparation for survival.

CHAKRA REVIEW

There is an enormous wealth of understanding about this great Eastern system. Here we are primarily concerned with the bodymind connection of each chakra, as its relationship with the physical body shows us how all illnesses have an energetic component and are affected by energetic imbalances. By associating a particular chakra with the related physical difficulty you can gain a deeper insight into the nature of illness. To do this:

- Mentally make the connection between the part of your body that is out of balance and the relevant chakra. (The questions at the end of each chakra description will help you do this.)
- Focus on the qualities of that chakra, then look within yourself to see how, energetically, you have been dealing with such issues.
- Then see if you can turn the energy around in order to embrace the positive aspects of the chakra.

1. *Mooladhara* or Root Chakra

The first chakra is energetically located at the perineum, halfway between the anus and the genitals. The level of consciousness here has to do with basic and instinctive qualities of survival, security, trust, and self-protection. It is connected to your history and ancestral energy, the sense of belonging to a particular family and having a valid place in the world. When this chakra is active or awakened, you can meet survival challenges with optimism and creativity. Your attitude will be one of trust in the world and acceptance of others. You will feel secure or "rooted," with a strong desire for life. If the energy is inactive, then your consciousness will cower in the face of difficulties and you will rely on others to solve your problems. You will fear being able to provide, whether financially or emotionally. There will be suspicion, paranoia, and personal greed, the "I come first" attitude. There may also be a fear of not belonging, of having no safety or support, even of being suicidal.

The physical connections to this chakra are found in the skeletal and muscular systems, particularly in the back, pelvis, and legs, as seen in back pain and sciatica. These areas are all related to your ability to stand your ground, to feel safe and rooted in the world. The attitudes you hold toward your family, work, and your ability to survive are all shown in the way you walk, the posture of the spine, the way you hold your head. Issues of support, of being held and sustained, are all found here.

This chakra is also related to the stress and fear that are found in the kidneys and adrenal glands. This stress and fear can cause digestive or bowel problems, such as irritable bowel syndrome or constipation. These issues are to do with trust, particularly in trusting that the world is not a threatening place and that it will support you. This chakra is related to all forms of creativity and manifestation. Where there is no ground or the soil is weak, then creation cannot flourish. When you are well rooted and firmly established in your place of being, then the flower within is free to blossom.

- Have you been experiencing a loss of security or loss of a sense of belonging?
- Do you feel "unrooted" or "ungrounded"?
- Do you feel stuck or unable to move forward?
- Do you have deeply held, unresolved family issues?
- Can you find a deeper place of security and trust within yourself and your place in the universe?

2. *Swadhisthana* or Base Chakra

The second chakra is energetically located at the base of the spine. It is connected to issues of desire, sexuality, and reproduction, as well as financial issues. Having secured your ground, you now need to deal with the details of living. This covers a vast area. It determines how you feel about intimacy, communication, sharing, relating, birthing and parenting, money, and the world of exchange, trade, or business.

As you emerge out of the realm of survival in the first chakra, the energy is now that of continuation of the species and of exploring pleasure, especially sexual desire. However, desire can lead to greed and the longing for more in the belief that more will bring greater pleasure. Sexual energy is often mishandled or abused, leading to guilt, shame, confusion, deceit, and relationship breakdown. Such conflict over sexual issues can give rise to problems in the genital organs and related areas.

Issues in this chakra also revolve around feeling inadequate financially, having a "poverty consciousness," or being unable to cope with the business world. There may be feelings of being impoverished compared to others, of devaluing yourself and losing self-esteem. This chakra can influence all or part of the reproductive organs, including menstrual issues, menopause, the lower back, the bladder, and elimination. It also relates to the lower belly, the core of your inner strength and emotional ground.

If the potential of the second chakra is undeveloped, it will give rise to excess exhaustion, low appetite, low sexual desire, feelings of helplessness, or an inability to cope. When it is open and developed it will give rise to feeling balanced and at ease with yourself and your sexuality, and able to function responsibly in the material world.

- Are you ignoring unresolved issues to do with your sexuality?
- Are you ruled by your desires and cravings?
- Are you being sexually used or abused?
- Are you fearful of survival, whether financial or physical?
- Can you find that place of balance within yourself, a place that is not ruled by cravings or fears?

3. *Manipura* or Solar Plexus Chakra
The third chakra is energetically located in the spine behind the navel and is connected to the power centre of the solar plexus and

the adrenals. Emerging out of survival and procreation, this is where the individuation process starts—the development of the ego, self-consciousness, and personal power. This is where you assimilate information and digest your world, where you feel fear, rage, or the need for control. The energetic connection is to the digestive system, which includes stomach problems and eating disorders such as anorexia or obesity, liver, gall bladder and kidney problems, or addictions—all issues of fear and control.

As this chakra is associated with power, it relates directly to your feelings about being worthy, valuable, likeable, and confident. When the third chakra is undeveloped, it gives rise to a false sense of power, with delusions of grandeur that cloud perception. It includes a fear of power or authority, of being intimidated, fear of trusting others, or a fear of responsibility. You have a weak sense of yourself; you need to be told what to do or need authority in order to act, rather than being able to take the initiative. This weak self-image can also manifest in a need to dominate others.

This area has tremendous energy, which used positively gives a purpose and direction to life. It is the energy of politicians and teachers, of entertainers and athletes, of people who want to get ahead. It is also the seat of intuition where you feel something in your guts. Taken further, this is the area of psychic awareness. However, this energy can be misused to exploit and manipulate others, as seen in dictators or those who lust for power, such as Hitler or Stalin.

The process of becoming an individual is one of finding your own inner power. This is not a power over others but is your personal authority and emotional strength. An open third chakra enables you to have a healthy, positive, and confident sense of yourself without needing to exert control over others.

- Are you over-critical, dominating, or controlling of others?
- Are you fearful of authority, or do you not trust anyone?
- Are you struggling with issues of self-esteem?
- Can you connect to an inner place of personal power that you do not have to impose on anyone else?

4. *Anahata* or Heart Chakra

The fourth chakra is energetically located in the spine, directly behind the centre of the chest. Moving from the development of the individual at the third chakra, this is where you evolve into a truly loving person by opening your heart and cultivating the deeper qualities of service and compassion, moving beyond your separate and selfish ego concerns to an awareness of community and the needs of all.

An undeveloped heart chakra is seen in a closed or cold heart, unable to warm to others or to truly care about yourself. Everything is sensual and sexual, or rational, logical, and intellectual, but the inner-heart feeling is missing. There is a lack of depth and warmth. You may have feelings of being unlovable, a fear of loving, or a holding onto past pain with a lack of forgiveness, creating untold misery. There may be bitterness, jealousy, or deep sorrow. Instead of love there is aggression and guilt, hard-heartedness, prejudice, or bitterness.

The heart chakra is associated with the thymus gland, heart, and lungs, hence the connection between lungs and sadness. Conflicts manifest in breathing difficulties, asthma, bronchitis, or pneumonia, in heart conditions such as angina and circulatory problems, and in breast problems.

An open heart chakra is an infinite source of love and compassion—the more the heart opens, the more love fills your being. This is about awakening to a real love for yourself that enables true forgiveness, and about developing a genuine and profound loving-kindness and compassion for all beings.

- Do you have emotional issues that are keeping your heart closed and affecting your ability to love?
- Do you dislike yourself?
- Are you holding on to past hurt and feeling unable to forgive and let go?
- Can you enter into a deeper level of acceptance and forgiveness for both yourself and for others, so that your heart can open and heal?

5. *Vishuddhi* or Throat Chakra

The fifth chakra is energetically located in the neck, directly behind the throat, and influences the larynx and the thyroid gland. From an awareness of others and the development of loving kindness, this is the place where your true voice is expressed. In Indian mythology the swan with its graceful long neck represents this chakra. According to tradition, the swan is able to discriminate between milk and water, between truth and ignorance.

The fifth chakra is associated with the throat and mouth, and with expression and assimilation. The throat is both the entrance to your whole being, through which you take in nourishment, and the exit point for your thoughts and feelings. A throat chakra that is undeveloped will restrict that flow of energy, hindering your ability to receive nourishment or to express yourself. You will likely express negative emotions, lie, cheat, or insult. It may feel as if you have no voice, that you are not being heard, or perhaps you are fearful of speaking up for yourself. This is seen in all throat, mouth, and teeth problems, also neck and jaw trouble and thyroid problems.

This chakra is also related to addictive behaviour. When you repress your feelings or ignore deeper issues of pain, you need a way to keep them down. Addictions, such as over-eating, drug abuse, or alcoholism, easily serve this purpose.

The throat chakra forms a bridge between the head and the body, the mind and the heart. When it is open, it energetically opens your whole being, enabling clear communication, and a flowing of energy between your mind and heart. Then there is a balance of wisdom and compassion, of thought and feeling, of giving and receiving. When this chakra is open you can transform negative to positive, poison to nectar, thereby healing the inner wounds.

- Are you fearful of speaking up and making your needs known?
- Is the reality you are swallowing causing you emotional pain or difficulty?

- Are you repressing deeper issues of pain through addictive or deceptive behaviour?
- Can you connect your mind with your heart and body, so that a true healing can occur?

6. *Ajna* or Third Eye Chakra

The sixth chakra is energetically located behind the centre of the eyebrows. Symbolized as a third eye, this chakra is the eye of wisdom that looks from within and sees the truth. It is associated with the mind and the development of higher consciousness, and in particular with the development of perception, intuition, and insight. Where the ego was so predominant in the solar plexus, here the ego is dissolving as consciousness expands beyond the individual self. This is the eye that sees through the limitations of human existence to the transcendent wisdom of the awakened mind. Insight is the key here.

A closed third eye chakra is seen in a lack of self-awareness or any sense of higher consciousness. There may be a fear of the inner self or anything introspective or spiritual, leading to nervous behaviour, paranoia, or distorted images of reality. This results in fixed, closed, or prejudiced thinking patterns and attitudes, and a resistance to new or different ideas, especially spiritual ones. Negative, critical, or prejudiced attitudes are felt in every part of the body, so this chakra affects the nerves, the senses, and the immune system, as well as brain disorders, senility, headaches, eyesight, and hearing.

The balance of head and heart is essential for complete awakening. The wisdom of the mind gives direction to the compassion of the heart, just as compassion gives depth to the clarity of insight. One without the other is incomplete—insight without feeling, or compassion without discrimination.

It is also necessary to distinguish between the mental energy that can lock you into the intellectual levels, and truly spiritual energy that opens you to the brilliance within. Through the third eye chakra you have the ability to penetrate into the nature of reality and to discover the truth within yourself. This is not an intellectual pursuit.

- Are you fearful of others, or closed to the way others think and feel?
- Do you tend to hide behind your intellect?
- Do your belief systems limit your openness and acceptance?
- Can you open your mind to different ways of thinking and to deeper parts of your own being?

7. *Sahasrara* or Crown Chakra

The seventh chakra is located at the top of the head and is seen as the ultimate human experience, where the individual self dissolves into cosmic consciousness. Personal desires are purified, and all activity becomes selfless. This is not so much the end of the journey as the beginning of the real journey with the emergence of the true human. When this chakra is not awakened, it is reflected in a strong ego and a resistance to spiritual growth, which can lead to depression and sadness, for life seems to have no meaning. Faith is lacking, whether in an external God, guru, or the divinity within. Without faith there is emptiness, a vacuum or spiritual void.

The energy associated with this chakra is that of surrender: the full surrendering of the ego or the individual self to the divine self that is limitless and all-embracing. It is associated with the whole physical body, as this chakra affects every aspect of your being, and with all psycho/emotional issues that are connected to a loss of purpose, meaning, or direction.

- Are you depressed or has life lost real meaning for you?
- Do you feel an inner emptiness or loss of direction and purpose?
- Can you enter into a deeper place of surrendering your self-importance?
- Can you find a place of divinity within you?

ACCIDENTS HAPPEN

Some people believe there is no such thing as an accident, as everything that happens is seen as having a meaning or purpose. My own feeling is that accidents do happen, and at the same time we can learn from the result of the accident. For instance, they often happen at times of stress or chaos, or when you are going through a period of change. At such times you tend to pay less attention to yourself, often ignoring messages from your body or your intuition. You are likely to be distracted and become prone to mishap or physical disorder.

If you have had an accident in recent years, explore the parts of the body that were most affected. Look back to any tension there may have been before the accident happened. See if there are any connections to be made. What does the affected area represent? What is its function or purpose? Was the affected area already in a weakened state? Did the accident stop you from doing something, and were there benefits to that? How did the accident change your life? Are there any benefits in this? John Taylor had just such an experience:

"I went from climbing the corporate ladder to falling off a ladder at home, while trying to fix the gutters. But breaking my back and having to lie still for six months was the best thing that ever happened to me! I actually had an excuse to stop, to get to know myself, to get to know my children. We had long conversations together, something I had never had time for. All my defences were down, I was vulnerable and weak, but that let them get closer to me. Before, I was way too protective to show my feelings. By the time I could walk again I felt as if I had been reborn, that I had a whole new life. That accident was such a blessing!"

CHILDREN'S ILLNESSES

Generally, children's diseases—such as chicken pox or measles—are an essential part of building immunity for the rest of life, but it is interesting to note when such illnesses occur, perhaps at a time when the child needs extra rest, attention, or love. Honouring these needs will speed recovery.

Other children's illnesses, such as problems they may be born with or develop at an early age, are not so easily explained. One school of thought says it is due to the mother smoking or drug-taking during the pregnancy, both of which have been found to be detrimental to the growth of the foetus; or because of emotional conflicts between the parents, which the unborn receives through the mother's emotional imbalance. Another school will say that it is due to unresolved issues in the child from a past life, or from a combination of the parents' and child's past lives, finding resolution in this life. There may be much truth in this, but we can only speculate. What is important is that the child is working through something now, in this life, so it is here where the healing is needed.

Children cannot express themselves easily, and so any illness or physical difficulty may well be expressing a difficult time at school, getting bullied, feeling disliked, or conflicts with friends or family. Pay attention. It may be very important for the child to talk about his or her feelings—perhaps to a counselor, teacher, or someone else outside the family.

An ill or disabled child is often blamed for family problems. But blaming the child or the condition does not resolve the issue. This is where you need to look at your own attitude, behaviour, and feelings, and how these may be affecting the child or the family dynamics.

PUTTING IT ALL TOGETHER: SYMPTOMS MEAN CHANGE

From all of the above you can now get a clearer and more complete picture of your own bodymind. Begin by noting where the difficulty is and what the function is of that particular part—what it actually does. For instance, the arms are for lifting, carrying, expressing, creating, caring, etc. Then add the side of the body, the left or right, and the qualities associated with that side. Then add the nature of the tissue structure involved, whether it is hard tissue that has been broken, soft tissue that is inflamed or irritated, or fluids that are pouring out or swelling up. And most importantly, how does it feel inside? How does a sprained muscle feel or an upset stomach? Find the words to describe how it feels, and see if those words are describing something about you.

Although you may be able to see quite clearly what your symptoms are saying, or even to intuitively guess their meaning, accepting the truth of them is not so easy. After all, a symptom often expresses an issue that you have been ignoring, denying, or repressing, so acceptance means accepting this unwanted part of yourself. Sometimes it seems easier to just keep everything the same, even if you lose your health in the process. In Marc Ian Barasch's *The Healing Path*, George Melton describes how he went from one form of sexually transmitted disease to another, not wanting to look at what the message might be until: "One day I woke up with AIDS ... the one disease my body manifested that couldn't be cured with a pill. It forced me to go beyond the physical and find the things inside me— the self-hatred and fear—that I had been dying of for a long time."

In the same light, a young man suffering from acute pain came to Dr. Joan Borysenko's Mind/Body Group at the New England Deaconess Hospital. The pain had kept him living at his parents' house. It had also prevented him from fulfilling his career potential or having a relationship. As he became proficient at relaxation and breath control, the pain began to ease. However, he was then confronted with a far more difficult situation. "Now I don't know what to do with myself," he said. "I'm twenty-seven, and I've never moved out of my parents' house. I don't know how to relate to women. I should probably go back to school, but I'm too scared. I don't know how to live any other way. I think I want my pain back."

Illness gives you the chance to look at your behaviour and the pattern of your life, at what your real feelings are and what you want to do about them. Recognizing the meaning of your symptom is the beginning of the journey, the first step toward understanding yourself more deeply. After that has to come the commitment to releasing the old and opening to the new. You have to really want to get well. The body is trying to regain wholeness, to heal, but it is going to be hindered if, beneath it all, you are holding on to the illness for more subtle motives. Making a commitment to your own healing gives you the courage to change.

FOUR
LISTENING TO THE
BODY SPEAK

As we saw in the last chapter there are a number of different "maps" you can use to guide you in understanding the body-mind language, such as the function of the part involved, on which side of the body it is occurring, etc. But more important than any of these is your own intuition or inner sense of what something means and feels like. This will develop as you become better acquainted with the terrain, and will begin to arise naturally the more you focus your awareness inward and expand your perception. "When I stopped praising myself for self-torture and began listening to my body, I found that there was wisdom in my cells to exceed anything my bewildered doctors could offer," wrote Martha Beck in *O: The Oprah Magazine*. "Listening to its 'language' improved every aspect of my life … As your physical and mental selves begin to understand each other more completely, you may find (as I did) that the symptoms of chronic disease go into remission."

We all hold different stories in our bodies. Just as we all have our own unique voice, so each body has its own means of expression.

For instance, feeling that you are not getting the support you need or that you are weighed down with responsibility may manifest as difficulties either in the back or in the knees and ankles, the weight-bearing joints. It is different for each of us.

Discovering your own bodymind means paying attention to the details and listening to the body's communication. Your body does know what is going on, and you can learn how to listen to and interpret what it is trying to tell you. Listening to your intuition, your feelings, and your body is a gentle process of opening into awareness. In our everyday lives we are normally very distracted or externalized with thoughts flying off in many directions at once. To listen to yourself you have to first become internalized, with your attention facing inward rather than outward. This is essential, for your inner voice may be quite shy, quiet, or subtle and requires your full attention.

Patience is also needed here. You need patience to let your body speak to you, as it may not be immediately forthcoming with information. You need patience with yourself in understanding your body's language, as with each layer of insight your symptoms may vary. Pain may move to a different place, for example. And you need patience with your body as you may have long since released the repressed, denied, or ignored issues, but your body has not yet changed; the symptoms or illness have not yet disappeared. If you think about how your body is manifesting thoughts or emotions that have been repressed over a period of time, sometimes a long time, then it is not surprising that it takes a while to change, maybe even a few weeks or months after psychological or emotional issues have already been healed.

Listening to your body will also help you know what sort of healing help you may need. It may be emotional release or psychotherapy, it may be deep-tissue massage or herbal remedies, or it may be surgery or medicinal drugs. If a symptom is a "coming together," then usually each contributing factor will need attention, i.e., both the psycho/emotional and the physical. Uncovering the source of your difficulty and dialoguing with your body will help you determine what is most important.

There are a number of ways you can listen, such as through paying attention, dialogue, writing, visualization, and meditation.

PAYING ATTENTION

Also known as mindfulness, paying attention simply means becoming aware, watching and observing the present moment. When you are mindful in this way you notice the ground beneath you as you walk, the sound of the birds, or the feel of the wind. You are in the present moment rather than lost in thoughts of the past or future. You notice pain or discomfort without getting involved in the story surrounding it. You notice how you function, where your strengths and weaknesses are, what upsets you, where there are resistances or limitations, where your muscles tighten and hold your emotions. It may feel rather odd at first—you may never have tried being aware in this way before—but such mindfulness enables you to understand yourself more deeply. As Christine Evans describes it: "I try to just notice myself, without judgment. I notice that I feel sick when my ex-lover rings. I notice that I feel sad when my lower back is massaged. I notice the area between my shoulder blades that aches when I'm tired or feeling tense. I notice that the sick feeling, the retching and vomiting, is about not accepting how I really feel and not believing that I have the right to feel whatever it is."

Paying attention means watching, noticing, without comment. It doesn't mean judging, criticizing, or feeling guilty. You are just seeing yourself as you are, observing your body, your mind, and your feelings, and how they interact with one another. You will probably notice how much you avoid yourself, particularly your weak areas, or how often you want to change the subject, start fidgeting, remember something that needs to be done, or suddenly get very tired; how easily you fill your days with things to do so there are no empty spaces.

Pay attention to your feelings by watching how you respond to different situations and people. Watch your anxieties and fears. Notice your desires and how you manipulate events or people to get your needs fulfilled. See how your feelings stimulate different responses, or what is happening emotionally before you get a headache or your back starts aching.

As awareness grows you may find yourself confronting old patterns of behaviour or lost memories that have shaped your thinking. Bringing awareness to the interaction between your mind, emotions, body, and behaviour can open the door to whatever has been repressed, denied, or ignored and enables those energies to move out of the darkness and into consciousness. Sometimes that is all that is required. Shining light on what has been hidden means acknowledging it, accepting it, and bringing it into the wholeness of your being.

Becoming aware of yourself as you are is the beginning of accepting yourself. You can't accept something you are not aware of, and you can't become aware without paying attention, watching, and listening. The deeper levels are the most repressed. Becoming aware of and accepting your inner pain brings warmth and softness and release. It may be very hard at times. The tendency is to run away, to cover the pain up again. But it is there to help you grow. Always remember to breathe and soften.

Your body hears every thought you have and every word you say. It knows your moods, whether you are feeling glad to be alive, optimistic, and hopeful, or depressed, sad, and lonely. In fact it probably knows you better than you know yourself! So talking with your body is not as crazy as it sounds. There are many ways you can dialogue with your body.

Listening to Yourself Speak

One way to listen to yourself is to pay attention to the phrases you use that may be reinforcing your unconscious beliefs. For instance, if you have back pain, are you saying "I can't stand this," "My back is killing me," "I don't get any support," or "I have such a bad back"? Listen to your own conversations with others, and listen to how you think about yourself. Watch where your thoughts and words are limiting or even causing your physical state. Then ask yourself why you are thinking or feeling this way.

This investigation into your attitude toward your body is important not only to help you make it more positive, but also to unearth the inner places of repression, denial, or conditioned patterns of behaviour that led to this state. So much of how you are now is a result of what you learned from your parents or what you needed to do in order to survive, and those patterns are still affecting you. By paying attention and by listening to yourself, you can begin to get to the root of your attitudes and feelings. And from there it is easy to see what needs to change. "The greatest discovery of any generation," said Albert Schweitzer, "is that human beings can alter their lives by altering their attitudes of mind."

I used to care for the elderly. I had one client who did nothing but complain. Every time she opened her mouth it was to find fault with something, whether it was the food, the weather, her family. It didn't matter what the subject was, she would find something to gripe about. For the sake of my own sanity I decided not to respond to this. So every time she complained, I would say something positive. The conversation would go something like this:

"Terrible weather again."
"What a pretty dress you have on."
"Food is rotten here."
"Look at those lovely raindrops on the leaf."
"Can't find anything to wear."
"Did you hear that bird singing?"

And so we went on. I never knew if I was having any effect until one day I went into her room while she was talking on the telephone with her son. She was grumbling as usual when she saw me sitting by the door. Immediately, she said to her son, "Whoops, Deb is here so now I have to say something nice!"

Listening to Your Body Speak
Every symptom is the way the body communicates; it is like a word or a message. Remember that the word *symptom* means "to fall

together," so when you pay attention to the symptom and all the circumstances that have fallen or come together you will be able to "hear" what your body is saying. The symptom is like a doorway into yourself. If you understand what issue the symptom represents, then you can go through that doorway to the next one, going deeper until you find the originating cause.

Remember also that symptoms are the manifestation of something that may have started quite some time ago, perhaps two years or more. So let your inquiry trace back over time to see where feelings first began to get repressed, denied, or ignored.

When you listen to your symptoms you may not always get a clear message. Instead you may get a feeling or an image, and it may be one you do not fully understand, like a dream image. Just stay with it. It may change, or it may grow clearer.

Dialoguing

You can also dialogue or have a two-way conversation with your body. Start by sitting or lying quietly and go into a deeply relaxed state. You may want to put your hands on the area that is hurting. Focus on the pain or conflict and explore in and around it. If you can, also take your mind to the part of the body involved. Then hold a question in your mind such as, "What is this illness or difficulty trying to tell me?" or, "What does this part of me need?" It may take a while before there is a response, but just stay quiet and focused. Try not to "think" a reply, but allow any feelings, images, or responses to arise spontaneously. Do not judge or reject anything, even if you do not understand it, but acknowledge whatever comes.

If you receive an image, or you may just "feel" a response, then ask another question. You can begin to go back and forth and dialogue in this way with your area of difficulty, following each feeling or image with another question.

When you are finished, write down whatever happened so you can remember it and come back to it throughout your day. The practise of creative visualization will help you with this process. (See page 80.)

Affirmations

Affirmations are another form of dialogue and are a good way to shift hidden or fixed thinking patterns. Normally you confirm the negative aspects of yourself—your lack of love or health, your weakness or stupidity, saying things like "I can't do this" or, "I never seem to have enough energy," or, "I always get it wrong." Even by saying "I will not get angry," you are confirming that you are angry. In this way you create a thinking or behavioural pattern that maintains the original thought.

Conscious affirmations help to reprogram your thinking because they channel the energy in a different direction. Instead of maintaining the "I feel unloved" state of mind, you can turn that around and create an "I am surrounded by all the love I need" state. It is all too easy to give in to the old thought patterns, to slide into a mire of self-pity and depression. Affirmations are like the rungs of a ladder that enable you to climb upward toward sanity and self-acceptance.

Repeating an affirmation may feel very superficial at first, as if you are just repeating platitudes in order to keep reality at bay (especially if you are not well and the pain continues, no matter what you do). Remember, your body does hear you, so trust that it will work. It just may take time.

Affirmations not only create a positive alternative, but they also enable you to see yourself more clearly. For instance, if you want to lose weight you can create an affirmation such as, "With each day, my slender and healthy body is emerging." If you repeat this as you go through your day, then you will be far more aware each time you reach for a cookie or sweets—the action will be highlighted because it is no longer in accordance with the behaviour you are affirming. You will also notice that you feel better about yourself because you are affirming and supporting your desire to change.

Sending Love

Now that you know how your body responds to both negative thinking and to positive affirmations, you can also love your body, yourself, or the part or parts that are hurting most. Just pour loving thoughts into that part—thoughts as loving as you would feel for your loved ones. Embrace your body in love. Keep doing this and watch what happens. The second practise on the CD, "Bodymind Appreciation," helps you connect with the love in your body.

PUTTING SYMPTOMS INTO WORDS

If, as French psychoanalyst Jacques Lacan said, *"symptoms are words trapped in the body,"* then we can use words to release the meaning of the symptom. When a feeling is locked away inside, it can easily stay there, untouched and unacknowledged. When something is written down, it no longer needs to be held inside—it has been seen and heard—and so leaves room for the next thought or word to come. So one way to deepen your process of inquiry is by writing down everything you can about your illness or difficulty. Symptoms can be subtle, elusive, and indefinable, but the words you use to describe them can give vital clues to the deeper issues.

For instance, if you have a cramping muscle, what does the cramp feel like? Does it feel like it is clinging or resisting? Are the words describing a tightness or restriction in your life? If you have a pounding headache, describe the sensation. Do you feel that someone is pounding you? Or are you beating yourself up? If you describe arthritis as making your hand feel as if it is being pulled back from the inside, do you feel you want to pull back from what you are doing? Do you feel like a puppet, with someone else pulling the strings?

Paul had polio when he was a young child. He told me how, with the birth of his younger brother, he felt as if his mother had left him emotionally hanging. Later he remembered being in hospital following his illness and feeling as if his body was just hanging there, lifeless and helpless. Without realizing it he had used the same word twice to describe his feelings. This gave him the clues he needed to begin to heal the emotional and physical imprint from his childhood.

See if you can put yourself inside the part of the body that is hurting and find the words for the feeling. What words do you use to describe an aching, throbbing head? What words describe an ulcerated stomach? How does your runny nose feel? Do the "Bodymind Review" below to take this process further.

BODYMIND REVIEW: EXPLORING YOUR BODYMIND MESSAGES

Get a pad of paper and a pen, shut the door, lie or sit comfortably, and enter into a quiet place within yourself. As you answer the questions, write down any words or descriptions that come to you; let each word or thought lead you on to the next one. Write pages on a single question if you want. Don't worry if it does not make sense.

When you are ready, bring your attention to the area of the body that you want to understand more deeply.

- What is the **function** of this part of your body? Write down all the different things this part does, what it enables you to do, what it represents in your life. What words describe this function?
- What is the **nature** of your difficulty? Is it an inflammation, a broken bone, an infection, a nerve disorder? Is it sore? Hot? Stiff? Aching? For instance, if your back is to hold you upright and now it is sore, then is the soreness because you feel let down in some way?
- What is the **tissue** structure involved: hard, soft, or fluid? Does this tell you something about the part of your psycho/emotional self that is involved? Is it a core issue, a mental or emotional issue?
- Which **side** of the body is involved? What does this side mean to you? What words describe this side? Is your problem more to do with home and relationship issues or with work and financial issues?
- Which **chakra** is involved in this difficulty? Are there words that describe what that chakra represents for you?
- What **meaning** does this part of your body have for you? How do you feel about this part of you? Are there old memories here or hidden resentments?

- How does this part of your body **feel** inside? Can you find and describe the feeling inside your body? Is it angry, irritated, hurt, shy, worried, or sad?
- Are there any **benefits** you gain from your difficulty? Does it make you feel special? Does it make you feel loved and cared for? Does it mean you are a failure? Does it make you feel guilty? What effect is it having on your relationships? Is it getting you out of doing something? Or is it the best thing that could have happened to you?
- Can you imagine yourself **being well** again? If you are in a wheelchair, can you imagine yourself walking? If you are depressed, can you imagine being happy and laughing? How would you feel if someone offered you a cure right now? Be honest—this is important. Would you accept the cure? If you could be absolutely well, right now, what effect would that have on the rest of your life?
- And finally, ask your body what it needs to **be healed** and how you can help. What does it need you to do? Is it physical, psychological, or emotional healing or change that is needed?

Consider all that you have written. Can you see what your body is trying to tell you? What is there for you to learn here? Can you see where you need to start working with yourself, what areas or issues need to be brought to the surface? Really take note of the ways in which you have described yourself and your body and allow the words to sink in. Do they have other meanings? Do they have implications for other aspects of your life?

Bodymind Writing

Writing down feelings, thoughts, ideas, insights, and experiences is a very powerful way to connect with your healing, release meaning, and deepen your understanding. Be as candid and open as you can. This is just for you, not for anyone else. Writing opens the door to communication; without communication we live in isolation and fear. When you communicate with yourself, you discover a new friend, a playmate with whom you can explore your inner world. It is a way of letting the voice within you speak. These are just a few suggestions.

Try writing a dialogue with your illness or with a specific part of your body. You can even do this in the form of a letter. Write to this part of you and let it know how you feel: "Dear Cancer, This is how I feel about you ..." Tell it everything. But then let it write back to you! To do this, sit and breathe quietly and let an answer come on its own, in its own words, in its own way. You may be surprised to hear what your illness has to say. Go back and forth in this way. This process helps you see the illness or affected area of your body as a part of you, rather than being something you must get rid of. You soon see that your illness or difficulty also needs to be claimed and even loved.

Or you may want to keep a journal, writing each day or each week. Write about what happens and your response. Write about your feelings, your inner world, your health. Write about any treatment you are receiving and about your doctors. How do you feel about your prognosis? How has this affected your life goals or priorities? How has it affected the people in your life? Write about your parents, your spouse, your children, your work, your home life. You may want to focus on a particular issue, a feeling, a relationship, a conflict, or a part of you that needs healing, and write about how you feel, what you want to do about it, or how you would feel without it. Write your anger, hurt, or resentment; write your forgiveness, love, and concern. And, as you write, just let the words come freely.

Or you can start each page with a specific question. Write a statement at the top of the page and then let your responses flow. If you repeat this each week with the same issue, you will see how your responses change and evolve. For instance:

How I see myself is ...
How I feel about my body is ...
How I see my illness is ...

I am ready to release …
I am ready to accept …

Or try writing your autobiography. Take your time over this, entering into your memory objectively and honestly. Look at the whole of your life and write your thoughts and feelings. Tell your own tale. See the threads that connect each part of your life, that connect events with feelings, feelings with experiences. Try writing for at least twenty minutes at a time. As you think back you may find unexpected insights emerging, ones that deepen your understanding of who you are now.

CREATIVE VISUALIZATION

The power of visualization is enormous. Just as the body tends to speak in images, so you can create images to speak to your body. In one study, a group of healthy five-year-old children were told a story about a magic microscope that showed how the immune cells in the body fight germs; they were also shown a film with glove puppets acting out the roles of the different cells in the immune system. The children were then led through a relaxation exercise where they were asked to visualize the immune cells as policemen fighting off the germs. Saliva was collected before and after for analysis. After the experiment, the saliva was saturated with immunity substances at levels normal for fighting an infection.

Visualization can be used to communicate with your whole body, or to bring healing to specific areas.

Imagery for Communication

Visualization is a very effective form of communication to find what is physically happening and what your body needs for healing. In this practice (instructions below) you visualize yourself getting smaller and smaller until you are small enough to walk around inside your own body. Then you can go to the area that you wish to understand more deeply, where you can communicate with your body from the inside.

As you are communicating with your unconscious, the images

or words that arise are often dream-like or difficult to immediately understand. The body expresses your unconscious patterns, and you may find it difficult to bring these patterns into your conscious mind. If you persevere, the communication will open and you will come to understand yourself more deeply. Sometimes the images are obvious, sometimes more obscure, yet they always offer a clue to healing.

During one such visualization exercise, Linda, who was very addicted to sugar, went to her pancreas. There she saw a big dump truck offloading pure white sugar, burying the organ beneath it. This image alerted her to the seriousness of her addiction. In another example, Eric, who was suffering from overwork and stress, went to check his brain. He saw electrical sparks shooting off in all directions where power circuits were broken. He realised that he was very close to a complete power failure, such as a nervous breakdown.

There are times when the images take a while to make sense, as was the case with Pam, who had had chronic fatigue syndrome for 7–8 years. During the visualization she went to her heart. There she had the image that the walls were all encrusted with dried wax. She didn't understand this so later, when she was lying in bed, she went back to her heart. There she saw the wax begin to peel away and behind it was a door. When she opened the door she discovered a room full of gold. This image told her she had the power within herself to heal.

Visualization practice: talking with your body

This visualization enables you to communicate with your body, from the inside. (The full practice is available on CD from www.SoundsTrue.com). You can go to any part that you wish to understand more deeply, whether it is a physical, mental (mind) or emotional (heart) problem. If you are unsure, then scan your body and find a place that may be calling out to you for attention. This practice can be very informative so make sure to have paper and a pen, so you can write it down afterwards.

During the practice, allow any answers to your questions to

arise spontaneously. The body may use dream language to convey a message, so accept whatever images arise, even if you do not understand them at first. Practise for 15–20 minutes.

Letting go

Make yourself comfortable lying down. Take a deep breath and blow it out. Begin to relax, sinking into the floor, becoming peaceful. Start at your toes and move upwards to your head, relaxing and releasing each part. Now follow the flow of your breath and start to count at the end of each breath, from ten back to zero. Completely relaxing, letting go.

Journeying within

Visualize yourself getting smaller, until you are small enough to walk around inside your own body. Enter your body in whatever way appears to you, and find your way to the area that you wish to understand more deeply.

When you get there, start to explore the tissue structure of this area and the environment you are in: What size is this area? Is it so big that you cannot see the other side, or really quite small? What shape is it? What does it feel like? What texture is it? Is it soft or hard? Is it bumpy or smooth? What colour is it? Does the colour change? What temperature is it? Is it hot or cold? Does it vary? And how old is this area? Has it been like this for a long time, or is it quite recent?

Asking and listening

Explore the images that come into your mind, and let them communicate with you. Ask whatever questions you need to and listen for the reply, such as: What is this part of your being trying to tell you? Is it expressing a deeply hidden part of you that you are not dealing with or fully acknowledging? Does it relate to something from your past that is still unresolved? What is needed to bring healing? Is there something you need to do?

Allow the answers to come freely and explore them in your own time.

Completing and departing

When you are ready to leave, acknowledge what has happened and thank your body, promising to act on whatever has been asked of you. Take your time to find your way out and then grow big enough to fit back into yourself again.

You may wish to write down whatever happened. As with dreams, you may not understand it all, but let the images or words become a part of you until their meaning becomes clear.

Imagery to Heal

Visualization can be used to increase the healing process. However, it is very important to find images that work for you, not ones that make you feel uncomfortable. For instance, some people visualize their immune cells as ferocious animals, such as sharks, to help boost their immune system to kill off cancer cells. Others have found that visualizing their immune cells as warriors or knights in shining armour has a stronger response.

One of the drawbacks of using a "hunter and the hunted" image is that it makes the hunted into an "alien thing" that must be eliminated. Yet each part of your body is a part of your whole being, even cancer cells. One of the patients quoted in Stephen Levine's book, *Healing Into Life and Death,* came up against this problem: "As my immune system became more ferocious and I saw it attacking the tumours, it only seemed to intensify the tightness in my gut. Rather than using aggression to encourage the immune system, visualising white alligators (lymphocytes) ravaging rotten hamburgers (cancer tumours), I began instead to image sending love. What a relief not to stimulate hate in my gut, nor to fear myself there anymore".

Imagery that worked particularly well for another patient was seeing her immune cells as white hearts filling each cancer cell with a pure love liquid, and seeing the cancer cells as simply having forgotten about love, rather than seeing them as the enemy. In *Peace, Love and Healing,* Dr. Bernie Siegel suggests visualizations in which the diseased cells are ingested as a source of growth and nourishment. This encourages you to see the disease as a part of yourself that not only needs embracing and integrating, but could actually be beneficial.

Recently, an abscess in a tooth made me tune into my immune system. The image that came was of a host of really big women – big mammas! – all dressed in flowing white robes. The invading bacteria appeared as a gang of superficially tough young men who, at the sight of this advancing wave of large, white-robed women, cowered, trembled, and fell to their knees. Young girls came to lead the quaking men away. At the time I was going through a phase of thinking I could do everything by myself, of acting all tough and capable. What I really needed was to ask for help, to let more of my gentler qualities come through. The abscess was showing me where the request for help was getting stuck.

Imagery can help to mend broken bones, open blockages in arteries, heal wounds, or calm stomach ulcers. Visualize the particular area and focus on what form of healing is needed. For instance, visualize a wound being stitched together; imagine the wound closed and the skin healing without a scar. Or see some cooling balm being rubbed into an inflamed area, easing the pain and releasing the irritation or anger.

MEDITATION

Meditation is the key to all of the above ways of communicating, as it provides the quiet space in which such communication can take place. During meditation you meet yourself in an entirely new way. This leads to an increase in self-awareness and self-respect, a release of fear and self-judgment, and a greater ability to deal with repressed issues such as guilt or grief. Meditation creates the space for you to see how your mind works, how thoughts and dramas come and go. But instead of getting lost in the story and then feeling bad about it, you develop greater objectivity. You no longer need to identify with your story or the details; you are free to let it go.

Meditation is also an invaluable tool for healing. Traditional yogis who use relaxation and meditation techniques are known to reduce their risk of cardiovascular and nervous diseases by up to 80 percent. Dr. James Gordon, a clinical professor at the Georgetown School of Medicine, says, "I'll almost always 'prescribe' some form of meditation to them [his patients] along with any medicine I might give them. Meditation and medicine come from the same root: 'to care or to cure.'" Some hospitals are now even offering a meditation program as a part of pain management in order to release tension and resistance, to lower stress hormones, and to find a deeper place of ease.

There are many different meditation techniques, but they all have the same basis. Each is a means to quiet and calm the mind by focusing attention inward on a particular object or thought. This may be the breath, a candle, a mantra or sound, an image, or the development of a particular emotion, such as lovingkindness or forgiveness. This gives the mind something to do so that the constant turmoil of thoughts, dramas, and concerns begins to settle. Beneath those thoughts are ever deeper layers of inner quiet, creative energy, and clarity. The object of meditation is just to see but without attachment, to be the witness. At times it may feel as if you are witnessing a noisy and eventful drama; at other times it may get very quiet and you can hear a different silence that comes from within. Meditation focuses you in the present moment. Nothing else is going on, nothing else exists. There is a surrendering of resistance, a letting go of chaos, and an opening to clarity.

However, such a quiet space does not always come easily, so perseverance and practise are important. The mind is very good at finding all sorts of reasons why you should not be doing this; and if that doesn't work, then your body will start aching or getting pins and needles. Move your body if you need to, but stay firm with your mind. You are here—and it is only for a short time—to be quiet and to focus within.

MEDITATION REVIEW: BREATH AWARENESS MEDITATION
Find a comfortable but upright seated posture, in a chair or on the floor. Your back should be straight and your eyes closed.

Take a deep breath.

Let the breath out through your mouth. Spend a few minutes relaxing your body. If there is any tension anywhere then breathe into that tension and feel it release.

Pay attention to your breath.

Become aware of the natural flow of the in and out breath. Do not force or change your breathing in any way. Simply watch your breath.

Focus on your heart.

After a few minutes of watching the flow of your breath, bring your attention to the space in the centre of your chest—the heart space—and focus your attention on the movement of that place with each in and out breath. Just watch.

Stay with your breath.

Silently repeat the word "in" with each in-breath and "out" with each out-breath. In … out … in … out. Just watch the breath, focused at the heart space in the centre of the chest, and follow its in and out movement. If any thoughts arise, just see them as thoughts, label them as thinking, and let them go. If you find you are getting distracted, label it distraction, and let it go, always coming back to the breath. In … out … in … out. As you become more focused, your mind will become quieter and the space between your thoughts will lengthen.

Stay with the practise.

Continue for as long as feels comfortable—ten to thirty minutes. Then take a deep breath and let it out through your mouth. Slowly open your eyes and stretch your legs. Be aware of how you feel. Have a smile on your face.

FIVE

CURING A SYMPTOM OR HEALING A LIFE?

There is an important distinction to be made between curing and healing. To cure is to fix a particular part. Western medicine is particularly good at doing this, offering drugs and surgery so that disease, illness, or physical problems can be suppressed, eliminated, or removed. It plays a vital role in alleviating suffering. It is superb at saving lives and applying both curative and palliative aid. This is absolutely invaluable, and most of us avail ourselves of the tools of Western medicine at one time or another. However, the World Health Organization defines health as *complete* physical, mental, and social well-being, which implies a much more inclusive state of wellness beyond simply being cured of a symptom or illness.

This is where we enter the realm of healing. If you only look at what is wrong and try to get rid of it, you are ignoring the original cause of the illness, why it is there, what it can teach you, and how it is of benefit. Yet the illness or difficulty you want to be rid of may be the very thing you need to learn from. While a patient remains passive when cured by someone else, healing is an involved activity, less dependent on external circumstances than on the work you are prepared to do within yourself. "Healing can occur even when curing doesn't," said Bill Moyers in *USA Today*. "It is an acceptance of the unavoidable, a grace in living that escapes us if we are simply passive in the face of trouble."

For instance, you get self-involved with your pain: with anger, regrets, hurt, shame, or helplessness, until they become your means of identity: "I am an angry / shameful / helpless person." However, you can pamper your pain, or you can use it to understand yourself more deeply. You can indulge in guilt, or you can develop self-respect. This is the challenge. To heal is to meet that challenge; to embrace all of the parts you have ignored, denied, tried to push away, or eliminate, no matter how disturbing or painful they may be.

"The word *salvation* is derived from the Latin word *salvos*, which means heal and whole," says Paul Tillich in *The Meaning of Health*. "Salvation is basically and essentially healing, the re-establishment of a whole that was broken, disrupted, or disintegrated."

Healing comes when you make the choice to work with your vulnerabilities, to open to the challenge of change. It is recognizing that the illness itself is the way the body is dealing with underlying imbalances or traumatized energies, and it is the resolution of those imbalances. It is a letting go of resistance, of the armour or barriers that have been constructed, of the layers of self-protection, of ingrained patterns of thinking and behaviour, of repressive control over your feelings, of all the ways you have held on and of what you have been holding onto—putting others' needs first, not thinking about yourself, staying so busy there is no time in which to be alone, or focusing only on the material and denying the emotional and spiritual. Healing is releasing the holds, breathing into the space that is left behind. "So our path becomes a letting go of that which blocks the path," writes Stephen Levine in *Healing into Life and Death*. "Healing is not forcing the sun to shine but letting go of the personal separatism, the self-images, the resistance to change, the fear and anger, the confusion that forms the opaque armouring around the heart."

Healing does not guarantee a long and healthy life or even the release of symptoms, or any of the normal ways we think of as implying a cure. What it does do is bring together intention with our thoughts and feelings as they are manifesting in the body, so that an integrated understanding of the deeper levels of repression emerges. In this way you can become free of the limitations and resistances that are holding you in pain.

There is an innate intelligence in every cell in the body. It is the intelligence of all life, the intelligence of pure consciousness. However, if we ignore that intelligence and override it with resistance and denial, then we will suffer. One of the most common places that holds us back from embracing our repressed, denied, or ignored issues is fear.

FEAR AND FEARLESSNESS

Fear is an instinctive response when your survival is threatened, when what you believe in is undermined, or when the ground you are standing on becomes shaky and there is nothing to hold onto that feels secure or safe. Healthy fear is an important part of your defence mechanism. It maintains your alertness to danger; it keeps you on your toes. But unhealthy fear is neurotic anxiety that creates worry, panic, and non-specific tension: the "what if …" syndrome. Constant fear or dread can undermine relationships, increase stress, and is physically detrimental. Physical signs include trembling, sweating, sleeplessness, exhaustion, heart palpitations, shortness of breath, and dizziness.

Unhealthy fear is paralyzing. Every movement forward is undermined by doubt: the fear of what has happened or of what might happen, fear of being a bad person, fear that you are not good enough to be loved, fear of the pain in your heart, and fear that you are not strong enough to deal with it. We went to visit a young woman in the hospital who had become a quadriplegic as a result of an accident. We offered her some relaxation and meditation tapes, thinking this might help her relax into a deeper place of acceptance. But she refused, not because she did not want to relax, but because, "I know I am being punished for being bad, and I am frightened of what I might find if I look inside myself."

You fear being healed for fear that you will no longer be sustained or supported. You fear that if you give something up you will no longer be worthy of love. "If I give up a bad relationship, maybe no one better will come along. If I look for a new job, maybe I will get a worse one," writes Joan Borysenko in *Minding the Body, Mending the Mind*. "If I let go of my suspicion, maybe I will be hurt and disappointed by people. It is fear that masquerades as the need to control, a fear that deprives us of the chance to be free."

In other words, fear is about the future and about what might happen, what the next moment could bring or how change will affect you. Change is the very essence of all life, but when it is resisted it brings uncertainty and doubt. If that uncertainty is resisted it brings fear. If it is embraced it brings security and fearlessness in the deeper acceptance that nothing can be held onto, as all things are constantly changing. Recently, my husband, Ed, asked a twenty-eight-year-old Buddhist monk what he found hardest to deal with in his life, and he replied "uncertainty." A few weeks later we were with a seventy-one-year-old woman who had few possessions and no home of her own. The same subject arose, about how life contains so much uncertainty. "I love the uncertainty!" she laughed. "It makes life so much more interesting."

The unknown can make you feel fearful, but only by entering into it can you reclaim your power. The contents of your own mind might appear scary but it is where your healing lies. For fear is like a mask covering up deeper issues, perhaps ones of grief or anger. Only when you go through the fear can you bring healing to what lies behind it. As Bruce Springsteen said in a *GQ* interview, "There's a world of love and there's a world of fear too, and it's standing right in front of you, and very often that fear feels a lot realer and certainly more urgent than the feeling of love … It's about walking through that world of fear so that you can live in a world of love."

Sit quietly.

Breathe into your heart, opening and softening.

Find your fear.

When your breathing is steady and you feel comfortable and re-laxed, then go and find your fear. Find where it is in your body, where it is in your past, where it is in your present, where it is in your future, where it is in your mind and your heart.

Do not hide from fear.

Get to know it. Feel it. Breathe into it. Every time it arises, see it, smell it, hear it, touch it, taste it. Then breathe and release.

Follow the fear.

Where does it come from? What does it want? Breathe and release.

Ask yourself questions.

How does fear affect you? What does it stop you from doing? What does it make you do? How often have you felt fear but not been able to identify what you are fearful of?

Name your fears.

Fear maintains control by being nameless, so find its source and give it a name. Define and name it. And breathe into it and release.

THE HEART'S REMISSION

Healing is a journey of trust, of discovering your inner strength, and it demands your total commitment. It is a gathering of your lost voices and forgotten selves, an embracing of those parts of your being that have been hidden and denied. As you heal you find that your lost voices have a song to sing, that your forgotten selves want to dance and laugh. You discover a deeper meaning, a more honest and self-empowered salvation.

The original interpretation of the word *"meaning"* was to recite, tell, intend, or wish. This suggests that without meaning, life is like a blank page—there is no story to tell and nothing to recite. But meaning also implies significance and purpose, without which there is no direction, no mission. And no story with no purpose equals no reason to be here. Meaninglessness can thus cause lethargy, depression, hopelessness, and illness. Finding meaning gives direction and motivation, a reason for being that stimulates passion, optimism, strength, and well-being.

This is seen in the word "*remission*," used to describe a period of recovery, when an illness or disease diminishes. A patient is described as being in remission when their symptoms abate. Yet the word can also be read as "re-mission," to re-find or become reconnected with your mission or purpose. In other words, disease can diminish when you reconnect with a deeper meaning or purpose in your life.

Remission also has another, lesser-known meaning, which is forgiveness. This implies that healing can occur through forgiving yourself by accepting your behaviour and releasing your guilt, or through accepting and forgiving another and letting go of blame. The power of such forgiveness is enormous.

Remission arises through a blend of responsibility and passivity. It is essential that you take responsibility for your own behaviour, actions, words, thoughts, and lifestyle. No one else can do this for you. Taking responsibility means acknowledging that healing comes from within. You can then work with others to find the best way to promote your health. This may involve taking medication or having surgery, but it can also involve meditation, psychotherapy, chiropractic treatments, or dance classes. The difference is that you are responding to your personal needs. To be responsible is to be able to respond: to listen to those lost voices and bring to life your forgotten selves.

Action also needs to be balanced by non-action—doing by being. Many of us have completely forgotten how to simply be present with whatever is happening. Children have this capacity to flow with each moment without holding on or trying to control. But, as we grow older, we cling to control and power; we stop being and start doing. Very often those who experience illness followed by a remission find that healing occurs by releasing control and allowing whatever is to be—a return to that childlike place of trust and present-moment discovery, where we stop being human doings and become more truly human beings.

This attitude toward simply being is one of letting go of resistance and entering into assurance—releasing the logic of what appears to be right and opening to intuition and inner feeling. It is surrendering the need to be in control. This is not the same as feeling you are a victim of fate, that you just have to suffer your lot. Rather it is recognizing the interdependence and intricate relationship between each and every aspect of your world. "Surrender means the decision to stop fighting the world and to start loving it instead," writes Marianne Williamson in *A Return to Love*. "It is a liberation from pain. But liberation isn't about breaking out of anything; it's a gentle melting into who we really are."

Your body needs to be appreciated. Your long-buried memories need to be tenderly embraced. Your past sins need to be forgiven. Every part of your being needs to be loved, and it needs to be loved by you. Without that love your body becomes discarded, unwanted; with that love you are embraced and connected. When you take away the judgment, the shame, and the embarrassment, you discover an inherent easefulness.

A caterpillar is beautiful, with all its textures and colours and shapes and hairs and legs; it is exquisite, perfect just as it is. So can we say it is more perfect when it becomes a butterfly? It is not possible to measure perfection. You do not have to look perfect to be beautiful; you do not have to be acceptable to others to be acceptable to yourself. Getting angry does not make you bad; doing something you are ashamed of does not make you beyond forgiveness.

FINDING FORGIVENESS

As we saw earlier, the word "remission" also means forgiveness. Through forgiveness you are able to confront those places within that are holding on to past trauma and to release the pain. This is not always easy. You may not feel ready to forgive—perhaps the wound is still too painful or the anger too strong. You may believe that you could never forgive because the act committed goes beyond the realms of mercy. You may think that forgiveness is a way of abdicating responsibility for what was done, or that it ignores the intensity of the emotions involved. But a lack of forgiveness keeps the guilt, hurt, and rage eating away inside you, creating a protective armour. It locks you into the past, limiting your ability to change.

A lack of forgiveness shuts you out of your heart, whereas forgiveness opens the door. It liberates the past, like floodgates being opened; there is a wave of released energy, and you are lighter, freer as a result. It releases you from both the story and your pain, Forgiveness is saying, "I care enough about myself not to want to keep hurting, to keep carrying this pain around."

In a television program on forgiveness, Bill related the story of his grandmother's brutal murder. He was justifiably distraught and had become quite depressed. However, he decided to get to know the murderer, Paula, by visiting her in prison so he could understand why this terrible thing had happened. A year later he was able to say that, "Forgiving Paula did more for me than it did for her." It freed him of his hate.

Such forgiveness does not mean forgetting. It does not rationalize or explain away; it does not erase what was done or dismiss its severity, for nothing can change what happened. But it does defuse the situation; it releases the emotional charge. When you forgive someone they no longer have any power over you. It removes the barriers, the walls constructed in defence and anger. Forgiving someone takes away all the potency. There is no more fear; they can no longer hurt.

However, an attachment to pain can create tremendous resistance to forgiveness, for when you forgive you are not only releasing the story but also all the excuses for your suffering. There is no longer anyone to blame and no reason for the pain. And it is much easier to blame someone else than to take responsibility for your own state of mind. By not forgiving you have the perfect excuse not to change, not to let go. So you hold on to being wounded, to the "poor me," to the victim. Yet by holding on, you are constantly re-creating the hurt.

Forgiving others completes the past so that you can move on; it lets the past rest. There is a spaciousness in which you can breathe and feel and let love come in. With it may come great grief, sadness, and even a sense of emptiness or loss. Let these feelings pour through you; do not deny them expression. Beneath the grief lie your love, compassion, and tenderheartedness.

As important as it is to forgive others, so you also need to forgive yourself. This does not mean absolving yourself of responsibility for your actions, nor does it deny guilt. It is simply recognizing your humanness and completely accepting your vulnerability. To forgive yourself for past deeds, past words, things you did or didn't do. To forgive yourself in the present each time you don't get it right. To say "I forgive myself" again and again.

This means accepting yourself just as you are, with all your weaknesses, mistakes, and helplessness. You have to strip naked emotionally and start from there: bringing forgiveness to every part of your being, into your pain, into your fear, into your illness, into your shame, forgiving your childhood, forgiving yourself for being abused, for thinking you deserved to be punished or hurt, for the way you have treated others, for the guilt, for all the mistakes you have made and the hopelessness you have felt. The more you forgive yourself the more you will be able to forgive others.

Forgiveness takes practise, commitment, and sincerity. It is something you may need to do every day, slowly softening resistance, opening the heart, letting the love in. It means being willing to look at whatever feelings arise as you delve deeper and to accept those feelings as they are, without judgment. But, eventually, forgiveness removes the walls, and you are free to dance and feel love again. It is the greatest gift you can give to yourself.

FORGIVENESS REVIEW: OPENING TO FORGIVENESS

Start by deciding who you want to focus on: yourself or another person. These instructions assume that you wish to forgive yourself.

If you want to direct your forgiveness to another person, simply alter the instructions accordingly. As you do this practise, different issues that need forgiving may arise spontaneously. Let them come but let them go without getting involved with the details.

Find a quiet and comfortable place to sit.

For a few minutes just watch the breath entering and leaving your body. Sink into the rhythm of the breath as your mind becomes quieter.

Focus on the heart space.

Focus your attention in the heart space in the centre of your chest. Watch your breathing from this place for a few moments. You can visualize yourself here or repeat your name, so you feel a sense of your own presence.

Bring forgiveness into this heart space.

When you feel ready, silently repeat the words, "I forgive myself, I forgive myself, I forgive myself for …" Let all the things that you forgive yourself for arise in your heart space.

Be gentle.

Let yourself go back in time, forgiving and releasing. Do not hold on to any one incident—forgive and let go and move on. Remember to keep breathing with a soft belly. Breathe into any pain or guilt or shame that arises and keep releasing; "I forgive myself, I forgive myself."

Stay with the practise.

Let each issue arise. See it without judgment, without attachment. Acknowledge it fully, and then bring forgiveness to it. Some things will be easier to forgive than others. Keep chipping away at the hard ones and in time they will soften and release.

Release yourself gently.

When you feel you have done as much as you can, take a deep breath and let it out. Watch your breath for a few minutes, feeling the forgiveness pouring through your being, washing through you and releasing you.

LOVING LOVE

Forgiveness arises out of love, for, ultimately, love is the healer. Enough time is spent focusing on difficulties and pain, and it needs to be balanced by dwelling in and experiencing the positive things. They are there. You need only look. You can look at rain and feel depressed, or you can see it watering the plants and feeding the rivers that in turn give you water to drink. Seeing this, you can thank the rain for nourishment. The choice is yours. *Bring love alive: think love, talk love, read love, act love, walk love, breathe love, sing love, touch love, eat love, and sleep love.*

In the moment of facing possible death many people's deepest and only desire before they die is to say "I love you" to their loved ones. This happened to me: when I thought I might die all I could think was that I would not be able to tell the people who I loved that I loved them. But you do not have to wait until you are dying to say this. Say "I love you" at least once a day—even once an hour—to yourself or to someone else. Don't just think it but say it out loud. Giving love a voice makes it come alive, brings warmth, gratitude, security, comfort, healing. If you can't talk, you can write love. Write to those you love and tell them how you feel. Write words of love to yourself. Write poems or songs of love. Fill your head with words of love.

Touch with love. Let love shine through you as you reach out a hand to hold, caress, and soothe. Without touch babies can die and adults go insane. Touch everything with love, treating all things with respect. Walk with love, feeling the beauty of your body as it moves, feeling the love that the breath, bones, muscles, blood, nerves, organs, joints, and even the toes have for you, as they support and care for you throughout your day. Remember: your body loves you!

PART TWO
YOUR BODYMIND REVEALED

SIX

FROM YOUR HEAD
TO YOUR TOES

The body operates as a whole, each part connected to the other, communication flowing throughout. A pain in a toe may emanate from a pain in the back; a pain in the shoulder may be due to a problem in the pelvis. To understand each part we need to recognize its relationship to every other part. For instance, a difficulty with the knees is related to the function of the knees as well as to that of the thighs, the legs as a whole, the pelvis and back, even the neck, as well as the functions of standing or moving.

THE OVERALL PICTURE

The actual shape of your body can say a great deal about you. Although much of this may be inherited, there are characteristics that accompany specific shapes and postures. Just like a woodsman can read the history of a tree, a good bodymind therapist can read a person's life history through the formation and shape of the body structure, the places that are being held, its ability to move freely or where it is constricted, and the areas of tension.

Your body is like a walking autobiography, muscle and flesh formations reflecting your experiences, injuries, worries, and attitudes. Whether you have a timid posture, one that is bowed over and constricted, or one that is standing square and defensive, all are learned early in life and become built into your very structure.

Try taking a good long look in the mirror—naked! Are you standing straight and upright, or are you bent over or lopsided? If so, were you taught not to be straight with people? How does it feel to straighten up? Which side of your body is most dominant? Is your head held high or slightly to one side, as if to avoid a confrontation? Can you meet the world head on? What happens when you move your neck? Are you stiff and unbending or do you move with fluidity and ease? Do your joints move freely? Look at the way you hold your muscles or joints. Are they locked into position, holding back your feelings? What do you need to do to release them?

Is the top half of your body bigger or smaller than the bottom half? The top half of the body is your more sociable and personal side while the bottom half deals with practical and worldly issues. A strong or heavy top with thin or weak legs tends to indicate someone who is very sociable and friendly, self-confident, and extroverted, but who may be somewhat ungrounded, unsure of dealing with physical or worldly issues. Big or strong legs combined with a small or weak top can indicate someone who is very grounded and practical, sometimes too much so, with less energy going into communication or self-confidence; they are likely to lack playfulness and spontaneity.

Take note of where you have most physical difficulties and see how this part relates to the rest of you. Is it smaller and less energetic? Is it more rigid or tense? Is it more over-developed and puffed up?

If your body is aching, what is it aching for? To be held? To be comforted? If your body wants to move, where does it want to go? Follow the movement and see what happens. Where are the areas that hurt or don't function properly? How do they feel inside? Try drawing a picture of yourself, painting, or writing what your body is feeling.

Look carefully but without judgment—simply observe, get to know and make friends with your own body.

WHOLE BODY REVIEW

This is a great way to get to know your body better and to make friends with yourself. Remember—by getting to know your body you are also getting to know your mind!

Stand naked in front of a mirror.
You are looking at how your mind and emotions have formed your body.

Notice how balanced your body is.
Is one side bigger than the other? Is one half bigger or fleshier than the other?

Try to improve your posture.
If you can correct your posture, such as standing straight where before you were lopsided, does it make you feel different?

Continue your review.
Can you see where you are lacking vitality or if there are areas that seem stiff and unlived in? Can you see where you need to bring more love and acceptance?

Stick with the process.
Keep doing this until you begin to feel more comfortable and at ease with yourself.

THE BODY BEAUTIFUL
The Head

Welcome to Head Office. Here you receive input from all your senses and transmit that information throughout your body, while also maintaining hormone levels, metabolism, nerve functioning, breathing, communication, and just about every other function of the bodymind. The head is your centre of awareness, insight, intelligence, and perception. It forms a pivotal axis between heaven and earth, containing both your highest spiritual awareness and your more earthly individual self. Such a polarity can, if the opposites pull in opposite directions, create tension.

Notice how your head sits on your neck: Does it pull to one side? Does it tilt up and back or face downwards? Do you lead with your chin, as if pushing forward?

It is natural to think of your head as the centre of your being, while the body is there to provide a vehicle for the head and to give some pleasurable diversion. Your body gets covered with clothes and put out of sight, while the head is left open for communication and contact. But the body contains your heart and your deepest feelings. If it is ignored, then the result is a separation between head and heart, between thoughts and feelings. Below the neck becomes private and hidden; it is where you keep those feelings you want to remain secret. The body, therefore, contains all the repressed issues that are too unpleasant to be shown in public, while the head shows the stress of separation from the heart.

There are two areas of consideration: the skull or outer head, and the brain and central nervous system on the inside.

BODYMIND DIALOGUE: THE HEAD

The skull is the container for the meeting of the spiritual and the individual, or the abstract and the relative. A **crack or accident to the skull** can indicate a great longing to expand and grow from within that is being restricted by external circumstances, like a shell breaking to let a new being emerge. Or it may be due to a conflict between the physical reality and responsibilities of the world, and a deeper spiritual desire or motivation.

- Do you feel that your inner urges for growth are being blocked?
- Do you have creative urges that are not being expressed or that do not have an outlet?
- Is your desire to grow spiritually being thwarted?

Your brain maintains your entire physiological system through the hormones and nervous system. It is also where all your thoughts and feelings are translated into physical responses, so **damage to the brain** affects not just your physical body but also your whole expression. This is the most complex and extraordinary part of your being, the least understood and yet the part responsible for everything. Is the brain the mind? Is the mind separate? We can only guess. But within this area is the capacity to grow, from deepening insight to full enlightenment.

See also: Headaches, Mental Illness, Sinus Problems, etc.

The Face

The part of you that meets and greets the world first and by which you are judged, your face is representative of your innermost being. A huge amount of money is spent on making the face look attractive. Yet no amount of makeup can hide your every emotion, feeling, and thought—issues of self-confidence, self-dislike, guilt, shame, anger, fear, joy, suspicion, trust, hurt, jealousy, forgiveness, shock, repulsion, whether you are closed or open, trustworthy or sly, happy or sad. All of these will be seen in your expression or muscle formation, through skin eruptions, irritations, or disorders, and by your skin colour.

Your face also refers to your image or identity, so when you "lose face" it is a loss of pride or ego. If you have courage and inner strength then you can "face up" to things. Calling someone "two faced" implies that this person never reveals their true face, only a series of masks.

You may even have two faces: the one you show the world and the one you keep for yourself. But if you habitually hide behind a mask, then your facial muscles will become tense and distorted. Remember as a child being told not to make an ugly face in case the wind changed and then your expression would be locked forever in that position? Well if you make an ugly face too often then the wind may not change, but your muscles will become set in that position. The more you frown the more the muscles will take on that furrowed look; the more you smile the more your face will appear at ease.

Damage to the face may indicate a breaking of the mask that you show to the world, so the real you can be seen; or a deep conflict with the face you have been presenting to the world and a longing to be more honest.

- Does your face express the real you?
- Or are you putting on a mask, even a whole series of masks?
- Is the real you inside trying to emerge?

See also: Skin, Eyes, Nose, Mouth, etc.

The Neck

The neck is a two-way communicator, both physically and emotionally. Life-sustaining food, water, and air are taken in and swallowed, as is input from other people and the world. At the same time, emotions, feelings, and thoughts are expressed outwardly through the voice and lips. In this way, the neck forms a bridge between thoughts and feelings, between the mind and the heart, as well as between the mind and the physical body. It is, therefore, a natural place for a bodymind split, where one part of your nature becomes isolated from the rest: the more energy that is put in one area, the less tends to be put in the other. For instance, academics tend to be less physically active, while athletes tend to be less studious.

BODYMIND DIALOGUE: THE NECK
A mind/body split can create tension or even rigidity in the neck.

- What constriction does your neck need to be released from?
- Do you need to listen to your feelings?
- Do you need to speak your heart?

- Or do you need to put less energy into thinking and more into physical exercise?

Problems in the neck may indicate a rejection of the body, perhaps due to past abuse or because of a disability: there may be a lack of energy moving through the neck into the body, a lack of relationship with who you are as a physical being.

- Do you feel your body as vibrant and energetic?
- Or does it feel like a stranger, unfamiliar, even unknown, something you drag around with you?

The neck holds the head upright so you can look forward, maintaining dignity and courage. A **drooping head** implies a hopeless, giving-up attitude, an inability to face what lies ahead. The neck also allows the head to move so you can see on all sides, embracing a larger reality than just the one in front of you. This implies an openness of mind and acceptance of others' views. **Stiffness** indicates resistance, usually to other ways of thinking; it is as if you are wearing blinders and cannot turn your head to see from the sides.

- Can you only see your own point of view?
- Are you feeling prejudiced or resistant toward someone?
- Are you becoming narrow-minded in your attitudes?
- Or is someone being a "pain in the neck," perhaps by asking too much of you?

A stiff neck may also indicate an inability to make a decision: literally not knowing which way to turn. Such stiffness limits the amount of feeling and communication passing between the mind and body. If you have a stiff or painful neck, it may also be due to TMS (tension myositis syndrome) and a cramping of the muscles, in which case see the section on back pain, page 118.

The neck contains your voice box, so it is intimately connected to your mode of expression, with a stiff neck limiting the amount of feeling that can be expressed from within.

- Are you holding back your feelings?
- Are your feelings too strong to express?
- When you cannot move your neck freely, this implies stubbornness and rigidity. What is needed to ease your neck?
- Is something or someone emotionally strangling you?

See also: Respiration, Digestion

The Shoulders

Here you carry the weight of your world, of your relatives, of the work you are doing. Responsibility is a word that weighs heavily here, as do duty, mortgage payments, sick children, and demanding mothers-in-law. Problems with the shoulders may also indicate avoidance of your own issues: being so busy dealing with your obligations to others that you have little time for yourself.

This area of the body is your doing centre. From your shoulders, your doing and creative energy flows down your arms and your hands, where it emerges in what you do in the world. This applies to the work you do as well as the way you live your life—what you do with your time, do with your relationships, or do with your feelings. The shoulders get **tense and rigid** when you are not expressing your real needs, when you are doing something you would rather not be doing, when you feel you have too much to do, or when you feel scared of reaching out and want to pull back into the safety of doing nothing.

If you are doing something that does not interest you while a deeper longing stays locked inside, then your shoulders may well be holding that repressed yearning. Can you find expression for what you really want to do? Tension restricts the flow of energy and feeling. In the process of putting others' needs first, your own activity may be stifled. The shoulders are where that "doing energy" becomes blocked. See what small changes you can make in order to start releasing any blocked doing energy.

The muscles correspond to mental energy, so you manifest that energy as knotted and tight shoulder muscles, for they contain so many burdens and longings. The heart energy comes up to the shoulders and out to manifest in your arms, in hugging and touching, caring and sharing. It should be a smooth expression, but often there are blocks along the way, causing pain and stiffness—if you are hugging the wrong person, or feel your advances are being rejected, or you are fearful of intimacy. This can manifest in a **frozen shoulder**, an indication of where emotional coldness is affecting you, either coming from another to you, or from you toward someone else.

Shoulders get **raised** in fear and anxiety. If this continues over a period of time the shoulder muscles begin to lock into that position. As the posture develops, so does the attitude that goes with it. **Hunched shoulders** are overwhelmed by the burden of life's problems. They also indicate a desire to protect the heart or chest by closing in. **Shoulders that are pulled back**, pushing the chest outward, indicate false strength, often hiding feelings of fear or inadequacy with a false bravado. Pulling the shoulders back is also a way of holding back feelings, especially ones that yearn to reach out to touch and caress.

BODYMIND DIALOGUE: THE SHOULDERS

Painful shoulders may mean that you are carrying too much on your own.

- Do you really want to say to other people, "Please look after me, please give me some caring and nurturing"?
- Have you been carrying other people's problems for too long?
- Is there something or someone you need to put down?

Pain, stiffness, and tension in the shoulders indicate a resistance, perhaps to the responsibilities you feel you must maintain, or the pressure that is put on you to perform.

Is it possible for you to offload some of your responsibility, so you don't have to do all the weightlifting?

The Arms

Arms are for action and expression. They enable you to hug or push away, to touch and caress, to show love or anger, to express your needs, to open your heart or close off in defence. Open arms are saying, "Here is my heart, come and share it." They are an expression of fearlessness and acceptance.

When you fold your arms, you are closing them across the heart, putting a protective barrier between yourself and others. The message is clear: "Stay away, keep your distance, intimacy not appreciated." There is nothing as off-putting as folded arms; they are a more effective "No Entry" sign than any words could be! Each time you notice yourself crossing your arms, try opening them instead and watch how it feels. Try spending time each day with your arms open and relaxed.

Some years ago, Ed and I were at a meeting with our publishers. They owed us some money, and we were there to collect it. However, as we sat around the table I noticed that everyone, including the two of us, had our arms crossed. I knew we would never get our money that way. So I opened my arms and, as I talked, I reached across and touched the shoulder of the man next to me. A few minutes later he opened his arms and slowly everyone began to relax and soften. And yes, we got our money!

Arms enable you to create and communicate, to bring your ideas and words to life. The shoulders extend down into the arms, extending the doing energy into action and into the world. Arms manifest all your inner desires and longings.

- Are you doing what you want to do?
- Are you doing something you should not be doing?
- Are you extending yourself too far, or holding yourself back?

Arms are also weapons. You can use them to attack, deny, reject, or repel. You can push away or you can pull close; you can hold and embrace. Is there something or someone you need to let go of? Arms lift, carry, transport, and bear, but sometimes the load gets too heavy and they ache or feel sore. Are you carrying too much?

BODYMIND DIALOGUE: THE ARMS

The arms express the energy coming from the heart out to the world through hugging, touching, sharing, and caressing. So problems in the arms may point to issues or conflicts having to do with intimacy and the expression of feeling.

- Are you holding back your feelings for fear of their acceptance?
- Can you open your arms to embrace others and share your love?
- Watch your body language when you cross your arms and be aware of what you are non-verbally saying.
- Notice the relationship of fear and love to closed and open arms.
- Notice this in others when you are talking with them.
- Try opening your arms and watch how it changes your attitude, even if you are in a difficult situation.

Weak or tired arms imply an inability to let feelings or energy flow outward. There may be a sense of being unable to take control or make decisions, an inability to grasp hold of life or a timidity of expressing real feelings. It may also show an inability to express your needs.

- Do you feel it is wrong to reach out for what you want or need, whether emotionally or physically?

Stiff or painful arms indicate a resistance to activity or expression.

- What are you holding back from sharing?
- What feelings are locked in your arms?

A **bruised arm** indicates that you are hitting some form of resistance, or you are feeling beaten up by someone or something. A **broken arm** indicates a deep level of conflict with your activity.

- What does the broken arm stop you from doing?
- What does it enable you to do?
- Does it stop you from hugging someone?
- Does it stop you from going to work?
- Does it stop you from being the caregiver?

See also: Bones, Muscles

The Elbows

Joints give movement and flexibility. If you did not have flexibility in the middle of your arms, you could not reach your mouth in order to eat, you could not hold someone close, you could not play the violin, or express yourself when you talk. Your elbows enable you to open your arms to embrace your world. Elbows give grace to your movement but they can also be used as a weapon, as when you elbow someone out of the way. Or perhaps you are being elbowed out of the way by someone else?

BODYMIND DIALOGUE: THE ELBOWS

The elbows enable you to respond with energy and vigour (as in "elbow grease") but can also express conflict about what you are doing.

- Do you feel capable or competent enough?
- Are you asserting yourself too much?
- Are you becoming too inflexible in your attitude?
- Are you fearful of expressing your heart energy?

Tennis elbow is an inflammation of the joint, implying that something is making you irritated, hot, and angry about what you are doing.

- Are you feeling resentful that you are working harder than someone else?
- Is there a fear of opening to the future, embracing that which is ahead of you?

The Wrists

The wrists connect thought with the impulse for activity. **Stiff or painful wrists** limit a whole range of activities—driving a car, eating, writing, or expressing your feelings.

BODYMIND DIALOGUE: THE WRISTS

If your wrist hurts, there is an activity you are resisting, avoiding, wishing you were not doing, or perhaps feel restricted from doing. A **sprained wrist** implies a mental conflict with your activity.

- Do you feel pressured, or under strain?
- Do you feel unable to do what is being asked of you?
- Are you being pulled in different directions?

A **broken wrist** indicates a very deep level of conflict over what you are doing, or what is being done to you.

- What is broken inside you?
- How does your broken wrist affect your activity?
- Do you want to stop what you are doing?
- Are you being stopped?

See also: Joints

The Hands

Children develop their mental capacities by working with their hands. In adults, when brain activity diminishes, as with a stroke, so does dexterity. The hands are where you create, so they represent all the ways you do things and all the feelings you have about what you are doing.

We touch each other with our hands. Touching is fundamental to life. Without touch we feel unwanted and insecure; we may even stop developing. In one study, baby monkeys, separated from their mothers by a sheet of glass so they could see them, hear them, and even smell them, but could not touch them, had retarded growth.

You are connected through touch. You bring healing through touch, releasing loneliness and pain. Are you longing to touch or be touched? Conflict in your hands may be showing that you want to reach out and touch but fear or insecurity is holding you back.

Stiff hands indicate a stiff or resistant attitude toward your activity or expression of feelings. **Painful hands** imply that what you are doing is causing discomfort, or something being done is hurting you. Is someone cramping your style? **Arthritic joint pain** in the hands often implies an overly critical attitude about what you are doing, or what is being done to you. Conflict arises because your nature is to reach outward, but the energy is turning in on itself.

Excessively **sweaty hands** indicate that you are feeling nervous, anxious, even scared, about what you are doing. Very **cold hands** may show that you are withdrawing feelings from your activity—perhaps withdrawing love or emotional involvement—or are feeling fearful of participating or being involved.

BODYMIND DIALOGUE: THE HANDS

The hands go ahead of you to meet the world. They symbolize how you are handling life or are being handled. They are the most outward expression of the heart energy, where you touch, caress, show love, or form a fist and express dislike.

- Are you touching the right person? In the right way?
- Do you really want to punch someone?
- Are you feeling resentful at giving someone else a hand and then not getting the help you need?

Hands are "wrung in anguish," "gripped in desperation," or "clenched in anger," perhaps enacting the movement you would like to make toward someone. You can "let things slip through your hands" or you can grasp them, perhaps too tightly.

- Are you fearful of letting go?
- Are you holding on to someone too tight for fear they will leave?
- How strong a grasp do you have on your world?

The Fingers

The fingers show you where you are being insensitive to subtler or smaller issues. The thumb has to do with control and power, as well as anxiety and fear. The index finger is pointed when you blame someone else, perhaps without recognizing your own involvement.

BODYMIND DIALOGUE: THE FINGERS

Fingers, which are extensions of your hands, stretch out into the world and often get damaged before other parts of your body.

- Are you extending too far?
- Are you reaching out inappropriately?
- Are you moving too quickly and in the process not being aware of the details along the way?

If the fingers are becoming **bent or crooked**, follow that movement and see where it wants to go.

- What is the movement trying to tell you?
- Does it make a fist and, if so, does the fist want to hit out at someone or something?
- Do the fingers point away, as if reaching out to new areas of experience?
- Are they going off in different directions, as if unity of purpose has been lost?

The Back

When animals evolved from being on all fours to standing up, all the weight of the upper half of the body, no longer supported by the arms and the hands, came to rest on the lower back and pelvis. Try bending forward at the waist and then slowly lift yourself back up. In this movement you are becoming a human. The spine is the pillar of your being, giving you support and strength, uprightness and dignity. It contains the central nervous system and the central blood supply, and therefore your every thought, feeling, experience, response, and impression is registered here. Yet at any one time upward of five million people are disabled from chronic back pain in the United States alone, while vast sums of money are spent each year on medical treatment and lost productivity resulting from back trouble. Many cases of back pain begin with an injury or weightlifting problem, but, if you look carefully, you will also find psycho/emotional issues that have caused tension, weakness, or contraction, prior to the injury.

Upper, Middle, and Lower Back

Issues of survival are connected to the back: the responsibility of earning a living, carrying your own weight, being the "backbone" of the family, or standing on your own. Thoughts like "I'm not being supported" or "I'm being let down" can translate into back pain or weakness. You can stand up for yourself and walk tall, or become bowed and bent over by the weight of your burdens. Is there someone or something putting pressure on you? Do you feel overloaded?

BODYMIND DIALOGUE: UPPER, MIDDLE, AND LOWER BACK

The **upper back** is the reverse side from the heart. While the front side looks all nice and friendly, the back is where repressed anger, rage, resentment, feelings of guilt, shame, or fear get put. Even people get put here—the memories or feelings to do with someone you want to push away, deny, or ignore. Are you turning your back on someone or something?

The upper back is connected with expression through activity—energy moves up from the heart to the shoulders and down the arms—and with any obstacles to that expression. Issues of fulfillment, lost dreams, or resentful compromise may be found here.

- Are you compromising so much that you have become "spineless" or powerless? Unexpressed feelings can contort the muscles or bones. Tight muscles may be loaded with rage or longing. Do you feel as if you have your back against the wall?
- Are you up against difficulties?

Like the pivot of a seesaw, the **middle back** holds the balance in the centre of the body. It allows you to bend and move in different directions, representing your ability to be psycho/emotionally flexible. Difficulties here will reflect an inner stiffness or holding on due to a fear or inability to move with events.

- Where are you feeling stiff or rigid in yourself? This area is about decision-making. Problems here can indicate that you are locked in indecision, caught between your own needs and demands from others.
- Do you want to assert yourself more and make your needs known? Resentment is also found in the middle back. How many times have you "bent over backward" to help someone, or "put your back into something," only to find that when you need help it isn't there?
- Do you tend to let people walk all over you?

The middle back corresponds to the solar plexus and the third chakra. This is an area of power. You can use that power to dominate and control, or you can use it to enhance your own sense of self, your inner confidence. Disharmony here can indicate power issues or weakness, often activated in the process of discovering your place in the world. The lure and promise of power are extremely seductive; once tasted it is hard to say no. However, the energy of this area is also closely related to corruption and manipulation.

The **lower back** expresses all the weight and responsibility of being human. It supports the weight from above, just as you carry the weight of responsibility of your world. If there is no one to help with the load, no sense of being supported, this part of the back may give way.

- Have you tried asking for help?
- Is someone being a "pain in the back" because they are causing you more work when you really need their help?
- This part of your back keeps you upright. If it is hurting, do you feel let down in some way? When you stand up straight, the abdomen is exposed and unprotected, so there may be a tendency to bend over to protect this delicate area. Are you feeling particularly vulnerable?
- Do you want to curl up and hide?

This area also has to do with survival, security, and self-support. If you are feeling insecure—perhaps unable to meet other people's expectations—then the pressure may be felt in the lower back.

- Do you doubt your ability to support yourself?
- Are you feeling isolated?
- Are you trying to do too much? As the nerves that flow down the legs issue from the lower spine, pressure here can create pain or numbing sensations in the feet and legs, affecting your movement forward.

Back Pain

Most of us believe that a painful back is due to damaged structural issues, such as a herniated disk. Although this may be the case, enough research shows that it often is not. For instance, the *New England Journal of Medicine* reported a study showing that the vast majority of people with healthy, pain-free backs had some form of structural defect, such as a herniated disk, while many of those with chronic back pain showed no abnormalities at all. In other words, a structural defect is not necessarily a cause for concern, and even if an injury has occurred the back will usually heal quite quickly.

"Most people with back pain see several doctors and are told to rest, take medicine, or use a variety of devices to 'protect' their backs," writes Dr. Christiane Northrup. "The bad back industry is now so huge that entire businesses are devoted to selling a variety of chairs, furnishings, and other devices designed to help you protect your back. Surgery is often recommended, as well. And far too often, this can make the problem worse, if the underlying cause is not addressed."

It would appear that most cases of chronic back pain are actually caused not by spinal problems, but by muscle tension and spasm. This is not to be dismissed: it is extremely painful. Such muscle tension is caused by emotional tension, and the deeper that emotional tension is explored the more the story behind the pain is revealed. It may be a story of anger, fear, exhaustion, of trying to prove something to someone, of denial, of a lack of forgiveness—whatever it is, it is in the back because it is well hidden there. But it also hurts.

While I was revising this book my own back was in deep pain and I had sciatica for about a year caused by intense muscle spasm. It did not surprise me. In the previous five years we had moved four times, the last move being from England back to the United States. My stepfather had become senile and had been in a nursing home for a year before he died, so one of those moves had been to live nearby and support my mother. A family member had had a nervous breakdown. We had been traveling a huge amount for work, and I was exhausted. Too many boxes, too many emotional dramas. I needed to just be still, so my back made sure I was.

As I found my ground and released deep layers of emotional stress, the muscles in my back relaxed. In the healing process I had numerous deep-tissue-massage treatments and unearthed emotional conflicts with family members, fears of abandonment, issues of vulnerability and surrender, and places of deep anger. Just as tense muscles are holding back emotional tension, so those emotions may be "re-experienced" when the muscle tension is released.

This muscle tension syndrome was first recognized and named **tension myositis syndrome**, or TMS, by Dr. John Sarno. He recognized how tense muscles and emotions reflect each other: just as you clench your jaw to hold back tears, so you tighten stomach, back, or buttock muscles to hold in or resist other emotions. This is a prime example of the body speaking your mind as stress finds an expression through muscle stress, and it can gather unnoticed for some time—even years—before it is felt physically. This is especially the case with *repressed* emotional tension. If you cannot release, or do not even acknowledge that such tension is there, then it has to find a voice through your body.

Research has shown that people with chronic back pain unconsciously tighten back muscles when emotionally upset. When muscles remain tense for long enough—as when different emotional issues have piled up enough—they become very painful. When you add the tension created by the pain and the fear of what might be happening then you soon get caught in a cycle of pain.

"When we are under psychological stress, our muscles become tense," write Drs. Siegel, Urdang, and Johnson in *Back Sense*. "Eventually this tension leads either to muscle spasms which are intensely painful, or to dull aches. When such back pain persists … we may become frustrated or angry. These feelings further tighten the muscles, lead to more pain, and the cycle is off and running."

Issues can easily build and gather over the years without your conscious awareness. For instance, if you experience any form of psycho/emotional **shock** or **post-traumatic stress**, then it tends to get deposited in the spine. This may not affect you at all. But if you then have another experience that is equally traumatic or difficult, the energy will go to the same place in your spine and recovery may be harder. Eventually, it may only be a small incident that triggers your back to collapse. As painful or difficult experiences gather, they affect the muscles and weaken the energy flow, eventually causing pain. This pain is a direct response to the psycho/emotional pain being held in your unconscious.

Healing TMS comes through recognizing the role emotional stress is playing, particularly anger and fear; finding ways to release and heal it; deep relaxation of the muscle tension; and resuming physical activity, such as walking, so as to loosen and release the muscles.

See also: Pain, Sciatica

BODYMIND DIALOGUE: BACK PAIN

As the back is out of reach and out of sight, so this is the perfect place for hidden or repressed emotions or issues that you don't want to deal with, because if you can't see them, how can anyone else? Most especially, there may be layers of unconscious rage being held in the muscles of your back.

- Is there something you have pushed away that you need to acknowledge and accept?
- Are you "pushing back" your feelings, particularly rage, grief, or guilt?
- You talk about having a "bad" back, as if it has done something wrong, but is it the back that is bad or the stuff you have dumped there?
- What would it have to do to be a "good" back?
- Is something "holding you back" from moving forward?

If you are suffering from any kind of back difficulties, ask yourself these questions:

- Are you trying to do, or having to do everything yourself without being able to ask for help?
- Do you feel unsupported or let down by somebody?

- Are you fearful of what lies ahead in the imminent future?
- Is your inflexible spine indicating an inner, emotional stiffness?
- What psycho/emotional stress is manifesting as stress in your back?

Through the spine and central nervous system every part of the body is connected and networked. It is the backbone that holds the skeleton together. Spinal issues are therefore connected to central issues that affect every part of your life. Muscular back problems, such as **stiffness**, show resistance and inner struggle. Perhaps there is a resistance to what is coming next in life, or you feel you cannot continue doing everything without more support. If it is a **posture** problem, then you need to look at your standing in the world.

- Are you standing upright, or are you bent over?
- Do you need to straighten your life?
- Do you feel weighed down by other people's psychological or emotional burdens?

A **slipped or herniated disk** primarily has to do with feeling pressured, as the weight of the spine puts pressure on the jelly-like substance around the disk and causes it to **prolapse**. Disks are like shock absorbers. With inappropriate pressure they get squeezed out of line.

- Do you feel pressured to live up to someone's expectations?
- Are you putting undue pressure on yourself, perhaps trying to keep yourself strong and upright, while not showing your real feelings?
- Is the weight of responsibility too much to bear?
- Do you feel unsupported?

A **broken back** indicates a deep split, a deep conflict with your purpose or place in life, a tremendous inner conflict that undermines your ability to carry on.

- Are you trying to go in two different directions at once?

- Do you feel unsupported, alone, even abandoned?
- Do you feel unable to stand up for yourself?
- What burden was so great that it finally broke your back? What does a broken back enable you to do, or not do?

See also: Bones, Muscles, Nerves, Pain

The Buttocks

Although seemingly soft and spongy, the buttock or gluteal muscles are often the most clenched and tense muscles in the body, for it is here that you can hide any tension and nervousness you may be feeling by literally sitting on it. Although that tension is hidden from view, its effect will be felt throughout the body. Consistently tight gluteals will throw off your posture causing spinal distortion and backache, and they can affect the functioning of your bowels, leading to constipation or irritable bowel syndrome. Deep issues of power and control also found here.

BODYMIND DIALOGUE: THE BUTTOCKS

Just for a moment, right now, check the muscles in your backside. Are they relaxed? Or are they clenched tight? If so, consciously relax them and notice the difference in your attitude.

- What are you sitting on, repressing, or holding down?
- What energy is being held in your backside?
- Are you sitting on feelings of insecurity?
- Are you sitting on a need for support and comfort?

The buttocks area also has to do with elimination and release. The experience of being potty-trained as a child can have a marked effect on the rest of your life, especially on your ability to feel relaxed and spontaneous as opposed to tight and constrained. For small children the only area of control they have is with food, either by refusing to eat or refusing to use the potty. Control and power issues are therefore often held here.

- Are you fearful of spontaneity, of letting go?
- Do you need to hold the power and be in control?
- Tension here may be related to your parents and their expectations. Do you feel you have to do what your parents want?
- Do your parents interfere with your decision making?
- Are your parents a "pain in the butt"?

This area is also related to issues of sexuality and intimacy, and fears or tensions that can hold these muscles tight. Here, also, are issues related to your sense of being grounded and safe in the world, supported, and secure.

See also: Muscles, Constipation

The Chest

In your chest are all your life-giving organs—your heart, lungs, liver, and stomach—making this central part of your body the most vital. (For Breasts, see Chapter 15.) The chest represents your public image, strong and powerful, or weak and retracted. It is where you point when talking about yourself, the place you most commonly refer to as "I" or "me." You don't point to your head or belly and say this is me; you point to your heart.

The heart is the feeling centre of your being; here are found the depths of your passion, love, grief, and forgiveness. When you feel love, it is in the heart not the head. Difficulties in the chest tend to indicate issues to do with your feelings toward yourself, such as deep issues of self-worth or self-centeredness.

A **puffed-up chest**, which is pushed out to make it look bigger and more powerful than it really is, often hides a deeper doubt or insecurity, as seen in the military chest. The military are taught to lift their shoulders back and push their chests out in a posture of false bravado, like a bird puffing up his feathers to impress his mate. This puffed-up chest creates an image of strength and power but is often just a protective armour hiding an inner vulnerability.

A **weak or concave chest** indicates a lack of self-identity, as if you have not really found yourself yet. The "I" inside is still unformed. There may be an emotional timidity, a shyness of expression and need for reassurance. This posture indicates a depressed, sad, or helpless attitude, which can be uplifted by deep breathing. The breath is not only vital to life but also for releasing tension and letting go of inner stress. When you breathe deeply, it opens the chest, and you can open your heart without fear.

BODYMIND DIALOGUE: THE CHEST
You can test these ideas for yourself:

- Experience the body language of the shoulders and chest by letting your shoulders droop and round over your chest. Watch how your feelings change, how you feel sadness, depression, or hopelessness in this posture.
- Now move your shoulders back and push out your chest like a puffed-up bird and see how this brings up feelings of bravado and valour.
- Now let your shoulders relax; keep them open and just breathe into the centre of your chest for a few moments, feeling your heart opening with each in-breath. Notice how this brings feelings of peace and easefulness and even love.

The Ribcage
The ribs surround and protect the organs in the chest, so they are like your sentinels, guarding your inner being. If you have **bruised or broken ribs**, you need to ask yourself if you have "let your guard down" and allowed someone to get closer than you would prefer, or perhaps you are feeling vulnerable or exposed. At the base of the sternum (breastbone) is a tender place of sadness that connects you to your emotional heart.

BODYMIND DIALOGUE: THE RIBCAGE
The ribs have to do with boundaries and limitations.

- Are you clear about your boundaries, about how far you want to go, and how much you can give?
- Do you try to please everyone and fail to look after yourself in the process, thus going beyond your capabilities?
- Do you need to be more protective with your feelings so you are not abused or misused?

The Diaphragm

A large flat muscle in the chest, positioned below the lungs, the diaphragm is essential for the breathing process. It enables you to breathe in deeply and take life into yourself and, in releasing that breath, to let go of tension or stress. A stiff diaphragm that causes **shallow or restricted breathing**, creates a block between the upper realms of thought and mental activity, and the lower realms of emotion, intuition, and sexual energy.

Difficulties here indicate a resistance or fear of sharing your deepest feelings. By drawing a line here, you can keep your more intimate personal issues separate from the world. Control and power issues are also focused here, especially control over others. Deep belly breathing relaxes the diaphragm, relinquishes the need for control, and releases any feelings that are being held back.

The Abdomen

Within this area are your intestines, kidneys, and reproductive organs, covered by a large sheath of muscle stretching from the ribs to the pubic bone that protects the front of the body. This is a major feeling centre, so **tightly held abdominal muscles** show a sense of vulnerability or fear of intimacy; they are a way of warding anyone off who may be getting too close. They indicate a fear of feeling, for the gut is a centre of emotions. By pulling in the muscles you are able to hold back the feelings that lie behind them. Conversely, **loose and soft abdominal muscles** imply a lack of uprightness and dignity, an inner dissatisfaction and yearning, or a lack of care or self-respect. There is a sloppy letting-go, a "who cares" attitude that often masks a deeper unhappiness or lack of satisfaction, or a real longing to be cared for.

In the middle of this is the **solar plexus**. This area balances the two sides of your nature—the introvert and the extrovert—seen in the upper and lower parts of your body. The chest and upper part is more focused on the "I" and personal issues, while the pelvis and lower part reflect social and sharing issues (such as sex and birth).

Within this solar plexus area there is great power. The Chinese refer to a point approximately one to two inches below your navel as the centre of chi, or life force, and call it the *hara*. By focusing your awareness at this point you are able to tap into a tremendous resource of energy. This power source is not about having power over others, but it connects you to the core of your own personal power or inner strength. Practitioners of the martial arts, such as karate or aikido, find strength and focus by concentrating their awareness in this area. If the hara is strong and balanced, you cannot be pushed over.

ABDOMEN REVIEW

Take a few moments now to get in touch with your hara.

Stand upright.
Keep your feet a few inches apart, arms by your sides. Take a deep breath and let it go.

Tune in to the hara.
Bring your attention to about one inch below your navel. As you breathe in, imagine you are breathing into this area. You will need to take long, deep breaths. Let your belly muscles soften and your abdomen expand with each breath.

Watch how you feel.
Watch the growing sensation of quiet strength and inner harmony.

Stay with the practise.
Continue your deep breathing for a few more minutes.

The Pelvis and Hips

Giving you balance and stability, the pelvis forms a pivot between the upper and lower halves of your body, balancing the realm of action and creation above with the world of direction and movement below. Within this area an enormous amount of activity takes place. Here, you make love, give birth, digest food, and eliminate that which you've finished with—all actions connected to security, survival, communication, and relationship.

The pelvis forms the beginning of the moving energy that goes from the hips down the legs and into the feet. Whereas the feet represent that moving energy in the world, the hips represent your feelings about the movement you are taking or are about to take within yourself. Fear of this movement, such as how you may survive on your own after the loss of a loved one, concerns about having to move home, perhaps a fear that there is nothing to move toward, or a fear of where you are going, may show itself in this area. The hips are one of the most common places for the elderly to break—this age group is also the most likely to feel fearful of the immediate future.

As the hips are the centre of movement, they also symbolize your ability to let go of the past and enter into new areas. Nature is in a constant state of change, so when you resist change you are resisting the flow of life itself. However, change is not always easy. Retirement, divorce, getting a new job—these can all be scary propositions.

The hips are a favourite place for **weight gain**, happily blamed on gravity. However, as this area contains the genitals, weight gain is often connected to the unconscious desire to keep sexual intimacy at a distance. Beneath those excess layers there may well be hidden memories or repressed feelings that are being kept well out of sight. If excess weight applies to you, explore your sexual feelings. See where healing is needed.

As much as this is the area of birth, so the pelvis is involved with your relationship with your parents, particularly with your mother. Like the shoulders, the pelvis is connected to carrying the weight of your world and it is here that a woman carries a child. As you grow older, you may find that symbolically it is where you are now carrying a parent—that you are now becoming a parent to your own parents—or feeling emotionally unable to stand on your own. As you grow from a child into adulthood, the movement takes you away from your parents into an independent life. Yet often that movement can be loaded with emotional issues or parental pressures. This area will reflect those inner conflicts.

BODYMIND DIALOGUE: THE PELVIS AND HIPS

A problem in the hip area indicates an inability to let go of the past, or a feeling of being unable to stand on your own. **Stiffness or pain** in the hips can indicate that the challenge of change is causing a desire to hold on to how things have been, until eventually you become immobile.

- Does it feel like the ground is no longer sustaining you?
- Is something making you concerned or scared?
- Are you due for retirement and feeling fearful about how you will find a purpose to life without work?
- Are you concerned about how you will be able to manage financially?

The area of the hips also contains your sexuality, which is about intimacy and trust in a relationship. **Intimacy** can give rise to enormous doubts and uncertainties, leading to a breakdown in communication.

- Are you fearful of letting someone get too close?
- Has past hurt caused a withdrawal of energy from this area?
- Do you want to go in your own direction, to move away from the relationship?

See also: Bones, Intestines, Genitals

The Legs

The legs are responsible for your movement in the world, the direction you are taking, and your ability to stand, walk, run, dance, and move. The legs carry you forward in life, moving you through the world. They give you stability and connectedness to the ground, each step reassuringly confirming that the ground will support and sustain you, hence the sense of disorientation or a sudden jolt of consciousness when you slip or miss your step, as if the world has suddenly stopped behaving in the way it should.

When the ground you are standing on or the direction you are going in is uncertain or fraught with conflict, this can be seen in the movement you make as you walk. There is a big difference between someone taking small, uncertain steps and someone taking large, confident strides. One person may trip and stumble as they go, another may move purposefully and gracefully. Get a friend to watch you walk and tell you what you are doing—see how that reflects in your life. Are you stumbling and tripping your way forward.

BODYMIND DIALOGUE: THE LEGS

Strong legs give stability and the power to stand up for yourself, but **over-developed or very muscular legs** can be so firmly grounded that it is hard to be spontaneous or to move with lightness and ease.

- Are you holding on to something too tightly?
- Are you fearful of change?
- Has the rug been pulled from under you once too often?

Under-developed or weak legs represent insecurity.

- Do you feel unsure of your place in the world?
- Do you feel overwhelmed by worldly issues?
- Do you find it hard to be alone?
- Is there a fear of commitment?

Locked into the **thighs** are issues to do with the past, such as parental problems, traumatic childhood memories, anger, or resentment. This area is closely associated with sexuality and intimacy, which you initially learn from your parents' attitudes. Like your arms, the language of your legs being either open or closed speaks volumes.

By holding them together you protect your sexual organs, while opening the thighs means you are open to sexual possibilities.

If there is any fear or resistance then it is often found in **tight muscles** or layers of **excess fatty tissue**, like a protective wall hiding your real feelings. Women often develop excess weight in this area after having children.

- Have your sexual relationships changed?
- Has parenting brought up painful issues from your own childhood?
- Are you trying to hold on to things as they are?
- Does the future appear scary?

The volition for movement starts in the thighs and moves down to the feet, so in the **lower leg** that energy is getting close to manifestation. In other words, this area represents your feelings about the direction you are about to take, the movement that is imminent. This area is also related to your standing and position in life.

- Would you rather be going in the opposite direction?
- Do you feel insecure or uncertain about the direction you are going in?

Very **tight calf muscles** imply a clinging to the past and a resistance to what lies ahead. Or you may be feeling unsupported and are therefore holding on tight to ensure that you can stand up.

- Are you trying to hold onto things as they are?
- Does the future appear scary?

Bruising a leg indicates that you are knocking into something, or you are going in the wrong direction and need to re-route.

- What are the obstacles standing in your way?
- Are you fearful of what lies ahead?

A **broken** leg signifies conflict on the deepest level, about where you are going, or if it would be better to go in a different direction.

- Are you being pulled in two?
- Do you feel unable to stand up for yourself?
- Have you lost your standing?
- Do you feel unsupported?
- What is happening to your movement in the world?

See also: Bones, Muscles, Back, Pelvis

The Knees

The knees enable you to move, dance, run, and to stand straight. They are therefore connected to pride, obstinacy, self-righteousness, arrogance, and ego, as well as surrender, grace, and humility. Try walking without bending your knees and see the arrogant, stiff attitude it represents. By bending the knees you can release and express your feelings. Too much pride and you will stumble. Remember: pride comes before a fall! Arrogance makes you stiff and ungracious, whereas surrender enables you to bend and move with dignity.

The language of the knees is immediately obvious, for here you kneel—an act of humbling yourself to a higher power or authority. The knees allow you to bend, to concede, to give, especially to give way, to be humble. In kneeling you relinquish the ego and embrace humility; without this ability you become stubborn, proud, inflexible, self-righteous. But when the knees give way too quickly, knocking and trembling with fear, then you need to rise up and claim your place in the world, developing greater self-esteem and confidence.

The knees are like shock absorbers, taking the strain between the weight of the body above and the ups and downs of the terrain below. The knees are major weight carriers, so if that weight becomes too heavy the knees may show the strain. This weight may not be physical; psycho/emotional weight can be just as heavy.

Water in the knee indicates a holding of emotional energy, particularly a resistance to surrender, or there may be too much emotion to cope with and the weight is being carried in the knees.

An **inflamed knee** indicates that something or someone is making you feel irritated or angry, and you will not give in!

A **dislocated knee** shows a resistance to giving way. The knee can no longer take the pressure, so it collapses and you are unable to maintain your standing. To dislocate is to lose.

- What ground have you lost and what do you need to do to regain it?
- How can you reclaim your balance and dignity?

See also: Joints, Bones

The Ankles

The ankles enable your entire body to stand upright and walk, a feat that is extraordinary given their narrowness and fragility. If an ankle slips, your whole body falls to the ground. Support is the key word here, as the ankles reflect the support you depend on, not just from others around you but from the inner support system you have built for yourself.

This inner system consists of the psychological and emotional beliefs that give your life meaning and purpose—the emotional support of your loved ones and religious or spiritual convictions. If any of this is taken away, doubted, or questioned, then there is nothing to hold you upright. This can happen when you experience extreme shock or trauma, or when you feel rejected or betrayed.

BODYMIND DIALOGUE: THE ANKLES

As the ankles are essential to your uprightness, they tend to collapse when your sense of being "held upright" also collapses.

- Are your beliefs being questioned?

- Have you lost your support system?
- Do you feel "cast adrift" with no ground to stand on?

The ankles also enable you to move with more flexibility, but like the knees, they are weight-bearing joints, so problems here may be due to the psycho/emotional or physical weight being too much to carry.

- Do you feel weighed down by difficulties or feelings?
- Can you lighten your load?

A **sprained or twisted ankle** indicates a lack of flexibility for the direction you are going in. The strain is too great, causing the energy to buckle or twist, to go in all directions at once.

- Are you being pulled in different directions?
- Do you need to change direction?
- What needs to be untwisted, unraveled, or redirected?
- Has your support system been questioned or undermined?

Swollen ankles indicate a holding of emotional energy, an emotionally holding or resistance to letting go.

A **broken** ankle indicates a very deep conflict about the ground you are standing on and support for where you are going.

- Do you need to go in a new direction, and are you resisting making the change?
- Are you questioning your underlying beliefs?
- What has damaged your ability to stand up for yourself?
- What does the broken ankle enable you to do?
- What does the broken ankle stop you from doing?
- Have you finally reached your breaking point and can no longer stand something or someone?

See also: Joints, Bones, Legs

The Feet

Such small things to carry such a big person above! How your feet do the job, every day, with so little complaint, beats me. The feet are remarkable, as through them you can connect with the whole of your body—nerves and meridian lines begin and end here, and pressing reflexology points in the feet can stimulate each one of the organs.

The feet support and carry you, while going first into the world, extending your moving energy outward. It is a sign of growing up when you can "stand on your own two feet" and not be dependent on someone else. "Putting your foot down" means not letting someone take advantage of you. You "put your best foot forward" as you step into the world with courage and confidence. If you "dig your heels in," it implies that you are holding on tight to reality, your stubbornness indicating a fear of change.

If your direction is unclear or you are unsure of where you are going, then you may walk with your feet turned inward because you do not know which way to go, or outward because all directions appear possible. The former is the more introverted expression, the latter the more extroverted.

Your feet also indicate how you feel about where you are going. If, for instance, there is fear of what lies ahead, perhaps due to old age, illness, emotional or financial insecurity, then the **toes may curl** or the **feet become sore** so that you cannot walk easily. This stops you moving forward, as if you are trying to stop the future from happening.

Cold feet indicate the blood is not flowing freely, and as the blood corresponds to the circulation of your love, this implies you may be pulling back or withdrawing from an emotional situation, or you are feeling emotionally unclear about the direction in which to go. Very **sweaty feet** indicate nervousness or an excess of emotion about your direction. **Swollen feet** mean you are holding on to fearful or frustrated feelings about your direction, or the weight of your emotional burdens is too much to bear. **Peeling skin** on the feet implies that you need to let go of old mental patterns so that new directions can emerge.

The arches on the feet correspond to the solar plexus or middle of the body, the balancing place between the more introverted, self-centred part of your being and the more extroverted or social part. **Flat feet** indicate a lack of boundaries between your private, more personal life and your public activities, as well as a sense of rootlessness or restlessness, as if you are moving over the surface of life without being grounded. **High arches** tend to indicate the opposite: your boundaries are so firm that your private and public worlds hardly meet, almost as if you have two lives, which may, at times, lead to you appearing separate or aloof to others.

You may be extending too far or too quickly and find your **toes** keep getting bruised or bumped. The toes are like the fingers, concerned with the details or smaller, more immediate issues, so make sure you are not missing the details in your desire to move forward. The toes also extend outward first, so they get to test the water before the rest of you dives in, though they are most likely to get knocked or trodden on when you are pushing forward too quickly or in the wrong direction. Those who **tiptoe** through life may be fearful of making their presence known and of coming down to earth.

Bunions on the side of the big toe are usually caused by wearing the wrong shoes. However, this may also indicate that you allow others to make decisions for you, rather than taking responsibility for yourself—such as when buying a pair of shoes that fit! A bunion can develop if you find yourself in a relationship where you have surrendered decision making to someone else, as the big toe is connected to issues of authority and personal power.

SEVEN
MOVING PARTS
The Bones, Joints, and Muscles

Together the moving parts—the bones, joints, and muscles—create the framework within which you live. This structure enables you to move. It allows your thoughts, ideas, beliefs, and feelings to find expression, determining whether you walk with a confident, joyful step or drag your feet behind you. Just as your emotions affect your physical state, so physical movement elevates your emotional state. Exercise creates a positive and vibrant feeling, while a lack of exercise soon depletes your energy, leading to lethargy and depression.

The Bones
It is through the bones that you exert your independence and find your place in the world. This framework is developed from early childhood onwards. (Remember all that milk you had to drink to "strengthen your bones"?) And just as the bones form the foundation of your physical being, so family and home security form your foundation as a child. In this way, the skeleton contains feelings of

safety, trust, belonging, and security, as well as repressed issues of abuse, insecurity, or survival. These are issues connected to the first chakra, and to the hard tissue structure (see Chapter 3).

Bone marrow nourishes you with essential minerals, salts, and nutrients and produces vital immune cells, while the hard outer tissue forms a strong and resilient framework upon which your whole being is built. Bones are the densest form of energy in the physical body. Like the rocks in the earth, they support and sustain. They enable the muscles to move, and the muscles in turn help to move the fluids, giving life to your whole being.

You can live with a reduced amount of muscle or fluid, but you cannot live without bone. In the same way, you are not truly alive without being in touch with the deepest part of your psycho/spiritual being, with the inspiration and impulse that give life meaning. Just as the bones support your physical being and give life to the muscles and fluids, so your core beliefs give you constant inner strength and support, while finding expression in your lifestyle, behaviour, and relationships. Problems with your bones, therefore, represent conflict within the very core of your being.

Osteoporosis

Osteoporosis causes a loss of bone mass, making the bones brittle and liable to fracture. Due to changes in the hormones, this condition is most common in women after menopause. Osteoporosis implies a thinning of the life force flowing through the bones, perhaps due to a sense of giving up, of feeling helpless or hopeless.

BODYMIND DIALOGUE: OSTEOPOROSIS

After menopause, especially if this coincides with children leaving home, a woman can believe her reason for being has gone, and there is no impulse to create a new direction, or to find a new purpose.

- Do you feel a loss of purpose now that the potential for motherhood is over?
- Do you feel you have lost your womanhood or femininity?

- Have you lost your dreams and longings?
- Have you found a direction for yourself that is just for you, and not related to being a mother or wife?

The strength of your bones is at stake, as is the strength of your core feelings, your inner purpose for being. The bones are connected to spirit, so you need to raise your spirit, to bring it into action, rather than let it fade away.

- What can you do to bring more vibrancy and spirit into your life?

Broken Bones

As bone issues are about core issues within yourself, so a broken bone indicates a deep inner conflict, a breaking into different pieces. For instance, a broken ankle or leg indicates the conflict has to do with the direction you are going in. It's as if you are being pulled in two opposing directions, or that the ground you are standing on is not supporting you as fully as you need it to. A broken arm indicates a deep unease about what you are doing and how you are expressing your feelings. Or perhaps you are doing or giving too much? Have you reached breaking point? Are you going in one direction yet inside longing to go in a different one? Are your loyalties being divided? Do you feel fractured, split, or broken into pieces?

BODYMIND DIALOGUE: BROKEN BONES

A broken bone means you have to stop whatever you are doing. Make a list of the ways it has changed events or relationships.

- What can you no longer do?
- Did you really want to do those things?
- What do you have to do instead?
- Is that what you really need to do?
- How has the broken bone affected those around you?

- What core issues within yourself are in conflict?
- Do you need to stop and reevaluate your direction or behaviour?

A broken bone usually forces you to rest and ask for help. But perhaps this is what you really need: to be cared for and given extra attention. Having a rest provides an opportunity to look at where you need more strength and flexibility.

Joints

The bodymind language is very clear here—joints enable you to freely express yourself: their job is to *join up* your thoughts and feelings with your actions. Through the joints you can run and jump, hug and caress, punch and push away, or paint and play the piano; you can move easily or awkwardly, with grace or discomfort. Joint issues are, therefore, connected to the expression of your feelings through your movements, and any conflict you may be experiencing with those feelings will be apparent.

Try walking with stiff knees or rigid ankles, talking or hugging with unbendable elbows, and you will soon see how the joints speak your mind. **Stiff joints** reflect an inner stiffness, a resistance to sharing, a locking away of your real feelings. Where have your thoughts become rigid or your feelings so unacceptable that you cannot share them? As the whole purpose of the joints is to move, so stiff or unbending joints have lost their purpose and meaning.

BODYMIND DIALOGUE: JOINTS

For pain or stiffness in the joints, ask yourself these questions:

- Do you think your feelings are inappropriate to share?
- Do you feel misunderstood?
- What has become stiff and inflexible within you?
- Where have you lost your purpose, your direction, or your ability to move with the flow?
- Who or what is making you so angry, irritated, or critical?
- Can you be more accepting, more fluid or expressive?

Inflammation of the Joints

The most common difficulty with joints is inflammation, indicating hot and angry feelings trying to find expression.

BODYMIND DIALOGUE: JOINT INFLAMMATION

As this inflammation is connected to movement, expression, and communication, it indicates a resistance or conflict with what is happening, a build-up of angry or irritable emotions, or an inability to say what you really want to.

- What is making you so sore or inflamed?
- What is making you feel so hot or fired up inside?
- What is so irritating that it is restricting your expression?

When the joints are sore or inflamed then the feelings being expressed are often critical, irritated, or inflexible ones, so you need to release the cause of those feelings.

- What is needed to loosen the joints?
- More forgiveness? Acceptance or more love for yourself?

Joint Stiffness

If the joints become stiff or unable to move, then where has your thinking become rigid or unbending, critical or dismissive? Rigid joints become useless—they lose their purpose, which is freedom of movement—and the relationship between emotion and expression is lost. Stiff joints imply that you are not expressing your deeper feelings; there is lack of freedom, or a holding on to old ways of being.

Osteoarthritis

Arthritis is a degenerative joint disease, and osteoarthritis is the most common form. In this condition the cartilage deteriorates and hardens, and bone spurs can develop, sometimes with pain and deformity. It is mainly prevalent in the elderly as a result of usage over the years, occurring in younger people as the result of abnormally shaped joints or structural damage due to overuse.

The inflammation implies a build-up of toxic thoughts or attitudes, such as anger, irritation, or frustration, either with yourself or someone else; as well a grinding away, a slow eroding of the ability to move the joint and therefore to share, express, and emote. It's as if you are slowly becoming less appreciative, expressive, caring, or tolerant. Arthritis is often associated with an overly critical attitude (uptight and unrelenting) and with bitterness or resentment (which brings stiffness and pain) as attitudes wear away at your joy and appreciation.

Osteoarthritis occurs mainly in the weight-bearing joints and the hands, so here you can also look at issues of resentment toward the load you are carrying, your responsibilities, and how your personal life may be slowly eroding beneath your obligations.

BODYMIND DIALOGUE: OSTEOARTHRITIS

If you have osteoarthritis, it is important that you ask yourself what is causing such irritation or bitterness. Blaming others is not the answer, for the deeper cause lies within.

- Do you feel out of control of your life?
- Do you want to regain control?
- Do you want someone else to take control for you?
- Are you getting so deeply frustrated or irritated that these feelings are limiting your ability to be gracious or loving?
- Do you dislike spontaneity and find it hard to relax?
- Is it difficult to receive?

Arthritis brings up issues of control, as you slowly lose control over your joints.

- Do you find it hard not to dominate or demand attention?
- Do you feel controlled by someone or something?
- Is life making you angry or resentful?

- What is wearing you down so much?
- What can you do to release some of the tightness in your life?

Rheumatoid Arthritis

Rheumatoid arthritis is an autoimmune disease in which your immune system attacks the membrane of the joints due to an abnormal rheumatoid factor in the blood. It can affect the whole body but is particularly prevalent in the hands, wrists, feet, ankles, and knees. The joints can become swollen, red, and painful. It means that movement and expression become very limited, as the joints become progressively more rigid and painful. The bodymind symptoms indicate there may be repressed anger. Many people with this condition have previously been very active, such as athletes who can channel their energy into sport, but this does not necessarily resolve the underlying issue, for when they retire they have nowhere to put those angry feelings.

BODYMIND DIALOGUE: RHEUMATOID ARTHRITIS

As the rheumatoid factor is in the blood, this indicates the emotions are very involved here, especially the expression of love. An autoimmune difficulty implies the immune system is attacking you, instead of an external antigen.

- How have you become your own enemy?
- Are you denying feelings of love, caring, and tenderness and instead becoming overly self-critical or judgmental, dismissing those feelings in your heart as unimportant?
- Do you feel stuck in a negative or criticizing mode?
- Are you feeling resentful or bitter about something or someone?
- Do you lack assertiveness and, feeling inhibited, find yourself unable to express yourself in the way you really want to?
- Are you destroying yourself with guilt or shame?
- Do you have a tendency to undermine yourself through criticism or a lack of self-respect?
- Due to the condition, arthritics often have clenched fists—is the fist really indicating a desire to hit someone or something?

• Is it hate that is replacing love?

Movement is essential, especially going with the flow and allowing change to happen. Life is movement, so the more stuck you are, the more lifeless you may become. However, most important is finding your heart and expressing it, sharing your love, and in this way becoming your own best friend.

See also: Autoimmune

Bursitis

Bursitis is an inflammation of the fluid-filled sacs in the joint, usually in the elbow or knee. It can be brought on by excessive use, as in "housemaid's knee" or "tennis elbow."

BODYMIND DIALOGUE: BURSITIS

Excessive use may not be the only cause for bursitis.

• Is there a deeper resentment at having to work and not getting the help you need?
• Are you doing something or going in a particular direction that is not true to you, causing you to feel resentful or angry?
• Do you feel you are not being appreciated?

Dislocation

To dislocate is to lose your place. Having lost your place, you cannot move forward easily; there is pain and uncertainty as to how to proceed.

BODYMIND DIALOGUE: DISLOCATION

Putting a bone out of joint indicates that you are feeling deeply put out, have lost contact with your centre or core, or perhaps have lost your standing or place in the world. It also signifies difficulty in expressing your feelings.

- Do you feel put out about something?
- Is the direction you are going in causing confusion or uncertainty?
- Is your activity contradicting your inner feelings?
- Do you feel pushed out of place?
- What do you need to do to get realigned, to reconnect with the flow?

Gout

Gout is caused by an accumulation of uric acid in the joints, often in the big toe. Uric acid is normally removed by the urine, which is the body's way of releasing emotions that are finished with, or no longer needed, so they do not poison your system. If you do not release these old emotions they begin to get stuck, to solidify and crystallize, causing rigidity and inflexibility.

BODYMIND DIALOGUE: GOUT

Gout is an expression of being stuck. Because it is also more common in the elderly, holding on to the past is also often a contributing factor.

- Do you feel stuck in your present direction?
- There is also anger involved, as the joint gets very red and swollen, full of hot emotion. Can you find the emotion, what it is that is unmoving?
- If you cling to the past, you are unable to move forward. Are there past issues that are very important to you?

Muscles

The soft tissue in the body is found in the muscles, flesh, fat, skin, nerves, and organs. While the hard tissue in your bones is most closely associated with your core beliefs, the soft tissue reflects those core beliefs in mental activity and thought patterns: remember, *as you think, so you become; as you have become, so you can see how you have been thinking.* Past memories, conflicts, traumas, experiences, and feelings are all found in the soft tissue, as are repressed anxieties, fear, guilt, levels of self-worth or self-esteem, joy, vibrancy—all reflected in the condition of the organs, flesh, and particularly in the muscles. As you change, so the soft tissue reflects this change, whether through tight or floppy muscles, gaining or losing weight, fatty deposits, nerve disorders, skin eruptions, or organ deterioration.

Muscles absorb and respond to tensions and feelings. If they do not relax sufficiently following stress, then the tension accumulates and causes deeper, longer-lasting damage. If this continues over a period of time, the muscles become set and fixed in this restricted form. This is where you "hold" issues, emotions, and trauma. Frozen anger, fear, or grief create a kind of body armour, which further blocks and holds back feelings, locking the musculature into fixed positions. In this way, a depressive or fearful attitude becomes built into the physical structure, which in turn maintains the mental attitude. To bring change you need to work from both sides—to release both the physical structure and the psychological patterning.

The muscles enable all the bodily systems to function, such as circulation, digestion, breathing, and nerve impulses. Their freedom of movement is essential for optimum health. When the muscles are restricted, whether through tension, tightness, or lack of tone, your energy will be unable to flow smoothly, and you may suffer from related problems. Stress release and emotional expression are therefore essential for muscle ease. Exercise is also vital—it not only releases muscular tension but psycho/emotional tension as well.

Muscle Stiffness
Muscle stiffness can be caused after you exercise hard. The following day there is an excess build-up of lactic acid in the muscles. The only answer is to exercise some more to get the lactic acid moving. But stiffness can also be due to not having enough exercise, especially in the elderly. Here it indicates stiff and tired thinking patterns, stubborn and resistant attitudes.

Stiffness shows a desire for things to stay as they are, a holding on to the past. There is an inability to bend or adapt. Not being able to bend means you become rigid and then brittle.

- Do you need to let go a bit more, to be more spontaneous, playful, and loving?
- What are you feeling so stiff about?
- What are you holding on to, or needing to let go of?

Muscle Pain

The normal reaction to pain is to try to eliminate it. But pain is saying something. It is your unconscious speaking loud and clear: a feeling or issue is being repressed or resisted, and it is creating tension. Mental attitudes and emotional tension affect the energy flowing through the musculature and can easily cause pain or limit movement. Muscle pain tends to indicate that psychological pain—anger, fear, insecurity, guilt, or even self-punishment—are being expressed through the body. It signifies an aching or longing for something or someone, a deep desire for movement or change, but also an inner resistance to such movement. Physical pain can also act as a great distraction from dealing with deeper psycho/emotional pain.

Pain tends to restrict or limit movement, especially if you are told to stay still. Yet physical movement enables expression of emotion. In not moving, your emotions—often the very ones that are trying to find expression through the pain—may also become immobilized and stuck. Exercise, where possible, is essential. Keeping the muscles and joints moving will not only help them to heal but will also help your feelings to keep flowing.

Pain can be all-consuming; it is easy to lose touch with who you are, apart from the pain. And it is easy to get stuck in a cycle of pain, as pain creates resistance and resistance creates more pain. The breath can be used to ease into pain, to soften and release restrictions or resistances. A number of hospitals are now offering pain-relief clinics based on relaxation and breath-meditation.

Look closely at what your pain is saying:

- What movement do you really want to make?
- Are there any benefits to your pain, such as extra attention?
- Can you find the inner pain behind the physical pain? See if you can find out what it is telling you by entering into the pain, rather than running away from it.
- Use your breath to help you—breathe deeply and gently into the area as you relax and soften any resistance. What inner pain is being expressed here?
- What are you really aching for?
- What does your body need you to do to release the tension?
- Do you need to scream, to cry, change direction, or hold someone close?

See also: Back Pain, Pain

Cramps

Cramps occur when a muscle tightens and goes into a spasm. Not to undermine the intensity of the pain, but cramps can be as simple as a calf muscle cramping after exercise, or as complex as TMS (see Back Pain, Chapter 6), a condition in which the muscles in the back spasm so intensely that there is severe pain.

To cramp (as in "cramp one's style") is to limit or prevent full expression. This indicates a psychological cramping or holding; something or someone is making you want to hold on tight.

- Are you fearful of what would happen if you let go?
- Are you fearful of what is coming next?
- Perhaps you want to shrink back from it?
- Are you anxious about what you are doing?
- Find the place that is feeling cramped or tight and breathe into

it to release the pressure. What unconscious psycho/emotional cramping needs to be released in order to feel greater freedom of movement?

Sprains and Strains

A sprained muscle indicates energy going in different directions and getting twisted or wrenched as a result. The cause is usually a fall, indicating the need to pay attention to the path in front of you, to the details, or that you cannot realistically tread two paths at the same time.

BODYMIND DIALOGUE: SPRAINS AND STRAINS

Sprains and strains occur when a muscle gets pushed beyond its normal limits and cannot handle the pressure. It is showing you that you have limits and that you need to respect them.

- Where are you getting emotionally wrenched?
- What needs to be untwisted and clarified?
- Are you feeling stretched beyond your limit by something or someone?
- Are you getting strained or pressured?
- Is there a mental strain you cannot deal with?
- Are you trying to do too much to please everyone, and, in the process, ignoring yourself? What needs to be unraveled?
- If it is in the ankle, is the ground too weak to support you?
- Is the direction you are going in creating conflict and confusion?
- Or are you trying to go in two directions at once?
- If it is in the wrist, are you doing the right thing, or is your activity creating uncertainty?
- How can you release the strain in your life?

See also: Wrists, Ankles

Torn Muscles and Tendons

Similar to sprains and strains, in torn muscles and tendons the stressing of the muscle has gone further, to the point of being torn. This symbolizes a mental conflict that is creating a painful wrenching inside, perhaps a conflict of values, or the need to make decisions that might cause a rift.

BODYMIND DIALOGUE: TORN MUSCLES AND TENDONS

Tendons link the muscles to the bone and therefore enable expression of your attitudes and tendencies: *rigid tendons indicate rigid tendencies.*

When tendons get torn, it indicates that you are being pulled in too many directions at once.

- Is something tearing you apart?
- What do you need to do to bring the different parts together?

Hernia

A hernia is a weakening in the muscle wall that allows an organ or fatty tissue to move out of position. A **hiatus hernia** occurs when a part of the stomach becomes trapped above the diaphragm (the flat muscle that separates the chest from the abdomen) and can be caused by exertion or injury. **Inguinal hernias** occur in the groin and are the most common of hernias, most often in men, where a section of the intestine protrudes through a gap in the abdominal muscle wall and forms a sac. Heavy lifting, straining, or excessive coughing can cause this.

A hernia indicates a weakening or collapse of psycho/emotional energy, often because you try to cope with too much at once and collapse under the weight; or you strain to do everything right and therefore push yourself too far (perhaps motivated by guilt or anger); or you feel weakened by inner fears and anxieties, so there are no reserves of personal strength. This is connected to over-anxious thinking patterns and fearful mental states. In the process your guts spill out—you lose your psychological control, strength, or courage.

Some boys are born with a hernia, due to the descending of the testicles. Very often this clears up in childhood. If it recurs later in life, see if there are any childhood issues coming to the fore, or a change in living conditions giving rise to fear or insecurity.

A hernia may indicate that an inner longing to explode is being restrained. This puts a strain on the muscle, so that it implodes rather than explodes.

- Do you need to be contained in some way?
- Are you resisting someone else's control?
- A hernia can also imply that you are pushing away a part of yourself. What is that part?
- What do you need to do to reclaim that part of your being?

EIGHT

CENTRAL CONTROL
The Nervous System

The nervous system is the transmitter of information as well as being the movement controller determining your body's coordination. It has two working systems: the automatic nervous system, which maintains automatic functions such as heartbeat, digestion, and breathing; and the central nervous system, which conveys information throughout every cell of the body. The brain is the main centre of control. The left hemisphere of the brain is predominately linear, rational, logical, rapid-fire thinking, and corresponds to the right side of the body; while the right side of the brain is visual, creative, sensitive, illogical, and corresponds to the left side of the body (see Chapter 3).

Information is disseminated in a number of ways. Firstly, there is an electrical communications system whereby input is transmitted along nerve pathways, with neurotransmitters jumping from one neuron to another. The functioning of the brain, mental activity, behaviour, and the central nervous system are monitored by billions of neurons, or nerve cells, linked through these synapses. Secondly, there are neuropeptides or chemical messengers that transmit information directly by way of receptor cells and binding substances known as ligands.

Neuropeptides are found clustered in the limbic system—the part of the brain that deals with emotions—in the heart, the gut, the immune system, and throughout the nerves. They connect with receptor cells, hundreds of which are found on the outer surface of every cell—there is a lock-and-key effect—and the information is transmitted through the receptor into the cell. That information then influences the behaviour of the cell. In other words, neuropeptides form an inter-cellular language that communicates with every other system, constantly transmitting information. More importantly, it is the neuropeptides that link the limbic system with the rest of the body: they transmit your emotions, translated into chemical messengers.

The nervous system is, therefore, more than just a series of pathways that let you know when something is too hot to touch. Nerves take information from the physical body and transmit it to the brain, receive a response, and take that back to the body. But they also receive information in the brain from your emotions, thoughts, and feelings and transmit this throughout to the appropriate cells. All of this is about communication: communicating between your own body and mind, as well as between yourself and the outside world.

As in a telephone exchange system, there are numerous communications going on at the same time, crossing and interchanging with each other. A fault in any one area can affect other areas, creating a blockage or system failure. In the light of this, nervous disorders can be seen as times of a breakdown or change in that flow of communication. Fear, panic, shame, anger, hate—all these can undermine the normal functioning of the nervous system, leading to debilitating nervous conditions. In the same way, joy, happiness, lovingkindness, and forgiveness can increase your well-being, leading to a balanced, calm, and healthy nervous system

The nerves are also responsible for physical movement, just as are the muscles and joints. Without full communication, the message to move or behave does not get through. The breakdown area may be in the brain, as in multiple sclerosis, a condition in which the nerve sheath is damaged and the message distorted, or in the body, as in a pinched nerve or damaged nerve ending. If movement is impaired and the flow of energy distorted, there may well be a corresponding stress from overwork and a need to rest or even collapse for a while; or there may be depression, loss of purpose, an apathetic attitude, or a deep fear of what lies ahead in life. This is particularly noticeable in the elderly when being moved from their own home to a nursing or rest home. The move is often followed by a partial collapse or mild stroke, indicative of a fear of confronting their immediate future.

NERVE REVIEW

The nervous system responds to your every thought and feeling.

- Become aware of this by watching how your physical response changes depending on your mood or circumstances.
- Become aware of where you are holding or expressing nervous tension in the body, as seen in pain, ache, weakness, or tightness.
- Watch what happens to your nervous response if you relax or repeat positive affirmations. Does the pain or tightness diminish?

Pain

Pain in any part of the body is a signal that something is off kilter. You are stretching too far, going in the wrong direction, trying to do too much on your own, or repressing too many psycho/emotional issues, so that the flow of communication is damaged. The normal reaction to pain is to want to get rid of it, to stop it, or obliterate it. Yet if pain is an indication that something is wrong, then it is also an indication that you need to pay attention and hear what it has to say.

Invariably, the area of physical pain is representing a psycho/emotional pain. When you stop and listen, further pain can be avoided. For instance, straining your back may well occur because of lifting a heavy weight. But beneath that strain can be layers of resentment that no one is helping you, that you always have to do things yourself in order to get them done. And beneath that can be a sense of emotional loneliness, a longing for attention or care, a fear of the future, or perhaps your inner child trying to prove how capable you really are to parents who are not paying attention to you. It is easy to blame the accident for the pain, for facing the inner pain is more demanding. However, the two are inextricably linked. Finding the inner pain or hurt will go a long way in releasing the physical hurt.

Where there is pain you will find resistance—resistance to the physical pain, resistance to the confines and limitations imposed by the pain, resistance to the circumstances in your life, and further pain caused by the resistance itself. Resistance is obviously the key issue here: whatever is happening, you are going against it in one way or another. All this leads to you wanting to numb the pain or tune it out. But pain does not just go away, whether physical or psycho/emotional; it demands to be dealt with, or it will simply reappear in a different form.

One way to deal with pain is to surrender to it, to give in, to really feel it, to soften to it, to find its core and enter in. To sink into it as rain sinks into soft earth. "Several laboratory experiments with acute pain have shown that tuning in to sensations is a more effective way of reducing the level of pain," writes Jon Kabat-Zinn in *Full Catastrophe Living*. "You are trying to find out about your pain, to learn from it, to know it better, not to stop it or get rid of it or escape from it." Softening to pain releases resistance so that the pain is no longer an enemy but becomes a teaching friend, showing you where to go next.

Acceptance of the pain is also vital, as fear only makes the pain worse through added tension—fear of being ill, fear of not being able to work, fear of being an invalid. By entering into the pain you confront the fear. Ask the pain to tell you what you need to know, to show you why you are holding on so tightly. Open yourself to letting go. Pain usually makes you hold your breath in an attempt to counteract the tension. Breathing into the pain, especially deep breathing, enables the muscles to relax and the tension to release. This will help the pain recede.

The causes of pain can vary, and a medical diagnosis may help you understand what is happening. However, emotional tension and stress are known causes for muscle tension, spasm, and nerve pain. The nerves are like wires that connect the brain with all parts of the body. As such they relay information from the brain to the muscles to make them move, but they can also relay information to make the muscles spasm, or to limit blood flow so that muscles become oxygen deprived. When that happens, you will be in pain. Remember, emotional and psychological tension can cause nerve and muscle tension.

BODYMIND DIALOGUE: PAIN

Pain makes us realize just how impermanent we are, how fragile the body really is. Confronting your own vulnerability often reveals a need for love and attention, a nurturing that you may have been longing for without realizing it. Pain indicates that you are holding on tight, so you need to work at releasing and letting go.

- Are you unable to ask for help?
- Are you feeling trapped by negative feelings, such as revenge, resentment, guilt, or shame?
- Is there someone or something you are holding on to?
- What part of your inner being is hurting so badly?

See also: Back Pain, Muscle Pain

EASING THE PAIN

Here's a technique that can help you deal with pain and discomfort.

Find a comfortable place to sit or lie down.
Begin to breathe deeply and gently, taking the breath into the pain, consciously softening the edges, breathing out tension and breathing in ease and acceptance.

Let the pain soften with the breath.
Let the pain talk to you. Let it tell you what emotional tension is

affecting you, and what you need to do to release it. With each out–breath, let the pain go.

Headaches

You probably spend most of your time in your head, especially if you are a thinking, creating, talking, rationalizing, organizing, repressing, analyzing, speculating, deliberating, contemplating, hiding-from-your-feelings type of person. For many of us, head activity feels safe and normal, while heart activity can feel risky and unpredictable. So you hang out in your head, making it appear like you have everything together and are really quite sane and intelligent. Until you get a headache. And then you are reminded how vulnerable the human body really is, and how easily stress and pressure and unacknowledged feelings can start to get painful.

There are many causes of a headache. It may be due to a hormone imbalance at times of menstruation or menopause, because of an infection such as a cold or flu, because of a more serious illness, or because your head is stressed out and exhausted from being overused. In this case it is saying stop, you are going too fast, doing too much, something is getting forgotten or repressed in the process, and you need to take stock. Tension is rising in the body and is affecting the blood vessels and limiting the flow of oxygen to the head. It's time to chill out.

BODYMIND DIALOGUE: HEADACHES

Headaches that occur on a regular basis need to be checked, as they may be due to something else going on in the body. Keep a diary of the food you eat in case it is the result of an allergy. Keep a dairy of your psycho/emotional environment. Describe the headache, its location, duration, and severity. Describe your feelings prior to the headache. In this way, you can build a picture of what is happening, especially if there is any repetitive behaviour or attitude.

• Are you resisting someone or something?

- Are you putting too much energy into your head while forgetting your heart?
- Are you trying too hard to be perfect?

Check the following list for more causes.

Causes of Headaches

Too much time spent in the head. The key here is excessive strain and tension from long hours on the computer, too much paperwork, or trying to do too many things at once. You know what you need to do.

Pushing yourself to achieve. Over-achievers can be prone to headaches, as there is the danger of becoming "top heavy" and losing touch with feelings and playtime. Remember to connect with feelings.

Repressed feelings. Failing to deal with feelings can create a build-up of energy in the body, especially feelings of anger, rage, frustration, fear, anxiety, worry, and a lack of confidence or self-esteem. Get more in touch with your inner self.

Rigid personality. A stubborn or arrogant attitude, prejudice, or intolerance can lead to tight tendencies and tight tendons in the neck. This is often combined with a controlling or overly powerful personality. Deep relaxation and letting go of control will help.

Avoidance behaviour. A desire to opt out, to avoid circumstances, to retreat into your own private world, where no one can reach you, ultimately leads to problems. Remember, relationships are about communication.

A lack of exercise. This translates into a lack of fresh oxygen into the blood and lungs. You are getting stale. It's time to breathe more deeply outdoors.

Food or chemical allergy. Keep a diary to observe the relationship between the foods you eat and physical symptoms.

Migraines

Migraine headaches can last for many hours and include nausea, vomiting, and the need for complete rest in a dark room. Most experts believe that a migraine is caused by blood vessels on the surface of the brain expanding, causing the area around them to become inflamed and irritated. However, why that should happen is another story.

Expanding blood vessels imply imploding emotions, such as anger and irritation. This also restricts the oxygen flow, which implies a restriction in the life-force, a holding back from full participation, a desire to push away what is happening and completely retreat. Such a restriction is usually due to tight muscles in the shoulders and neck.

It is important to track down the originating cause, as often it can be as simple as a food or chemical allergy. Keeping a diary of food eaten and places visited will soon show if this is the case. The most common food allergies are to chocolate, cheese, wine, and coffee. Environmental allergies include chemical intolerance, such as reacting to carpet glue. Also check out the following list.

Causes of Migraines

Fear of failure. This fear is often due to having high expectations of yourself and the fear of not being able to meet those expectations. Where do such expectations come from, your parents?

Issues of control and power. Keeping tight control over yourself, your feelings, or your environment limits spontaneity and creativity and causes tight muscles, leading to a lack of oxygen supply. Breathe and relax. Let go of control.

Repression of feelings. If you hold down the hot emotions, such as frustration, anger, and rage, the heat soon rises in your emotional body. There may also be the repression of sexual feelings or inappropriate longings. What feelings are you keeping so tight inside?

A fear of participation and involvement. There may be a desire to retreat into your own private world. What or who are you hiding from?

A way of getting attention, care, and love. This is especially the case if you don't know how to ask for that love directly.

HEADACHE REVIEW

Both headaches and migraines can be helped enormously through diet, deep relaxation, breathing, visualization, and meditation. Taking a painkiller may numb the pain, but it does not heal the cause.

Keep a journal.
This will help you determine the cause: diet, stress, or repressed feelings.

Breathe.
Try lying still in the dark and softening resistance, breathing, and gently entering into the core of the pain. Keep breathing and softening. As you enter the pain you may be able to see its cause and what is needed to bring healing.

Pinched Nerve
Here the language is of being squeezed, compressed, or gripped tight, as if someone or something is constricting your normal flow of energy. This may be due to excess stress or emotional tension making the muscles contract around the nerve.

BODYMIND DIALOGUE: PINCHED NERVE

Find the place in your psycho/emotional being that is so tense or holding so tightly that it feels squeezed.

• Do you feel trapped by someone or something?
• Are you unable to take the pressure?

If a nerve is pinched for long enough then it will likely become numb, which reduces the pain. A painful nerve is more likely to be an expression of a deeper psycho/emotional pain.

See also: Pain, Back Pain

Sciatica

The sciatic nerve is the main nerve running from the centre of your back down your leg. Sciatica is a condition in which that nerve becomes inflamed and creates a deep pain down its entire length. This may be due to a herniated disk putting extra pressure on the nerve, in which case you need to ask what is pressurizing you so much or putting such a burden on you that you are feeling squashed or squeezed. But it is more likely to be caused by muscle tension (TMS), which is a direct expression of emotional tension. For instance, the sciatic nerve passes through the piriformis muscle, which can spasm and entrap the nerve. Because the muscle tension is caused by emotional tension that does not imply your pain is not real, sciatica can be excruciating.

Nerves have to do with communication and sensitivity. Sciatica implies that there are emotional issues affecting the back and legs, and that these are deep, inner issues. These may be issues to do with being able to stand up for yourself. Perhaps something is happening that you cannot take anymore, and it is making you want to go in a different direction. Or perhaps you desperately need more support and cannot cope with everything on your own any longer.

BODYMIND DIALOGUE: SCIATICA

Sciatica may indicate a doubt or fear about where you are going and your ability to cope with what lies ahead.

- Are you concerned about where you are going and what is going to happen?
- What inner emotional pain are you sitting on or holding back?
- Is someone or something restricting your freedom to move?

- Are there financial or emotional issues putting pressure on you or weighing you down?

See also: Pain, Back Pain

Fibromyalgia

Fibromyalgia (FM) means pain in the soft fibrous tissues in the body. It is a newly recognized illness featuring widespread chronic pain, stiffness, tenderness, deep fatigue, and sleep disturbance. It can come and go and is of indeterminate length. The exhaustion may be so draining that it can make it hard to function, either mentally or physically, and there appears to be abnormal sensory processing, which increases the pain experienced. There also appears to be a strong connection to Chronic Fatigue Syndrome (CFS)—some experts say the two are simply variations of the same thing—as FM also has a possible post-viral cause and the two illnesses share many of the same symptoms. (See also Chronic Fatigue Syndrome.)

Pain is never easy to live with and should not be underestimated in its debilitating effect. However, from a bodymind perspective, it is also the place to start in understanding this illness. Here, we find a lowered tolerance to pain, probably due to a dysfunctional sensory system. This lowered tolerance says that repressed psycho/emotional tension is affecting you to the point that it is distorting your perception, which in turn is lowering your tolerance (or patience), creating a deep inner pain. This is a repressed resistance to your circumstances, a longing to pull back, as your tolerance for what is happening, whether in yourself or in your world, is close to non-existent. This is affecting your entire nervous system, giving rise to sleep disorders and other ailments. The deep fatigue indicates a longing to give up, an exhaustion from having to cope or carry on beyond your limits. Fibromyalgia often has muscle tension or TMS at its core.

As with CFS, this illness implies a loss of purpose or direction, and a loss of spirit. It is as if the desire to participate and enter into life has drained away, leaving you without intention or motivation.

See also: Pain, Back Pain (TMS)

Numbness

Numbness is due to damaged nerves or distorted messages from the brain and implies a withdrawal of feeling from that particular area. This may be because the feeling is too intense to deal with, or too strong to release, and suggests that not feeling anything or a lack of participation is emotionally safer.

BODYMIND DIALOGUE: NUMBNESS

Numbness indicates a detachment from feeling, even a giving up or hopelessness. It may be caused by stress or pressure, making you want to stop, withdraw, pull back, and especially not feel.

- Is there someone or something you don't want to feel?
- What part of you are you pushing away?
- Are there feelings you have withdrawn from inside yourself?
- Do you have long-lost hopes or dreams?
- What needs to happen for you to be able to accept that part of you, to bring it back to life?

Paralysis

Although there are various reasons for paralysis, such as injury, virus, or stroke, the message the body is giving is much the same. Paralysis implies an inability to continue the way you are. Something has to change, to concede, to surrender. This is often associated with issues of power and control, the need to dominate or rule, in contrast to a world that is essentially fluid and uncontrollable. The result is a system that gets jammed or overloaded with stress. Or there may be an intense fear of what is happening, of what lies ahead, and, therefore, a pulling back and resistance to any forward movement. Paralysis means no movement and, therefore, no expression of feelings.

Paralysis also means being dependent on others, having to be cared for and looked after, which is the exact opposite of being the one in charge. It can be very hard to accept such a situation, giving rise to tremendous bitterness and anger, which only adds more tension to the body.

Epilepsy / Seizure

This is where the brain has a seizure, linked to an electrical or nerve disorder. It may be **grand mal**—a complete loss of consciousness with shaking and convulsions and a falling to the ground, with possible frothing at the mouth and biting of the tongue—or **petit mal**, which is far less severe, being a break in consciousness for only a few seconds or longer. Seizures are seemingly unpredictable, but there can be links to previous head injuries or birth traumas. Alcoholics and drug addicts have a higher incidence of epilepsy. Causes may also include metabolic imbalances.

By its nature, an epileptic fit represents an internal breakdown triggered by unexpressed pressure that overloads the circuit. It is as if you are being "seized" by emotion. If you are unable to express your inner fears, insecurities, or concerns, whether real or imagined, the pressure will build up inside until there is an overload. Such a break in consciousness implies a separation between relative reality and your inner perception.

The separation may also be between yourself and the divine, for epileptic fits are known to occur during mystical states of emotional frenzy or devotion, as if the level of ecstasy being experienced is too much for the human brain, and a circuit break occurs.

NINE

SURVIVAL MODE
The Stress Response

Although stress was explored in some detail in Chapter 1, it is so important and integral to our daily lives and state of health that it warrants a chapter of its own. The effects of stress—which include anxiety, panic, doubt, lack of self-confidence, depression, and a host of other emotions—are such that stress is invariably at the root of every state of ill health and affects every part of our being: psychological and emotional as well as physical.

A caveman out on a hunt or a soldier on the front line needs the stress response in his body in order to have the energy to fight. The anticipation of the life-or-death experience puts his entire physiology into a state of red alert. This response is an important part of everyone's physiological makeup. Stress enables you to meet challenges, to push yourself into new areas of experience or understanding through heightening your awareness and focusing your concentration.

And all of this would be fine if you had a bear to hunt or a war to wage. However, the stress most of us are dealing with is not from life-or-death situations, but is the *distress* that arises from an accumulation of pressure from much smaller issues. Although each separate incident may appear benign, if your response becomes increasingly stressful so you are no longer able to maintain your equilibrium, then the body will translate this as life-threatening and put out the red alert. The stress response is activated when you are unable to adjust your behaviour or deal creatively with demanding circumstances. Changes are required in your normal coping mechanism, and you become more fearful, feel overwhelmed, or feel out of control.

Stress is a derivation of the Latin word meaning *"to be drawn tight."* By paying attention to your physical and psycho/emotional responses to various situations you can determine where you are becoming "drawn" into a tight or constricted psycho/emotional state and the effect it is having on your body. The circumstances may be as simple as when your child won't stop screaming, or as complicated as having to move house.

Stress has such a wide-ranging effect that it is hard to define which illnesses are stress related and which are not. Most conservative estimates suggest that 70 percent of all illnesses are caused by stress; others suggest up to 90 percent. Perhaps it is simpler to say that stress affects every part of your body, mind, and emotions. How pervasive and devastating it can be is seen in research done by the Centres for Disease Control and the National Institute for Occupational Safety and Health. Researchers found that in the United States up to $300 billion (£150 billion), or $7,500 (nearly £4,000) per employee, is spent each year on stress-related absenteeism or decreases in productivity, while 43 percent of all adults suffer from noticeable physical and emotional symptoms from burnout. Depression, which is only one type of stress reaction, is predicted to be the leading occupational disease of the 21st century, responsible for more days lost than any other single factor.

THE EFFECTS OF STRESS

The *stress response* is a physiological reaction that prepares your body to respond to the stressor. This begins in the hypothalamus, a small part of the limbic system in the brain that deals with emotions and feelings. This area also monitors the nervous system, the digestion, heart rate, blood pressure, and respiration. The red alert causes the release of adrenaline, cortisol, and other hormones that affect these systems. The hormones shut down the digestive system (to conserve energy), increase the heart rate (to increase energy), suppress the sensation of feeling (so you can be hurt and still keep fighting or running), and increase the rate of breathing. These systems then affect every other part of your body.

But what happens to the body when the stress response is experienced without any means of expression? When there is no animal to hunt or no war to fight in which to release the energy accumulating inside, where does it go? How does the digestive system cope with being suppressed once, maybe twice a day? Is it so difficult to believe that ulcers or irritable bowel syndrome are connected to high stress levels, that you get constipation, diarrhoea, or a loss of appetite? What happens to the urge to scream, to lash out, to find release from the tension? Is it surprising that marriages suffer, that alcohol and food addiction is rising, or that mental exhaustion leads to depression or breakdown?

Physical symptoms of stress include such digestive disorders as those mentioned above, plus ulcers, heartburn and indigestion, headaches, high blood pressure, palpitations, breathing problems (such as asthma or hyperventilation), overeating, exhaustion and insomnia, back or muscle ache, skin rashes (such as hives or eczema), excessive sweating, and nervous disorders (such as twitching, grinding teeth, or picking at skin). At the same time, cortisol has the effect of suppressing the immune system, so *all* immune deficient illnesses (from the common cold to cancer) can be directly or indirectly caused by stress.

As stress increases you become less psychologically and emotionally able to adequately adapt, causing you to easily overreact to issues, lose a clear perspective on priorities, get muddled or disorganized, or become increasingly depressed. Or you may rant or rage for no apparent reason. Most important is the feeling of being out of control, that events or demands are beyond your capacity, therefore failure is looming. You can get locked into repetitive self-criticism that only serves to reinforce your hopelessness. When the stress response continues over a period of time—with a regular release of adrenaline and cortisol, and the resulting physiological and emotional changes—you may begin to experience more serious problems.

Psychological and emotional disorders include increased anxiety and panic, irritability and frustration, irrational outbursts of hostility, power and manipulation issues, debilitating fear and insecurity, rapid mood changes, restlessness and nervousness, sexual problems (such as impotence and frigidity), addictive behaviour, memory loss, paranoia and confusion, as well as impaired performance, concentration, and efficiency.

Because the hormones that circulate as a result of the alarm signal have the effect of numbing your feelings, you may not even be aware you are getting stressed. In the battlefield you would be grateful for such numbness, but in ordinary circumstances this means that you may continue being stressed without experiencing the debilitating results until much later, when you collapse exhausted. It also means you are consistently out of touch with your feelings, which can result in serious relationship difficulties.

CAUSES OF STRESS

Few of us like to think of ourselves as stressed; we do not want to believe we could be so weak or that our circumstances are so debilitating. We like to think of stress as what happens to others, without realizing how susceptible we may be ourselves.

The most comprehensive study of the causes of stress was carried out by Drs. Holmes and Rahe at the University of Washington. They based their findings on the level of adjustment required for different circumstances, as the inability to adequately adjust is most likely to stimulate the stress response. Their Social Readjustment Scale placed the death of a spouse as the most difficult circumstance to adapt to, followed by divorce, separation, the death of a close family member, and marriage. In more recent studies events such as moving house, having a child, financial difficulties, illness of oneself or a close family member, redundancy, a new job, even taking exams, have also been rated very highly. To that list must now be added environmental stressors such as pollution, traffic, noise, and increased population, as well as a lack of connection with nature.

What must be remembered, however, is that as we all respond differently to circumstances. A divorce may be high on the list of stressors for one person, but it may be a welcome relief to another! The stressor itself may be any one of the big issues mentioned above as much as it may be an accumulation of little issues—an overcrowded train, spilling a drink, or too many bills coming at once. These are life issues that we are all subject to in one way or another, yet for some they will be stress producing, while for others they will not. The difference lies in your response, for although you may have little or no control over the circumstances or stressors you are dealing with, you do have control over your understanding of the situation and over your reaction to it.

In other words, the real cause of stress is not the external circumstances, such as having too many demands and not enough time to fill them. The real cause is *your perception of the circumstances*—whether that is a fearful, overwhelming, or challenging perception. It is also *your perception of your ability to cope*, as when you feel stretched beyond what you think you are capable of. And your perceptions invariably arise from your inner belief system about yourself—what you have come to believe you are capable of due to what you have been told or taught. For instance, if you were raised to believe you were good at certain things but not so good at others, then when you are confronted with the things you believe you are not so good at, you will invariably experience a lack of self-confidence and/or the inability to cope.

What you believe will colour your every thought, word, and action. As cell biologist Bruce Lipton says in his book *The Biology of Belief*, "Our responses to environmental stimuli [stressors] are indeed controlled by perceptions, but not all of our learned perceptions are accurate. Not all snakes are dangerous! Yes, perception 'controls' biology, but … these perceptions can be true or false. Therefore, we would be more accurate to refer to these controlling perceptions as beliefs. *Beliefs control biology!*"

In other words, believing that your work, family, or lifestyle is causing you stress and that if you could only stop it or change it in some way then you would be fine, is seeing the situation from the wrong perspective. Rather, it is the belief that something out there is causing you stress that is causing the stress. And although changing the circumstances certainly may help, it will only be temporary. Invariably, no matter where you go or what you do, you will be liable to stress until there is a change within your belief system that changes your perception of yourself.

There is also the misunderstanding held by those people who tend to live on the wire—such as those involved with sports or in competitive business—that we have to be stressed or "have an edge" in order to succeed; that the drive of competitiveness or ever greater challenges is needed to stimulate creativity and efficiency, and that without it our response would be too inert or passive. However, as stress actually diminishes performance rather than boosting it, there is a far more effective place where you are both fully relaxed and totally alert at the same time, as a truly relaxed state encourages greater creativity. In a relaxed state you have access to far greater physical and psychological energy levels. That is why stress-management is fast becoming an integral part of most forward-thinking businesses.

The greatest lesson you can learn from being stressed is that you can work with your stress response and develop a higher level of adaptability by changing your perception of yourself. You *can* change your beliefs! A greater belief in yourself, your capability, and a greater sense of humour so you don't take everything—including yourself—quite so seriously, will go a long way toward developing the relaxation response, which normalizes everything the stress response has upset.

Taking this quiz will to enable you to assess your stress level and see where you need to bring change. Sit quietly and have some paper and a pen handy. Answer those questions that feel most applicable to you and respond as fully and honestly as you can. This is not to create any judgment or blame, but to develop greater self-awareness.

About Your Work

1. Do you feel you have too much to do?
2. Do you often work overtime?
3. Do you believe you are capable of what is being asked of you?
4. Do you enjoy what you do?
5. Does your work environment feel depressing? Sad? Loud? Pressured?
6. How do you feel about your colleagues? Intimidated? Angry? Jealous?
7. Do you feel unfulfilled? Unacknowledged? Unrecognized?
8. Would you rather be doing something different?

About Your Family

9. Have you recently experienced a death or loss in the family?
10. Have you recently been married, separated, or divorced?
11. Has anyone in your family recently experienced a particularly difficult time, such as mental illness or trouble with the police?
12. Is anyone ill and in need of your care? And do you resent this?
13. Do your parents need you or worry you a great deal?
14. Have you been able to share any of these difficulties?

About Your Relationships

15. If your primary relationship is not a happy one, do you believe you have to stick it out regardless of your feelings?

16. Do you disagree about money? The children? Your life-style preferences?
17. Do you have sexual difficulties or differences?
18. Do you feel unable to stand up for yourself?
19. Did you grow up watching your parents having difficulties, either fighting or ignoring each other?
20. Do you find it difficult to be committed to a relationship?
21. Do you have anyone you can talk to?

About Yourself

22. Do you believe, or have you been told, that you are no good, hopeless, worthless, or incapable?
23. Do you get irritated or annoyed easily?
24. Do you always seem to be rushing from one thing to another without being able to complete anything?
25. Do you have an addiction of any sort?
26. Do you feel trapped and powerless to change anything?
27. Do you panic easily or feel anxious about the future?
28. Do you talk to anyone about your feelings?
29. Do you feel shameful about something you have done?
30. Are you angry about something that was done to you?

About Your Health

31. Do you get tired or run down easily?
32. Do you get any regular exercise?
33. Do you eat while doing other things, such as working, watching TV, reading the paper, or feeding the children?
34. Is television, alcohol, or food your main means of relaxation?
35. Do you have deep muscular aches and pains?
36. Do you drink more than two cups of coffee a day?
37. Do you spend any part of the day being quiet and reflective?

There are no right or wrong answers. Rather, use your answers to gain a deeper understanding of where you are not able to cope and what areas in your life need attention and consideration, and then find a way to express your feelings and needs. Changing your relationship to stress means changing yourself from the inside.

Trauma and Post-Traumatic Stress Disorder (PTSD)

Trauma occurs when an experience overwhelms your ability to cope. PTSD is the anxiety or mental disability that follows, particularly if those events are outside your normal range of life experience, for such experiences are the opposite of your expectations of what life should be like. The traumatic events most often associated with PTSD are rape and sexual molestation, physical attack and combat exposure, childhood neglect and childhood physical abuse, as well as being involved in a fire, flood, or other natural disaster, or being involved in a life-threatening accident. The effects of PTSD include nightmares, upsetting memories and flashbacks, emotional detachment, blame, irrational anger, distraction, excessive alcohol or drug use, impaired breathing, muscle tension and pain, headaches, and/or sensory and nervous overload.

The muscular pain occurs because the experience of a traumatic event usually makes you contract or pull inward in order to create some form of physical protection, but such contraction limits the flow of blood and oxygen to the muscles, thereby causing intense pain. The muscles effectively "hold" the memory of the trauma, and the tension and pain may continue for a long time after the trauma has passed. If another traumatic experience follows, even many years later, it will invariably be held in the same way and in the same part of the body, as this part is already weakened, making recovery that much harder. This is classic bodymind, where the muscles are expressing the tension in the mind.

As with repeated stress, trauma leads to an excess of adrenaline in the body that can then lead to adrenal exhaustion, depression, the inability to communicate, a rejection of normal society, and even thoughts of suicide.

Recovery from PTSD needs to be approached in three ways: by establishing a sense of safety in your everyday life, by releasing the held tension and resulting disturbance in the body, and through connecting the fragmented pieces in the mind in order to put together and integrate the story. As a traumatic experience is outside your normal range of experiences, the process of recovery and healing is also an opportunity to transform your normal perception of reality and to find a deeper meaning and purpose in life.

TEN

PROTECTOR OF THE CASTLE
The Immune System

One of the most complex and important systems in the body, the immune system is comprised of the lymph glands and nodes, the thymus gland, tonsils, spleen, and white blood cells. The main function of the immune system is to recognize foreign substances (antigens)—such as viruses or bacteria—and prevent them from doing any harm. This is the ability to protect yourself against illness. It is an awareness of the relationship between inside and outside, to what extent you are influenced by that relationship, and the ability to discriminate between what is you or is not you—between self and other than self. If the immune system is overactive toward external antigens, such as pollen, then an allergy can develop; if it is underactive, then an infection develops. If the immune system is overactive against an internal antigen, then it can start destroying the body, as in autoimmune diseases; if it is underactive, then abnormal body cells will develop, as in cancer.

The immune system works in two main ways. Firstly, when the system encounters a foreign substance (such as bacteria), an antibody is formed by B-cells in the blood. As each substance is dealt with, immunity develops against future invasion by the same antigen. Vaccination was developed on this basis. This is also how infectious diseases help build resistance and strength, and why childhood diseases like measles or mumps occur only once.

The second aspect of immune defence is cell-mediated immunity, which occurs through specialized cells in the blood. T-cells destroy the invading substance—helper T-cells sound the alarm, killer T-cells do the destroying, and suppressor T-cells sound the retreat when the job is done. Macrophages engulf the foreign cells and clean up the debris. T-cells originate in the bone marrow and are then sent to the thymus gland for maturation, before entering the bloodstream.

As their main job is to identify and destroy foreign substances, the immune cells have to be able to distinguish between what is harmful and what is harmless. This is the ability to discriminate between self and other than self, between what is you and what is not you. It is reflected in your ability to determine your own thoughts and feelings as opposed to adopting those of someone else. When you believe another person more than you believe in yourself, you are giving away your sense of individuality and surrendering your power. This makes you more vulnerable and liable to be affected—or infected—by someone or something outside of yourself.

The word "tolerance" is used to describe this discrimination between self and other than self, so that the immune cells only attack non-self substances. "Intolerance" is the inability to distinguish between these, so that the non-self actually appears as self and is not destroyed. Here, the bodymind connection is clear, and just as external toxins or substances can put such a strain on the immune system that it loses its tolerance, so excessive stress, grief, trauma, loss, or loneliness can push you beyond your coping or tolerance capacity to a place of incapacity or intolerance.

For instance, loneliness, divorce, and bereavement can all lead to a quicker death, as if the death were literally due to a broken heart. Many studies show higher rates of illness among people who have recently lost a spouse. At New York's Mount Sinai Hospital, tests showed that immune functioning in the partners of people who were sick was fine prior to their spouse dying, but after the partners' death immune functioning dropped alarmingly and could not be raised. The immune cells, although normal in number, were simply not working. "There is real evidence that in the first six months after the loss of a spouse, the remaining partner is in increased danger of succumbing to fatal illness," writes Colin Murray Parkes, former consultant psychiatrist at the Royal London Hospital, in *The Times*.

When Federico Fellini died, his wife was devastated and died five months later. A friend of theirs was quoted as saying, "She just seemed to have given up on life." It is as if the cells themselves are experiencing the grief and loneliness, conveyed from the brain to the immune system.

This is not to deny the impact of chemical toxins in the air, food, and water, which is enormous. The immune system tries to maintain harmony by tolerating and balancing internal states with external ones. If the external substances become overwhelming, or have abnormal patterns, then the immune system can get pushed beyond its tolerance level. In the same way, if the level of emotional toxins rises, this can also undermine its strength. Mental toxins, such as negative thoughts, can also have a detrimental affect. One researcher at Zurich University determined that negative thoughts or feelings could depress the immune system for hours.

BODYMIND DIALOGUE: THE IMMUNE SYSTEM

The immune system is adversely affected by stress, grief, depression, loneliness, and repressed feelings, and through a loss of a sense of self. If your immune system is low, it might prove helpful to find out where you are repressing your feelings and find constructive ways to release them.

- Have you lost your sense of individuality or confidence in your own beliefs?
- Have you been unduly influenced by someone or something else?

- Has your tolerance level dropped?
- Are you becoming increasingly intolerant?
- Is there a part of you that you have been ignoring or denying?
- Is there a psycho/emotional battle going on inside you?
- Have you been overly stressed, depressed, or worried of late?

THE GLANDS OF THE IMMUNE SYSTEM

The **thymus gland**, situated just above the heart, is primary to the immune system. In China it is known as a source of chi or healing energy. It derives its name from the Greek word *thymos*, meaning soul or personality, indicative of its relationship to the immune system, and its role in determining your sense of self. The thymus gland produces T-cells, which deal with bacteria, viruses, parasites, cancer, and allergies, and releases the T-cells into the blood system. It also produces specific hormones that help deal with infection and immunity. When excessive stress or trauma cause an increase in hormones released by the adrenal glands, these in turn inhibit the production of thymus hormones, leaving you more susceptible to infection and illness.

The thymus is also known as the seat of fire, because of its close connection to the heart. For instance, when you are in love, feel confident, or have an open and positive frame of mind, you will probably find it quite hard to get ill, as your T-cell count will be high. Conversely, when you feel depressed, lonely, or sad, your T-cell count drops and you can catch cold or get ill quite easily. As Dr. Norman Shealy says in *The Creation of Health*, "The new field of psychoneuroimmunology now suggests that emotions may be the final straw that causes the immune system to decompensate."

It appears that the emotional state of the heart can energize or deplete the thymus gland, which in turn influences the health of the immune system. In other words, a loving support system gives greater resilience and strength to resist outside influence or external invasion. The more love you experience, the better you feel about yourself and the less likely you are to be depressed. Laughter works just as well. Norman Cousins shut himself into a hotel room with dozens of comedy movies and laughed himself into a remission from cancer. If that emotional support system is weakened—whether through loneliness or loss—the ability to resist infection is also weakened. The immune system becomes exhausted, just as your tolerance for stress or grief becomes exhausted.

The **lymph glands** are another important part of the immune system. It is in here that foreign substances are ambushed and, hopefully, dealt with by the white blood cells. Swollen lymph glands—such as in the armpit or groin—indicate that the immune system is working to fight an infection. Issues to do with the lymph are, therefore, connected to fighting an "invasion" from somewhere or someone and being able to maintain your sense of self.

Included in the immune system is the **spleen**, which filters the blood to remove waste, old blood cells, and foreign substances, and infuses the blood with new immune cells. The word *spleen* means moroseness and irritability, so difficulties here indicate that, rather than filtering out the waste, there is a harbouring of old or stagnant thoughts and feelings. This creates disruption and an increase in irritability or indigestion. A strong spleen encourages clarity, compassion, and sympathy, as the blood is freed of negative influences.

AUTOIMMUNE DISORDERS

Normally the immune system is able to identify which substances are foreign or potentially harmful and which are harmless. When it starts attacking components of the body itself in the same way that it attacks foreign substances, then autoimmune diseases, such as rheumatoid arthritis or multiple sclerosis, develop. In these cases, the ability to differentiate becomes so confused that the self appears as the non-self.

BODYMIND DIALOGUE: AUTOIMMUNE DISORDERS

If you have an autoimmune disorder of any kind, the questions you need to ask are about how you have become an enemy to yourself, and/or to what extent you allow others to influence you, in denial of your own thoughts or feelings. These questions are not easy to answer, as they demand great honesty.

- Do you feel as if you are not really valid?
- Do you think you don't have needs?
- Are you carrying guilt, shame, or blame from the past that is wearing away your self-esteem or self-respect?
- Do you have an underlying dislike or hatred of yourself?
- Do you spend your time helping others but refusing help yourself?
- Are you overly critical of yourself?
- Do you constantly put yourself down?
- Is someone else wearing away at you, corroding your sense of worth?
- Have you lost your ability to discriminate?
- Do you let someone else determine what you think or feel?

Infection

Your lifestyle and environmental issues, such as hygiene, sanitation, and personal habits, can encourage infections. Smoking increases the risk of infection by lowering immune response, as does a poor diet. However, even if you live in the most sterile and germ-free environment, infection is still possible, as it is more than just the presence of germs or bacteria that causes an infection. There also has to be a weakness in the immune system. Think about it: one person in an office catches a cold, two others then get it, but two others do not. The contaminant is equally contagious to all five, so there has to be another factor involved, such as compromised immunity. Chemical stress weakens the immune system, inactivity weakens the immune system, and negative or upsetting emotions weaken the immune system.

The word *infection* can help you understand this more deeply. To be infected is to allow something in that affects you. It changes you in some way. You are no longer the same, as a result.

BODYMIND DIALOGUE: INFECTION

If an infection has occurred, you need to ask yourself how someone or something is detrimentally affecting you, to the point of weakening your ability to protect or defend yourself.

- Is someone or something making you feel intolerant, insecure, or fearful?
- What or who is causing you to lose your balance or tolerance so that your defences are weakened?
- Are you repressing deep emotions that may be compromising your immunity?

Inflammation

Inflammation occurs when the immune system is trying to fight off an invading harmful substance, causing heat, swelling, and pain.

There is a war going on between an invading substance and your inner being, and your immune system is fighting against the non-self in order to maintain balance. Perhaps you are failing to acknowledge this war within yourself.

BODYMIND DIALOGUE: INFLAMMATION

To be inflamed conjures up strong images of hot, fiery passion, redness, and anger.

- Are you feeling angry and fired up about something?
- An inflammation is swollen and sore—can you find what is making you feel this way inside?
- Is there a battle going on between what is acceptable and what is not?
- Is there a battle between your own beliefs or feelings and those of someone else?
- What or who has so penetrated your defences?

The Common Cold

You could get a cold from a number of different viruses that are floating around all the time, yet how often do you actually get ill? Perhaps a couple of times a year? The real reason you get a cold is not because of being exposed to someone else who has it, but because at the moment you encountered the cold virus your resistance was low and your immunity was compromised. Only when your immune tolerance is low will a virus be able to infect you. If your immunity is strong, then runny noses may surround you, but yours will stay dry.

There are many different versions of **the common cold**, although the symptoms usually include a runny nose, watery eyes, stuffy or painful sinuses, a sore throat, and sometimes a cough. A cold may start in the chest and move up, or start in the nose and move down. Stress may well be a cause, as it reduces immune efficiency. The stress may be due to overwork, in which case the cold could be trying to tell you that you need time off. Or it may be due to emotional issues, in which case you need to look a little deeper.

When you cry, your nose runs. When you have a cold, your eyes water. Colds, runny noses, and tears are all related—mucus and tears are both ways of releasing repressed or pent-up emotions. You may well feel the same helplessness and despair, the same need for comfort. So, if you have a bad cold, you may want to see if there is some crying or grieving you are repressing, some deep feeling that has been pushed aside.

Unshed tears will find their way into the nose, whether they are due to sadness, frustration, or guilt. A cold often follows the death of a loved one or some form of emotional shock, particularly when grief is not acknowledged. It may also imply that you have gone emotionally cold or are being cold to your feelings. Colds are common, just as it is common not to show how we really feel.

In addition, a cold may indicate a time of change and transition, when there is too much happening at once and you need to shut off for a while, slowing down your intake to allow for assimilation.

BODYMIND DIALOGUE: THE COMMON COLD

Remember that one of the ways to understand an illness is by looking at its effect in your life. In the case of a cold, this means that people will be steering clear of you and it is unlikely anyone will want to be too intimate!

- Is this what you really want?
- Do you need some time to yourself to adjust to something?
- Or is it the opposite: a cry for attention and affection because everyone seems to be taking you so much for granted?
- Do you need to get ill in order to be noticed and cared for?

Flu

There are a growing number of mutations and varieties of the flu virus now affecting the world. Flu can vary from simply having a high temperature and aching muscles to a more serious collapse of the immune system. That is why there is so much attention paid to getting an annual flu shot. However, the side effects of a flu jab can also be detrimental, so a safer alternative is to strengthen your immune health by avoiding or resolving stressful situations.

BODYMIND DIALOGUE: FLU

The flu bug will only affect you when your immunity is already low, so this is a good place to start looking for bodymind causes. The word *influenza* means to "come under the influence of," implying that someone or something is having a strong influence on you, perhaps making you doubt what you think or feel for yourself. This can undermine your sense of identity or purpose, and you need time to reconnect with your own feelings. Flu sends a clear message that time out is needed.

- What psycho/emotional issues have you been repressing?
- Have you been increasingly intolerant or irritable? What is disturbing you so deeply?

Tonsillitis

Both the tonsils and the adenoids, positioned each side of the throat, are a part of the lymph system, which in turn is the part of the immune system that helps to filter out harmful foreign substances. Tonsils and adenoids can swell when you have an infection and cause a very sore throat. As they are positioned at the point of entry into the body they particularly represent the ability to discriminate between what is helpful and what is harmful.

The tonsils are involved in protecting against infection, so when they become inflamed, as in tonsillitis, you need to explore what is causing such upset, irritation, or soreness. Tonsillitis is most common in children, indicating that the issue is usually about feeling powerless and unable to control what is happening. Children are invariably subject to change without choice or consultation, and they may not be able to express how they feel about this. They may feel vulnerable, exposed, angry, fearful, or insecure, and unable or unwilling to swallow what is happening. I had my own tonsils removed when I was eight years old, shortly after I had been sent to boarding school. Having the tonsils removed is one way of dealing with an uncomfortable situation, especially as it garners extra attention. But it also helps if the child can be encouraged to share and express his or her feelings directly.

BODYMIND DIALOGUE: TONSILLITIS

The tonsils swell up so much that it becomes hard to swallow.

- What or who is it that you are finding so hard to swallow?
- Is there something you are resisting?
- What is inciting such strong feelings?

Swollen adenoids normally occur in young children, blocking the nasal and ear passages. Swollen adenoids are also blocking the intake of information, whether through the throat or the ears, so attention needs to be paid to what is happening in the child's life that is so difficult for him or her to swallow or hear.

Allergies

When the immune system overreacts to a foreign body (allergen) that it perceives to be hostile, it creates an allergic reaction—sneezing, wheezing, watery eyes, skin rashes, headaches. The allergen is usually a substance that is hard to avoid, such as dust, cat fur, or pollen. It is therefore important to ask why the body is seeing a benign substance as an enemy, and why it is reacting so strongly. What is causing you to lose your tolerance over something that does not have any inherent life-threatening qualities? An irritant is irritating you, and it is making you irritable!

The physical reaction is one of defence and resistance, so the psycho/emotional cause of allergies will be connected to an inner need to withdraw, to put up resistances, not to enter fully into a situation. As most allergens are a part of daily life, it suggests a fear of participation, intimacy, responsibility or accountability. It is as if the external world has become an enemy, something to be resisted. Exploring what you are really afraid of, or what you are trying to avoid, will help you realize that the allergy is a symptom of something more ingrained.

BODYMIND DIALOGUE: ALLERGIES

An allergic reaction is very much like an emotional one, with weepy eyes, a runny nose, and difficulties with breathing.

- Are you overreacting to an emotional situation?
- What or who are you actually feeling allergic toward?
- Does your allergy affect your relationships?
- Is it really a cry for attention?

Seeing the world as hostile or potentially aggressive can be due to a repression of your own hostility or aggression. It is, after all, socially more acceptable to have an allergy than it is to scream or hit out! It also signifies an unwillingness to communicate, a withdrawal from connecting or sharing with your world.

- Before the allergy symptoms developed, were you feeling hostile or resistant to communicating with someone?
- Were you wanting to scream or shout?
- Did you feel yourself withdrawing inside, pushing those feelings down?

Cancer

Few illnesses have the impact on as many people as does cancer. Although the remedies are increasing, so is the number of cases, and the suffering is huge. Cancer develops when the immune system does not stop the growth of abnormal cells. Such cells are not unusual, but they are mostly dealt with without any interference to the rest of the body. In the case of cancer, the cells are not dealt with, and they multiply and gather. Medicine then attempts, often successfully, to annihilate such cells. As cancer is so widespread and seemingly arbitrary in who it affects, we need to look at the causes objectively in order to gain some deeper insight.

There are certainly environmental considerations. Toxins are consistently pouring into the ecosystem in the form of pesticides, plastics, hormones, and chemicals, all of which put an excessive strain on the immune system and may be active carcinogens. With the increase of cell phone technology, we are all being exposed to microwaves. Many of us are living and working in environments where there is little fresh air. We may get a limited amount of exercise. And our diet has changed dramatically since the invention of fast and packaged foods. However, we are all exposed to these potential carcinogens, but not all of us develop cancer. Rather, it would appear that it is a *combination* of both environmental and psycho/emotional factors that is most likely to have a detrimental result.

A cell that is abnormal has become wayward, even rebellious. It behaves differently than other cells. Rather than fulfilling its role in support of the whole it goes off on its own, like an isolated member of society, and forms a different system that begins to undermine the whole. In this sense, cancer reflects an aspect of the human condition: rather than being concerned with the welfare of others, we are more interested in looking out for ourselves, but such behaviour undermines the survival of us all.

Perhaps more significant is the loss of community and spiritual meaning in many people's lives. No longer do we live in extended families or close neighbourhoods; instead, it is estimated that by the year 2010 upward of 40 percent of adults will be living alone. We live in closer proximity to each other, but with less intimacy or community. We work longer hours, have ever-greater financial concerns, and we are not getting any happier. The rate of depression and the use of anti-depressants are rapidly rising. Loneliness, isolation, a lack of love or companionship—such factors can cause deep emotional and psychological stress, seriously undermining the immune system.

Alongside that, feelings that are pushed away, denied, or suppressed tend to become isolated and can cause unsociable behaviour. These feelings may go way back to childhood, and they may have given rise to a sense of guilt, shame, or unworthiness. For instance, deep feelings of aggression or hatred that are unacknowledged or denied can make you become timid or overly polite. The unconscious fear of releasing such aggression makes you keep a firm lid on yourself.

As we put all these pieces together, perhaps it is not surprising that an illness has developed that consists of cells going off and doing their own thing, in rebellion to the whole. These cells are a part of you, yet they have become separated, and from that place of isolation they begin to cause havoc. From a bodymind perspective, you therefore need to find that part of yourself that has become so separated, alienated, or rejected.

There are also some well-researched characteristics of the cancer personality as one that includes a suppression of strong emotions, particularly anger and passion; lack of assertiveness, especially in expressing your own needs; stoicism, avoidance of conflict; and appearance of niceness. Obviously, not all cancer patients have these characteristics, for cancer is nothing if not multifaceted and indiscriminate. There is undoubtedly a mystery factor involved here. But cancer has lessons for us all about our attitudes toward each other, about accepting and loving unconditionally, and especially about loving ourselves. Many cancer survivors have spoken about how their healing came as they began to honour themselves more deeply.

Most especially, cancer gives you the chance to re-evaluate, to take stock and be more honest about your feelings, and to clarify your priorities. Just as negative or repressed emotions compromise the immune system, so research (such as in Stanford University in the USA) has shown that therapy—particularly group therapy, where feelings can be released in a caring environment with the support of others—can make a huge difference to the healing process. Talking and feeling safe enable you to find those lost and alienated parts of yourself, to give them life and bring them back into the whole.

It is important to remember that cancer is not contagious, it is not some alien thing that enters the body and takes over. The abnormal cells grow within you; they are as much a part of you as any of your other cells. And if cancer represents an alienated part of yourself, then rejecting or isolating it further does not encourage healing.

Exploring the function of the part of the body involved will help you deepen your understanding. It is also essential to strengthen the immune system, which means strengthening the desire to live. Those who develop a fighting spirit, mental resilience, and vigor, and who do not reject themselves, appear to have a greater survival rate. This is about developing an "I want to live" attitude. Find your lost dreams and denied feelings and embrace them so that they may give you renewed life.

Visualization has been used very effectively to boost the immune system. It is natural to think of immune cells in terms of fighting and winning a war—soldiers on the battlefield, knights on white horses, warriors brandishing their spears, even killer sharks roaming the seas—as these images can boost the job of the T-cells in dealing with wayward cells. However, such images can also maintain feelings of fear and hate. Loving images have been found to work just as well, if not better, while also generating healing peace and ease. Images such as white doves bringing comfort, or hundreds of little red hearts absorbing all the cancer cells, can have a deeply healing effect.

See also: Imagery to Heal

Multiple Sclerosis

A complex illness, multiple sclerosis (MS) affects people in different ways. It even mimics and may be confused with other illnesses, such as CFS. Multiple sclerosis is an autoimmune disease in which the immune system attacks the myelin sheath surrounding the nerves, leading to a sclerosis—a hardening of the surface of the nerves. In other words, your immune system is seeing your own body as the enemy.

There are no known causes for this illness but plenty of theories. One recent idea is that it is due to a lack of Vitamin D. This is because there is virtually no occurrence of MS in the countries around the equator where there is plenty of sunshine—from which we get most of our Vitamin D. The further you go toward either pole and the less exposure to sunshine, the higher the incidence of this disease. This leads to an interesting bodymind analogy of being "in the dark" or of being unaware of your own feelings.

The effect MS has depends on the nerve damage that takes place, as either mobility nerves (movement) or sensory nerves (sensation and pain) are damaged. People with MS can experience numbness, nerve pain, difficulty moving, and/or deep exhaustion. This disease can vary with every person who experiences it, in length, duration, and severity, so it is impossible to predict its course. Approximately 25 percent of people with MS experience very mild symptoms, such as tingling or numbness that passes after a few days. About 50 percent have episodes that last from a few days to a month or more, with any number of debilitating symptoms, but that leave little noticeable damage as the nerves fully regenerate. This is known as relapsing and remitting MS. And about 25 percent experience progressive cycles of damage and remission, leading to greater deterioration as the nerves are unable to regenerate completely.

There is absolutely no doubt that stress plays a very big role in its occurrence, as seen in Anna's story. She has had relapsing/remitting MS since she was twenty-five years old. "I have had three episodes, each lasting about three months, and a few shorter ones, each followed by a full recovery. Every episode followed a period of intense stress (such as my marriage breaking down), close enough that the connection was obvious. After the third episode I went to stay at a yoga ashram, as I wanted to be in an environment where I could be quiet enough to talk to my immune system. I needed to find out what was going on. How had I become such an enemy to myself that my immune system was attacking my own cells?

"After a few weeks of processing and talking, I heard—loud and clear and much to my surprise—that I had not been looking after my own needs. At first this puzzled me, as I honestly believed that I did not have any needs. But I had to honour what my body was telling me. As I did, it was like opening a Pandora's box! Deep inside I discovered a whole heap of needs, left there like discarded dolls. One by one I had to acknowledge and listen to them, and I promised I would not deny them again. It took a while and a lot of learning, but I have stayed true to my word. And I have not had an episode since 1998, despite equally stressful times."

BODYMIND DIALOGUE: MULTIPLE SCLEROSIS

Multiple sclerosis is an autoimmune disease in which the immune system attacks your own nerve sheath, believing it to be the enemy, so this is the place to start looking for a psycho/emotional cause.

- In what way have you become an enemy to yourself?
- Are you recognizing and listening to your inner voice?
- Are you denying or repressing something to the point where you are losing your balance in life?
- Is there some past guilt or shame that is eating away at you?

(These questions apply to all autoimmune illnesses.)

To move is to emote, to bring to life your emotions and feelings. MS restricts and limits movement, implying that your expression of feeling (as in Anna's case: the assertion of her own needs) is becoming more and more withdrawn or held back. MS is most obvious in the way it affects mobility in the legs, making movement difficult or restricted.

- Are you feeling restricted or limited in the direction in which you are going?
- Do you feel you have to go in a direction that is not true to you?
- Do you want to retreat, to stop the movement forward and just be still?
- Are you finding it difficult to stand on your own, perhaps because you are not getting the support you need?
- Do you feel unable to stand up for yourself?
- Have you shut down your feelings in order to keep everything immovable, so you do not have to deal with change?

MS can make you feel powerless, out of control, with a loss of independence and direction. This can be both humiliating and difficult to reconcile. But this may also be where your healing lies.

- Is there a fear of failing as an adult and a desire to return to the safety of being dependent?
- Have you been too focused on your career?
- Have you been working so hard you became seriously stressed?
- Were you doing what you wanted to be doing, or was it out of ambition or the need to prove something?
- Have you forgotten yourself in the midst of your care for others?

Herpes Simplex

Herpes affects the genitals and mouth, with fever blisters or cold sores that burst and leave a crust. A particular characteristic of the herpes virus is that it stays with you for life and outbreaks are unpredictable. Unfortunately, it can easily evade the killer immune cells. The most usual time for an outbreak is following emotional stress or conflict, particularly around the theme of relationships, as herpes invariably brings any form of intimacy to a halt.

An infection in the mouth or the genitals implies that you want to stop what you are saying or how you are relating, as herpes means no one can get too close. This can also apply to work or financial difficulties (especially for men), with the pressure to succeed making you want to withdraw.

BODYMIND DIALOGUE: HERPES SIMPLEX

If you have herpes, there may be hurt, sore, or sad feelings that need to be released.

- Is there someone you feel sore about?
- Is the relationship a loveless one, only based on sex?
- Does intimacy make you feel fearful?
- Are you being asked to be intimate too quickly?
- Are you finding it hard to communicate?

Guilt can also be connected to herpes, perhaps guilt from past sexual activity, or the belief that you are somehow bad or dirty.

- Is someone or something reminding you of previous guilty or shameful behaviour?

Shingles

Shingles is caused by the *Herpes zoster* virus, which also causes chicken pox, and can affect adults and the elderly at times of immune weakness, as when you are stressed or emotionally traumatized. It affects one or more nerves, most often in the chest or in the face, causing redness and intense pain along the nerve pathway, where blisters can form and burst.

Shingles implies a deep anxiety, an inner pain that has been building up over a period of time. As the nerves are your means of communication, shingles is like a cry of pain demanding attention and tenderness, a rawness where you feel vulnerable and weak.

Your body is telling you to stop helping others and to start helping yourself, to ease the stress and tension, communicate your feelings, and to take time to nourish and love yourself.

Chronic Fatigue Syndrome (CFS) and Fibromyalgia

One of the more complex and puzzling illnesses to develop in recent years is **Chronic Fatigue Syndrome (CFS)**. CFS is puzzling because it appears to have no clear cause, such as one particular virus. It has a variable stay, lasting anywhere from a few weeks to several years. And it affects various unrelated parts of the body with symptoms as diverse as muscle weakness, muscle and joint pain, allergies, headaches, and debilitating exhaustion, although not everybody has the same symptoms. It tends to develop following an infection—such as glandular fever—when the immune system is compromised, indicating it could be of viral origin or due to an immune malfunction. However, it does seem to mostly affect younger people, predominately women.

Fibromyalgia (FM) is a companion illness to CFS. (Some say they are simply variations of the same thing.) It too has no known cause other than also being a post-viral infection. It has similar symptoms, although with more emphasis on pain, and affects a similar group of people.

Both CFS and FM make you stop, whether with exhaustion or pain or both. If you have either of these illnesses, there is little doubt you will spend some time resting. This is an important factor in your bodymind understanding. A large number of people affected by these types of illnesses—and there are many variations—are high-flyers already climbing their career ladders. If so, you may well be stressed, and this will certainly strain the immune system. But it may also be that you are going in a direction that is not true to your inner nature—as if you are going against the grain or against your spirit. And then you get stopped.

For others it is the opposite: they are not working, are depressed and inactive, and to some extent have already given up before getting ill. In either case it is as if your spirit is being ignored and it is crying out.

These illnesses seem to be symptomatic of the present age, as if they have developed in response to the increasing pressure to succeed, often at the expense of your own dreams or aspirations. Some common characteristics include thinking that you are not good enough and need to keep pushing to be better or achieve more; or a giving up and inner lassitude that represses any sense of purpose; a tendency to be image-conscious and self-conscious; a strong desire to be in control so that it is very difficult to ask for help; as well as a resistance to facing your responsibilities. So, on the one hand there is both a pushing for success and a fear of failure; and on the other hand, there is a loss of effort or self-respect.

It is interesting that in the United Kingdom this illness is known as **Myalgic Encephalomyelitis (ME)**. (There are some differences in symptoms but both CFS and ME appear to have the same overall characteristics.) More than any other illness, ME appears to generate an immersion in your own problems and issues and a need to talk about yourself: the "poor me" syndrome. The need to focus on yourself is perhaps due to a fear of being lost in the crowd, not being noticed or recognized, or because you want to be seen as special or different. It is as if the disconnection from your inner spirit or true self leads you to over-compensate by becoming excessively connected to your self-centred or superficial self.

BODYMIND DIALOGUE: CHRONIC FATIGUE SYNDROME

Perhaps the direction you have been going in is due to someone else's wishes or influence. Perhaps that direction is where you thought you were meant to be going, but something inside you is longing to express itself in a different way.

- Can you find that place?
- Can you find your spirit?
- Can you see how and why you can no longer go in the direction you were headed?

As there is no motivation or clear direction, all movement forward comes to a halt: muscles ache or collapse; exhaustion takes over. There is a longing to give up, to be free of all the effort it takes to be human. CFS and ME provide a hidden place where you cannot be reached, a shelter from the storm.

Acquired Immuno Deficiency Syndrome (AIDS)

When an invading substance enters the body, the immune system normally sounds the alarm and goes to work. However, when the HIV virus enters the body it not only invades the T-cells but it also shuts off the alarm. This leaves the body open to attack not just from HIV (which is the precursor of AIDS) but also from other antigens. The way this virus affects the body—by invading and even mimicking normal cells—implies an inability to discriminate between harmless and harmful energies, or to recognize potentially damaging circumstances, to the degree that you lose your personal power or "tolerance" and become overwhelmed by this other energy. The immune system loses its boundaries and becomes unable to distinguish between self and non-self.

In many ways AIDS represents our inability, as a society, to honour and respect each other equally. Its transmission is most prevalent in those areas of society that are regularly shunned by the mainstream: gays, drug abusers, the poor, and prostitutes. Having heaped judgment, prejudice, and discrimination on these people, we should not be surprised that an illness has developed that further removes any sense of dignity or pride.

From recent research it would appear that two of the main psycho/emotional characteristics that AIDS carriers share are a sense of victimization and/or a tendency to suppress emotions. For instance, even those gays who are open and honest about their sexuality know that society has yet to be so accepting, and the majority will spend many years feeling ashamed or guilty. For some, telling their parents of their sexual preference is the hardest thing they have to do. Others never feel able to do it, knowing the pain and guilt it will generate. Prostitutes and drug users live in fear of being caught, while the poor are victims of numerous political battles and social prejudice.

This disease also demands that we all explore our attitudes toward sex and relationships. With prostitutes and the majority of gays, changing partners is the norm rather than long-term monogamous partnerships. This is not a judgment on what is right or wrong, but sexual energy is a powerful and very potent energy, such that in some cultures it is revered as sacred. Perhaps AIDS shows us that we cannot misuse or underestimate this energy and that if we do then nature has a way of trying to stop us.

The fact that the HIV virus is transmitted through blood and semen can give us valuable insights into the bodymind relationship. Blood represents the circulation of love from the heart through all parts of your being, containing within it life-sustaining oxygen, while semen represents the expression of love from one to another, containing within it the potential for further life. Yet it is through these two essential life-giving fluids that a latent cause of death is transmitted.

Love and life are indivisible: without love, life has no meaning; without life, love has no expression. Without love—or a love of life—there is depression, hopelessness, an endless search for fulfillment. There may be self-hatred, self-abuse, anger, or fear that shuts you off from the feelings in your heart. Does the transmission of the virus imply that love is lacking? Does an inner defencelessness attract the virus, or does the virus create a defenceless emotional state?

And to what extent is the transmission dependent on being received? It would appear that to receive the virus there has to be a shared or similar physical and/or emotional environment. If there is no receiving pattern, no receptive place, then the virus is not transmitted. This is seen in the many cases where one partner is HIV positive but the other, despite unprotected sex, remains negative.

With AIDS has come the growing awareness of how love heals, as if the virus itself awakens us to see where the heart is closed. It is extraordinary how many AIDS patients, particularly in their last months or weeks, connect with unconditional love: families are healed; parents accept children who were previously rejected; friends and lovers openly care for each other; inner conflicts are resolved. I have seen few illnesses that focus so deeply on love. AIDS asks us to open our hearts to the beauty and dignity that is within each one of us. Singer Paul Krueger, a dear friend who died of AIDS as this book was being written, expressed this in the last song he wrote, "Finally Free":

> One day when I woke up in despair
> A rising sun broke the darkness there
> And on the horizon what did I see?
> A hundred of God's angels flying so high
> My heart took wing, my eyes could see
> The voice of my soul cried, I'm finally free!
> And then to my surprise
> Everybody flew to meet the angel band
> The people of hate and the people of peace
> All the opposites of the human race
> The Mother and the Father too
> The devils in me, and the angels in you
> And when the holy hour had come
> In freedom we flew into the sun
> We took no hate, we took no guns
> The game was over, the battle done
> Finally free, I'm finally free, I can fly like an angel.

There are also those people who have received AIDS accidentally—perhaps through a blood transfusion—and who do not fall into any of the above categories. It is at this point that our understanding of the implications of AIDS needs to expand. We need to recognize it as an illness of our times, a reflection of the harm we are inflicting on every form of life, not just ourselves. As we cut down the rain forests, pollute the oceans, and deplete natural resources, cases of AIDS, child abuse, cancer, and heart disease are rising. Perhaps nature is trying to tell us in the only way she can that the time has come to find a deeper level of tolerance and harmony, to realize that the way we are behaving, as a race, has become intolerable.

The energy of love is all-powerful; it should be the determining force of our lives. But, with our massive overpopulation and abuse of planetary resources we have become hostile and resistant to one another, more inclined to inflict harm than to share love. The ignorance of our essential connectedness is all too destructive. AIDS is a wake-up call for us all—not just those who are individually affected—to connect ever more deeply with love for one another.

ELEVEN
THE BREATH OF LIFE
The Respiratory System

The breath is the rhythm of inspiration and expiration that maintains all life. Both breath and spirit come from the same Latin root *spiro*—to inspire is to fill the body with breath and to fill the spirit with divine awareness. Without breath you are merely an inert physical form; without spirit life is meaningless. To be without breath is to die physically; to be without spirit is to die in your soul. When you die, both the breath and the spirit depart from the body.

The entire respiratory system represents your independence, your separate life, as well as your desire for life. From the nose to the lungs, the breath enters and fills you with oxygen and then leaves. The breath not only brings essential life, but its rhythm is used to calm and focus the mind—watching the in and out flow of the breath is the basis of most traditional forms of meditation.

The breath gives you life, yet it is not yours to hold. It comes from outside and, in so doing, demands that you stay aware of and participate in the world you live in. You cannot own the breath; you only have it on the condition that you give it away again. As you breathe out another breathes in: we all share the same breath, whoever we may be. You breathe the same breath as your loved ones and your enemies. You give, I receive. In this way there is a constant flow.

However, such a flow demands a trust that in letting go of the breath there will be another one to take, a trust that the world will support and sustain you, that you will not be let down. Bodymind issues to do with the breath, therefore, focus around feelings of insecurity and mistrust, especially if your birth was difficult or you were emotionally let down as a child.

Breathing marks your entry into this world. When you take your first breath you declare your independence, separate from your mother who has been breathing for you. So breathing difficulties may be connected to feeling unsure of that independence, or insecure in your ability to breathe—or live—for yourself. This may be due to an overbearing parent, usually your mother, or a partner in adult life who "breathes'" for you by dominating and controlling your life, thereby thwarting any attempt at your being independent.

With the breath there are no edges or limitations; each breath merges into the next. Difficulties are connected to boundaries, to feeling unclear about where you begin or end, so others can easily take over or breathe for you by influencing or dominating you. Issues of personal control can arise if you feel smothered or unable to breathe for yourself. There is a loss of personal power or autonomy, and this may lead to constricted breathing.

Every feeling you experience is reflected in the depth, length, and type of breath, from superficial and quick breathing at times of panic or stress, to deep full breaths when you are completely relaxed. Do you find yourself gasping for breath when you feel sad or angry? Anger makes the breath shallow and fast, while fear makes you either hold your breath or breathe very quickly. Sadness will make you gulp and gasp, and breathe irregularly. When you breathe deeply the chest opens, as when you are joyful and happy, and inner tension is released. As Kariba Ekken, a seventh-century Sufi, once wrote: "If you would foster a calm spirit, first regulate your breathing; for when that is under control, the heart will be at peace; but when breathing is spasmodic, then it will be troubled. Therefore, before anything, first regulate your breathing on which your temper will be softened, your spirit calmed."

You can transform how you feel simply by changing your breathing pattern. See this for yourself by practising the "Breathing Review" below and watching how your emotions change as your breath deepens. Just by shifting the focus of your breathing you can change your stress level—a direct bodymind relationship. When you breathe fully, you own your life and personal power. There is uprightness and openness, a natural dignity.

BREATHING REVIEW
Start by sitting or lying comfortably and closing your eyes.

Just watch your breath for a few minutes.
You need to take enough time to become familiar with your normal pattern of breathing. This is important.

Now breathe into the upper part of your chest.
Only the upper part should move. To do this the breath will have to be quite short and rapid. Watch as your emotions become panicky, stressed, even slightly fearful. Only stay here as long as it is comfortable. If you naturally breathe here, then become aware of how such shallow breathing may be triggering stress.

Now breathe into the middle of your chest.
Your focus should be around your heart or just below. This is a fairly normal place to breathe. Watch how your breathing deepens and your feelings change, becoming calmer, quieter. See if any other emotions arise. Stay here as long as you want.

Now breathe into your belly.
Aim for about an inch below your belly button. To do this you will have to take longer and fuller breaths. This means that the

diaphragm—the sheath of muscle running across your middle just below your heart—has to be relaxed. If this is difficult for you, do it lying down on the floor with your knees bent. Keep on breathing into your belly as long as you want to. See how your emotions become calmer and quieter, until you feel deeply at peace.

Breathing and Healing

You can use the breath to bring healing by consciously directing it to an area of pain or disturbance. Normally, we tense ourselves against pain, whether physical or psychological, and seek a way out through distraction or painkillers. But there is another way, and that is to breathe into the pain, to become more and more open to it. Breathing in this way releases resistance and tension and reduces the intensity of the pain. It also helps separate the physical pain from the emotional tensions or fears that often accompany it, so you can work more directly with the issues involved. To do this, consciously direct your breath into the painful area, feel the pain softening and dissolving with each in-breath, and release the pain and tension on the out-breath. Breathe and soften. This also increases the flow of oxygen and blood to the affected part.

You can use your breath to enter vulnerable and tender places within yourself. Keep breathing into and through any resistance. Use your breath to give you courage and fearlessness, to ground you in your present reality, to relax and find a deeper ease. Remember the phrase "soft belly" and repeat it to yourself whenever you need to. You cannot get tense or nervous if you have a soft belly, and as soon as you repeat the words it will remind you to relax and breathe. Softening the belly softens your resistance, limitations, and inner tension.

The respiratory system centres on the lungs, but also includes the nose, throat, larynx, trachea, and bronchi. It has an intimate relationship with the blood, as oxygen passes from the lungs into the bloodstream, while carbon dioxide comes from the blood into the lungs for expiration. This relationship becomes clearer in Chapter 12, on the circulatory system.

BREATHING AND HEALING REVIEW

Do this practise anytime, anywhere; eyes open or closed. Sitting on the train feeling tired and stressed—soft belly and breathe. Standing at the sink surrounded by dirty dishes and a screaming baby—soft belly and breathe. About to go into surgery—soft belly and breathe. On your way to an important meeting—soft belly and breathe.

The Nose

The entry point for the breath, the nose is where you inhale both the beauty and the repugnance of life. In yogic terms, the two nostrils correspond to the two sides of the brain and the masculine and feminine aspects of your energy system. Meditation breathing techniques, known as *pranayama*, use the closing and opening of the nostrils to deepen concentration.

The nose is also for **smelling**. You have a powerful aroma-recognition process built inside you, which is why you can be transported back to memories from childhood at the mere whiff of a familiar scent. But memories are not always welcome, so a **blocked nose** may be one way of keeping them away. However, smelling is not only about specific smells. Like the eyes, where you do more than just see, here you can "smell" a feeling or situation, as in "smelling a rat," which really means you are sensing that something is wrong. In this case, smelling is associated with your perceptive and intuitive abilities. So if your nose is blocked, perhaps there is some intuitive insight you would rather not acknowledge, or a deeper perception you are ignoring.

The nose also has an annoying habit of poking its way into other people's business and personal details. I'm not quite sure how it does this, but it certainly gets told often enough to keep clear! If you are experiencing nose problems, you may want to look at this aspect and see if you have been transgressing privacy rights and need to be a little more respectful.

The faculty for breathing is important here, as your feelings about taking in life are reflected in your ability to breathe in with clear, open passages. If your nose is **blocked**, do you really want to pull back or take some time out to yourself for a while? This is one way to put up a barrier, a blockage that stops the world from coming in.

- Are you blocking something within yourself, getting stuffy and airless in your attitude?
- Are you being particularly prejudiced or closed?
- What do you need to do to open up and breathe freely again?

Your blocked nose may be due to having a cold, but it could also reflect a need to release some deep grief or sadness. Feelings get locked inside, and they need to be aired. Unexpressed tears can find their way out through a **runny** nose: your emotions are literally pouring out of you. The language is easy to understand: blocked, stuffy, or runny. Which one applies to you?

- Where are you feeling emotionally blocked, or getting stuffy in your attitudes?
- Is there something or someone you need to run away from?

Sneezing is a natural reaction to an irritant, but when it becomes more frequent than normal, or occurs at specific times, it is worth exploring further.

An irritant can be an irritating person or a frustrating situation as much as it can be a piece of dust. I knew someone who always started sneezing whenever she was on the telephone with her mother.

- Is a situation or someone irritating you?
- Or is it "getting up your nose"?
- Are there unacceptable feelings arising that you want to blow away?

- Do you start sneezing when a particular person walks into the room?
- Are you sneezing because you are really feeling nervous?
- Look at the circumstances before you started sneezing. What feelings were being experienced or held back?

Hay Fever

This is one of the most debilitating allergic reactions, causing watery eyes, runny noses, itching, and redness. Certainly there are environmental causes here, especially when the pollen counts are high. However, hay fever is a very emotional response: all the waterworks are on, with an outpouring of fluids and a highly irritated physical state.

BODYMIND DIALOGUE: HAY FEVER

Allergies indicate an intense emotional reaction to external situations, a reaction of withdrawal, resistance, and fear leading to isolation, often induced by stress.

- Can you track down what you are actually feeling allergic to? What is it about this time of year that is so difficult for you to emotionally deal with?
- Is something causing this emotional outpouring?
- If this is the case, what is it you want to run away or hide from?

See also: Allergies

Sinusitis

The sinuses are the hollow chambers or air spaces behind and to the sides of the nose. They give the voice extra resonance. However, they are subject to infection and mucus and can be quite painful.

Sinusitis means you are feeling irritated or inflamed by something or someone, or even yourself, and this irritation is highlighting a sense of being emotionally or creatively stuck.

To breathe is to inspire, to take in new ideas. As such, sinusitis implies either a pushing away of that which inspires or nourishes, or an overload of mental work.

- Are you feeling blocked or limited, unable to break free of old patterns?
- Are you resisting inspiration or nourishment?
- Have you been doing too much head work and not acknowledging the need to play, be creative, or to listen to your heart?

Sinusitis is also connected to repressed grief and unshed tears, especially as there can be intense pain and a high temperature. The pain is expressing the inner anguish, the unexpressed grief accumulating inside; the temperature shows the intensity of feeling, the heat of emotion.

- What do you need to do to release the blockage, to become unclogged, unstuck?
- Is there a deep need to be loved?
- What other senses are being affected?

The Throat

The throat has a number of functions, so in order to identify its bodymind implication you need to be clear which function is involved. There is the digestive process and the act of swallowing food or reality; this has many ramifications, which are discussed more fully in Chapter 13. Here we are concerned with how the throat is involved with expression, as it is home to the larynx or voice box. Activated by the breath, the throat is also the link between the body and the head—the heart and the mind—so this is where you voice your feelings, express your ideas, speak your truth, bring your inner world out into the open or swallow it all down. It is easy to see the connection here with the fifth chakra, which is the centre of communication.

Expressing your emotions is not always easy. You may not feel it is appropriate (such as wanting to shout or cry while you are at work), that your feelings may hurt someone, that they won't be respected or valued, that you can't find the right words, or you may not even be in touch with what you are really feeling. All this can accumulate inside so that you end up holding back from saying anything, as when you take a big gulp and keep quiet; or you may deny and repress your feelings altogether.

The throat is also where you swallow other people's feelings and the effect of your daily reality. To swallow something is to appear to accept it, to "stomach" whatever is going on, to put up with it, even to tolerate it. Yet you may not feel tolerant toward what is happening. You may not want to swallow it at all.

See also: Chapter 13

Sore Throat

The throat is where you swallow the impact of what is happening in your life, so throat problems can arise when there is a fearful or irritating reaction. This is also where you express, or repress, your feelings.

BODYMIND DIALOGUE: SORE THROAT

A sore throat is a clear indication that either some reality you are taking in is making you feel sore or inflamed, or something you want to say is not getting said.

- Is something getting stuck in your throat?
- Are you tolerating something that is making you sore, irritated, annoyed, angry, or upset?
- Or is there something you really want to say that you are holding back?
- Are you really feeling sore while pretending that everything is fine?
- Is someone choking you, or do you feel choked by your own feelings?
- Can you find a way to express your feelings so you can release that blocked energy?

Coughing

Coughing is a reaction to a stimulus, usually a tickle in the throat or larynx. This tickle can worsen into an inflammation if the irritant continues.

BODYMIND DIALOGUE: COUGHING

Coughing is an attempt to clear the way, to get the irritant out of your system.

- What is causing you to feel so irritated?
- Is something or someone making you feel hot or angry?
- Are you being asked to accept or swallow something you don't want?
- Is something or someone making you gag?

Coughing may also be due to something you have said or wanted to say, as the cough mechanism is a part of the larynx.

- Have you said something that was hurtful?
- Do you now feel guilty or ashamed about it?
- Or are you longing to express yourself, to let out your feelings?

A **nervous cough** is a way of keeping the lid on inner fears or concerns. The feelings are right there, just behind the cough, but there is too much tension to release them.

If there is phlegm with the cough, or the chest is also sore, see Bronchitis, on page 214, or the Common Cold, Chapter 10.

The Voice Box

The larynx is your voice box, and your voice is your unique means of identification, as no two voices are the same. The way you use your voice conveys a great deal about your personality: whether it is gruff or loud, persuasive or overbearing, timid, soft, or caressing, high or low pitched. Try speaking into a tape recorder and then play it back and listen to your voice. What is the sound saying about you? The voice is your means of expression, of sharing who you are with the world. But expression depends more on tone and intent than the actual words used. Saying "I love you" with a voice full of venom invalidates the sentiment, in the same way as saying "I hate you" with a voice full of love. The emotion behind your words has a far greater impact than the words themselves.

Laryngitis happens when the larynx becomes inflamed, and you become hoarse or lose your voice completely. It may accompany a bad head cold, be due to excess anger, or it can arise when you are feeling particularly nervous about saying something. Losing your voice means nothing can be said, so you are emotionally safe. Laryngitis may also be due to feeling that you have nothing worth saying, as when a child is made to believe that whatever he or she says is unacceptable or worthless. It can also be due to feeling overwhelmed by someone or something—such as stage fright—that takes your power away. Or you may lose your voice after witnessing a traumatic scene, when there is an overwhelming terror of saying anything.

BODYMIND DIALOGUE: VOICE BOX

Difficulties in speaking occur when there is a suppression of feelings. This may be due to a fear of expression and extreme nervousness, always saying the wrong thing, or an inability to articulate your feelings clearly.

- Do you keep "putting your foot in your mouth"?
- Through the voice you express your needs. Does your request get "stuck in your throat"?
- Are you speaking for someone else and not finding your own voice?
- Are you speaking your truth or swallowing it back?
- Do you feel invalidated or overpowered?
- Have you witnessed something that has left you "speechless"?

Silence is golden, but it can also be a way of avoiding an issue, especially a contentious one with your partner.

• Could your silence be a form of manipulation?

Finding your voice implies finding courage and independence: you can speak for yourself, stand on your own, you know your own mind. **Losing your voice** implies that you have lost touch with your inner strength, your ability to speak up.

• What is it you really want to say?
• What part of you have you lost touch with?
• What inner voice needs expression?

The Thyroid Gland

This small gland, situated behind the windpipe in the neck, influences the chemistry of your whole body. It produces hormones for growth, cell regeneration, and repair; it maintains both metabolism and oxygen consumption. Many women (and it is mainly women) are diagnosed with **hypothyroidism**—one in eight below 65 years old, and one in five above 65. It is the most common thyroid difficulty and causes depression, weight gain, low energy, and sleep disorders. As a disorder it tends to appear around the same time as perimenopause, which can have very similar symptoms. It can also have similar bodymind causes, such as feeling a loss of personal power, purpose, or value.

BODYMIND DIALOGUE: HYPOTHYROIDISM

The thyroid gland's proximity to the voice box is most interesting, as hypothyroidism can be due to having spent many years "swallowing" or "stifling" your words or needs, until you are unable to fully express yourself. This is fairly typical for women who easily put others' needs ahead of their own and whose views or opinions are often deemed as less important. If this is the case, then finding your voice and learning to express your thoughts and feelings are vital.

- Are you able to speak up for yourself?
- Does your partner make all the decisions?
- Do you always put other people first, even denying your own needs?

The Lungs

To breathe is to take in and give out. You breathe in, knowing you can breathe out, and in breathing out you unconsciously know there will be another breath for you to take in. However, if there is any fear or lack of trust in this automatic process, then breathing difficulties may develop. Children who have been rejected or let down by their parents, especially by their mothers, can lose this trust; as can adults who have experienced abuse, life-threatening situations, or the loss of loved ones.

The lungs are symbolic of independence—inflating the lungs with air at the moment of birth creates an independent life. If this was a traumatic experience, it can influence the way you meet moments of transition later in life, and the extent to which you are able to breathe deeply and relax into change. In the lungs you manifest difficulties connected to taking life in or wanting to push it away; or living life for yourself rather than letting someone else have power over you. The lungs are also a place of sadness, of unexpressed grief and unshed tears, often accumulated over a long period of time.

Bronchitis

When the trachea (the windpipe) enters the lungs, it divides into the right and left bronchi, which look like an upside-down tree inside each lung. Here oxygen is transferred into the blood supply and exchanged for carbon dioxide. The bronchi become inflamed due to air pollution such as wood smoke, exhaust fumes, and particularly cigarette smoke, or from a throat infection. As the bronchi bring air to the lungs and take used air back out again, they act as mediators or communicators between the inside and outside world.

Bronchitis is an infection, indicating something or someone is affecting you; and it creates an inflammation, indicating irritation, soreness, anger, upset, all in the area of where you breathe in life.

Bronchial problems are often connected to being able to share what you are really feeling, as well as to issues of separation and independence, as here you breathe for yourself independent of anyone else. See if you can find the feelings behind the infection.

- What was going on before the infection began?
- What is it that is creating such an irritation and annoyance?

A **bad cough** may indicate that you want to bring something up or to "get something off your chest."

- Are you feeling overwhelmed or smothered by something or someone?
- As the lungs often contain sadness, is there a deeper sadness, grief, or guilt that the infection is masking?
- If it is difficult for you to breathe, what is holding you back from wanting to participate fully?
- Is there something irritating or painful that you need to externalize?

Asthma
An asthma attack can be provoked by bronchitis, by pollution, or by an allergic reaction to an external stimulus such as pollen, or even to crying or laughing. There has been an alarming increase in asthma over the past few years, especially in children. There is growing evidence that much of the physical cause of this increase lies in the corresponding increase in environmental pollution, particularly exhaust fumes, as cases of asthma are higher in places of more intense traffic.

However, pollution does not account for all cases of asthma. As far as the psycho/emotional connection to asthma is concerned, there are two main correspondences. One is your relationship to your mother, as the breath is symbolic of your separation from her. Over the last fifteen years, as pollution levels have risen, so also more and more children have been growing up in single-parent families; these children have to become emotionally as well as physically independent at an early age. Perhaps they have to breathe for themselves too soon. They may also feel emotionally insecure. Many children and young people feel an increasing fear about the future—about what they are growing up into—as housing and financial problems increase while education and work opportunities decrease. These social issues directly affect feelings about being independent and may therefore affect breathing.

The mother-child relationship is a deeply complex one, bound by the mother having "breathed" for her child throughout the pregnancy. For varied reasons, a mother may smother, dominate, or overwhelm, as if she is continuing to breathe for her child well after the child is born. In these cases, the boundaries between mother and child become blurred, leading to a repressed dependence on the mother.

Asthma attacks may be triggered by events that highlight the loneliness of breathing independently and that create a separation from mother, such as the birth of a younger sibling, graduation from school, leaving home, or getting married. The asthma attack is like a suppressed cry of longing to return to the womb. I knew a woman with asthma who had such a severe attack on her wedding night that her mother, who had just returned home, had to fly back across the country to be with her. The same thing happened after the birth of her first child. Her mother had been with her and went to go home, only to be stopped at the airport as her daughter was having another bad attack.

For adults, asthma may develop if you feel smothered by your boss, by too much work, responsibility, or over-demanding relatives, so that you feel unable to breathe for yourself, and unable to express your feeling of suffocation or helplessness. Stress further exasperates asthma, especially amongst middle management, the ones who are most likely to feel overcome by pressure to succeed as well as pressure to pay bills and provide for others. There is a feeling of having to do it all, a struggling for breath on your own.

This suppressed cry or longing to breathe freely is connected to the second aspect of asthma—the desire to express yourself but an inability to do so, leading to repressed feelings and even sadness. The out-breath enables you to speak; the inability to breathe out easily implies that this expression is being held back or impeded. Consequently, asthma has been called the "silent scream"—there is an inner crying, a silent scream of longing to emote, express, and share, to shout and even act inappropriately, but, perhaps through fear, childhood inhibition, or rejection, an inability to do so. Try holding your breath—breathe in but do not breathe out—and watch the emotions that arise. Usually there is a great longing to burst, to shout, and it is this repressed longing that can be seen in asthma.

Attacks can be triggered by emotional situations such as anger or heated feelings with a parent or lover, by being misunderstood, or through experiencing grief or loss. When a child is unable to speak for itself, that longing gets held inside, especially if expression is based on confusion or fear of the parents' behaviour.

BODYMIND DIALOGUE: ASTHMA

Asthma is an allergy, an overreaction of the immune system to an antigen. "Overreaction" may be the key word here.

- Is there something or someone who is causing you to overreact?
- Do you feel your boundaries have been lost?
- How can you reassert them?

This area is connected to your taking on a separate and independent life, so any doubts, uncertainties, or difficulties you may feel about being separate or alone can manifest here.

- Are you finding it difficult to assert your independence or boundaries?
- Have you recently ended an emotionally dependent relationship?

Hyperventilation

Hyperventilation is particularly associated with stress. It is estimated that one in ten people suffers from hyperventilation, a condition in which the breathing becomes so shallow and rapid that there is an excessive loss of carbon dioxide. The imbalance between oxygen and carbon dioxide upsets the body's acid/alkaline balance, creating faintness, dizziness, confusion, and feelings of unreality, panic attacks, headaches, tingling, or numbness. This is usually due to unconscious fear or anxiety.

BODYMIND DIALOGUE: HYPERVENTILATION

- What is the deeper cause of your concern?
- What are you really afraid of? Voicing your anxieties will help you to see them more clearly. Are you giving out too much and need to give to yourself more?
- Are you fearful of breathing deeply, of taking life in?

See also: Panic Attacks

Pneumonia

Pneumonia is an inflammation of the lungs, indicating that your immune system is highly compromised. So here you need to look at what might be weakening your immune response (see Chapter 10) and deeply inflaming your feelings, whether it is something you are taking in from outside, or something within that you are unable to express. There are hot emotions here, as well as pain and exhaustion depleting your energy.

BODYMIND DIALOGUE: PNEUMONIA

The act of breathing is the act of living.

- Are you feeling exhausted or overwhelmed by the burden of having to cope and keep going?
- Is there a longing to stop and take some time out?
- Do you need help but feel unable to ask for it?

- Do you feel knocked about, as if someone has "knocked the wind out of you"?
- Are you feeling a deep sadness that is not finding expression?

The relationship of breath to spirit is often seen in this illness, as mystical or spiritual experiences are not uncommon in those who have pneumonia. It can distort your relationship to the physical world, which is normally maintained by the rhythm of the breath, and this distortion can act like a window through to another level of reality.

TWELVE

THE RHYTHM OF LOVE
The Heart, Blood, and Circulation

The heart is the centre of the cardiovascular system, with a network of vessels taking blood around the body. Oxygen and other essential nutrients are taken to every cell via the arteries, while de-oxygenated blood is carried back in the veins. The heart is the centre of this system, and its symbolic relationship to love is deeply entrenched in our collective psyche. That the heart represents love is the one part of the bodymind we are all, universally, agreed upon. The blood represents the circulation of that love, the giving and receiving seen in the constant flow to and from the heart.

You are made of 94 percent water, and the bodily fluids, which include the blood, are constantly moving, shifting, and flowing. The fluids correspond to your emotions and feelings. Fluid issues are tenderness issues, to do with love and hurt, grief and passion, reflecting where your feelings are being repressed and locked away or are overflowing and out of control. The emotions give movement to your inner desires, longings, and beliefs.

As blood gives life through distributing oxygen and nutrients, so love gives life meaning and direction. With love and life come their opposites—fear and death. Love is expansive and all embracing, reaching out to other beings; while fear is contractive and exclusive, pulling back from participation. Love embraces fear, but without love fear becomes hate. Without love, life loses all meaning. When the heart stops, life goes.

The Heart

When you fall in love, you feel your heart flutter, beat loudly, or leap for joy; when you are rejected your heart breaks. You are called "heartless" or "cold-hearted" when you show no care or love, "big-hearted" when you extend your concern to others. When someone becomes your heart's desire you have "heartfelt" feelings. You "take things to heart" when they are emotionally evocative, or "talk heart to heart" about deeply personal issues. You love someone "from the bottom of your heart," but are only "half-hearted" about something when you are not emotionally involved. More importantly, it has to be a red heart, as seen in the thousands of valentine's cards sent each year. Red is the colour of love—a dozen roses do not have quite the same impact if they are yellow—yet few people realize this colour is also the colour of blood.

However, love rarely flows smoothly. Inevitably, in one way or another we all experience childhood conflicts, abuse, hurt, or loss, and if the pain is too big to deal with we lock it away inside. This serves to lock you out of your heart so that your ability to express your loving feelings is limited. If you become isolated from love, you become mistrustful, uncaring, shallow, hateful, prejudiced, and fearful. You also become closed to your own need for love.

Many boys are raised not to show their feelings, but to appear brave and strong. In adult life that can mean they are unable to express gentleness, caring, or nurturing qualities. Fear closes your heart so you are unable to feel love, as when you close your arms and pull back in defence. Love comes from the open heart, as when you fearlessly open your arms and embrace all. As Gerald Jampolsky said, "Love is letting go of fear."

From the heart all your passion, adoration, devotion, fear, anger, hurt, desire, yearning, gratitude, and joy are expressed: through your mouth with words and intonation and kissing; through your shoulders, arms, and hands when you hug, hold, caress, or push away; and through your sexuality, by caring and sharing.

HEART REVIEW 1

Spend some time each day getting to know your feelings.

Choose a subject.
It could be your partner, your children, your work, etc.

Keep a journal.
Each day start a new page with the words: In my heart I feel …
Then just let yourself write.

Write your heart out.
It doesn't have to make sense. No one else is going to read this; it is just for you.

Stay with it.
Keep this journal for as long as it takes for you to get in touch with your feelings and to be able to express them freely.

This is your emotional home, where all your struggles, anguishes, and hurts are felt, your likes and dislikes, longings and yearnings, and all those things that give you so much joy. They are all found here. This is seen in cases of heart transplants, as it appears that the likes and dislikes of the heart donor are often transplanted with the organ. One case I heard was of a middle-aged woman who developed a love for football and beer, things she had never gone near prior to her operation. Turns out the donor had been a football fanatic. In another case, Gaea Shaw, author of *Dying to Live: From Heart Transplant to Abundant Life*, found that after the transplant she had a great longing to swim and eventually trained for the U.S. Transplant Games and won several medals. And yes, you guessed it: prior to the operation she had never been an athlete, but she had been given the heart of an avid swimmer.

Learning to open the heart, to listen to, respect, and trust what you feel, is one of life's most powerful teachings. As Alexander Lowen describes in his book *Bioenergetics*, the heart is like a king, while the mind is like the king's advisors. The advisors go out into the world to see what is happening and then report to the king on the state of his kingdom. However, the king makes his own decisions based not on what each individual advisor might say, but on his own intuitive and deeper understanding of the bigger picture. That decision may appear illogical to the advisors, but it is invariably the fair and correct one. In other words, when you listen to your heart and make decisions based upon what it is saying, rather than what your mind is saying, then it is usually the right decision. Even though the heart may appear illogical or irrational, intuitively you know that it is more real and meaningful than all the arguments the head may use to counter it.

For the heart is more than just the centre of love, it is also the centre of your being, the place you point to when you talk about yourself. When you say, "You have touched my heart," you are really saying, "You have touched the deepest part of my being." The Native Americans, when they first met the white man, are known to have said how strange it was that, "The white man thinks with his head instead of his heart."

HEART REVIEW 2: BREATHING INTO YOUR HEART
Take a moment to stop reading and to breathe into your heart.

Sit comfortably.
Close your eyes and breathe naturally, breathing into the area of your heart—the heart space in the centre of your chest.

Feel this space gently opening.
Release any tension with each out-breath. Breathe in softness and openness with each in-breath.

Relax.
Continue this breathing pattern for a few minutes. Just breathe naturally, without effort, and let yourself sink into the heart space.

When you feel ready, gently open your eyes.

Heart Rhythm
As the heart is the centre of your deepest feeling, so its rhythm responds to those feelings, increasing at times of undue stress, emotional trauma or shock, fear, passion, elation, or joy. It should return to its normal rhythm as you relax.

BODYMIND DIALOGUE: HEART RHYTHM
An increased heartbeat that does not easily return to normal indicates the need for greater emotional equilibrium and inner relaxation, that stress, fear, and anxiety are affecting your balance.

- Are you easily upset or do you feel emotionally insecure?
- Where or what in your life is out of rhythm?
- What do you need to do to find greater stability and a calmer pace?

Angina
Angina means tightness and refers to the tightness of the chest experienced when a narrowing of the arteries prevents blood and oxygen from reaching the heart. It is usually triggered during exercise or by excessive mental or emotional stress, as both are times when the demand for oxygen increases so much that it outstrips the body's ability to respond, and there is a breakdown in the balance of supply and demand. Less exertive activities, such as smoking or overeating, can also precipitate angina, as can worry or anxiety, as these all tend to increase blood pressure.

Angina is a result of tight or restricted blood vessels, so it indicates an emotional state that is tight or "uptight" in your ability to give and receive. This applies particularly to receiving love and nurturing or being able to ask for help or advice. Instead there is a strong desire to stay in control, to do it all yourself. This reduces your inner resources, so when the demand grows the supply is not there: you have nothing to give. The tightness of the chest implies the conflict between the need to replenish and the inability to receive.

Perhaps you are ignoring your own needs, or feel unable to express your feelings, but the heart is now telling you that you must find a way of softening, of loosening that inner tightness. Angina may have no immediate damaging consequences, but it can lead to more serious heart attacks.

BODYMIND DIALOGUE: ANGINA

Angina is a red light, a warning that should not be ignored.

- Do you need to be in charge and find it hard to ask for help?
- Have you become hostile or aggressive, uncaring about others if they stand in your way
- Has making money or being successful become more important than walking in the country or playing with your children?
- Is too much being demanded of you, and do you feel unable to meet that demand?

Heart Attack

A heart attack is the number-one killer in the Western world, the incidence of which has doubled every twenty years since 1900. A heart attack is caused by a blockage of a coronary vessel supplying blood to the heart, a thrombosis, or a sudden spasm that causes the heart muscle to be starved of oxygen. It may be triggered by stress or emotional trauma, or from a long build-up of arterial deposits until the arteries can no longer function properly.

There are plenty of physical and lifestyle causes for heart attacks: overwork, excess pressure, and stress lead to a weakening of the entire system, but most importantly they limit the amount of time available for exercise, relaxation, play, or loving relationships. Too much alcohol debilitates the liver, immunity, and circulation; while smoking causes an 84 percent increase in adrenaline, which puts extreme stress on the heart. A diet rich in fat, particularly red meat and dairy foods, can cause a hardening of the arteries and increase the number of heart attacks.

Together these risk factors point to a lifestyle lacking in self-care, self-respect, and inner nurturing. This is usually due to the pursuit of material gain at the expense of emotional balance; a need to be in control, especially over your own feelings, perhaps because of painful memories, past hurt, or trauma; or because of grief, depression, and "broken-heartedness" due to the loss of a loved one. A cynical, self-centred attitude, with frequent anger or aggressive behaviour, is also identified as a high-risk factor for cardiovascular disease

If your focus is on work and achievement, then feelings not only get in the way but can appear to waste valuable time. So they get put on a back burner, and the heart becomes energetically cut off.

It is wonderful to witness how a heart attack can transform someone's life. Use this time to reassess your priorities and your relationships. Carrying on as you were before is asking for trouble. Your heart needs you to get in touch with yourself, with your passion and creativity, with the real reason for being alive.

BODYMIND DIALOGUE: HEART ATTACK

A heart attack implies that the heart is being "attacked" by a build-up of unexpressed hurt, loss, grief, or resistance to love. The heart is desperately trying to get your attention, to break down the limitations.

- Are you putting your heart in a cage so you cannot feel anything?
- Are you holding on to pain or hurt from the past, refusing to forgive?

Love is absolutely and essentially nurturing and life enhancing, yet easily dismissed as unimportant. Without deep, heartfelt involvement, life can appear meaningless. This leads to depression and sadness, a sense of not belonging.

- Do you need to put more heart into your life?
- Have you lost heart, or do you just want to give up?

Normally the blood flows continually; it has its own rhythm.

- Are you in touch with the natural rhythm of life that moves within you?
- Or do you regiment your life and fill every space with scheduled activity?

When blood vessels contract and go into spasm, the constricted circulation of the blood affects the heart.

- Are you focused so completely on work that the emotional side of your life is constricted?
- Are you suppressing your emotions so they take up less space in your life?

The Blood

The significance of the blood as the giver of life is seen in the images of spilled blood, of becoming "blood brothers," and of the use of blood in ritual and magic. Through an intricate maze of arteries, veins, and capillaries, the blood reaches every cell in your body. Blood consists of plasma, red and white cells, and platelets, and has a complete impression of your physical individuality contained in the DNA, the genetic code.

In the womb, your mother's blood comes in intimate contact with your blood through the placenta, as she provides you with nourishment throughout her pregnancy. In the same way her own blood came in contact with that of her mother. So within your blood is your history, your ancestors and their history, as is the potential for their illnesses and difficulties, their joys and laughter. However, you are also an individual, a separate entity, and your blood is unique to you. It contains your particular imprint and your interpretation of your inheritance. Blood issues are therefore connected to family conflicts as much as they are to issues of individuality, and where you may be experiencing a loss of your sense of self or your personal power.

Just as the blood contains an imprint of your physical individuality, so it also contains the deep feelings that form your emotional identity, and it is responsible for distributing those feelings throughout your being. There is normally an equal flow of give and take as the arteries carry blood from the heart outward (sharing the feelings in your heart with the rest of your being), and the veins bring the blood back to the heart (bringing what you receive from others). Any imbalance indicates a conflict with being able to give or receive, or issues to do with emotional involvement and the expression of love.

BODYMIND DIALOGUE: THE BLOOD

If you are having issues with your blood, then ask yourself the following questions:

- Has the circulation of love in your life undergone a recent change, such as a separation or loss?
- Are you either withdrawing emotionally or wanting to pour forth feelings that you cannot?
- Are feeling depressed or disinterested in life?
- Have you had a recent conflict with your family or loved ones?
- Are you allowing yourself to receive nourishment and love?

Blood Pressure

Blood pressure represents your energetic relationship to the pressures and tension around you, and how that may be limiting your behaviour, as represented by the walls of the blood vessels.

Blood pressure generally rises at times of stress, passion, or strenuous activity, and in a healthy person it will normalize soon afterward. **High blood pressure**, also known as **hypertension**, is an unhealthy response to increased pressure and stress and can lead to more serious conditions, such as a heart attack or stroke.

Low blood pressure suggests that there is little or no energetic input. There is a resistance to meeting challenges; an inability to stand on your own without feeling weak or collapsing, leading to an ineptitude when confronting responsibilities or dealing with difficulties.

Low blood pressure may also occur when you are deeply relaxed, as in meditation. In this case, it is not due to a resistance to life, but to a letting-go of all resistances and a merging with life.

BODYMIND DIALOGUE: BLOOD PRESSURE

As the language suggests, high blood pressure represents your own high-temperature emotions, feelings that are boiling inside. But like a pressure cooker, they are not being released. High blood pressure is usually accompanied by manic activity, indicating that there is an attempt to avoid those hot and intense feelings by staying very busy. However, ignoring them will only lead to further emotional pressure. It is essential that you learn how to read the signs before damage is done, and to connect more deeply with what is seething just below the surface. These are hot emotions.

- What is getting you so heated?
- Are you applying the pressure yourself, or is it coming from outside you?
- Are you trying to avoid something that is making you angry or upset?

If you have low blood pressure, there may be a sense of being overwhelmed by the demands of life. This is a powerless or hopeless response to pressure, an inability to meet life face to face, a giving-up attitude. Love does not flow strongly here.

- Do you feel unable to cope with the demands on you?
- Do you feel overwhelmed?

- What do you need to do to connect with greater reserves of inner strength?

Circulation

Poor circulation, which in its worst form is known as **Raynaud's disease**, usually affects the extremities—the feet, hands, ears, and nose. The parts affected become pallid and/or purple and invariably numb and cold. It also causes **chilblains**, which are swollen, red, itchy, and hot areas.

Poor circulation is normally associated with cold weather when the blood contracts, followed by a sudden warming. But it is equally connected to an emotional coldness or withdrawal. It affects those parts of you that go out into the world first and farthest: the toes that point in the direction you are going, or the fingers that reach out to touch or hold. As the blood represents the circulation of love and life, poor circulation implies a weakening of that force, as if there is too little blood to reach into every part or too little love to meet the need. Or it may be a withdrawal of your love, perhaps through fear, through a change of heart or a change of direction, a weakening of love, or a desire to emotionally pull away. You may be in a relationship that, deep inside, you know has to end and you are already emotionally withdrawing. Or perhaps you are receiving a coldness from someone and you are pulling back in order to protect your feelings.

BODYMIND DIALOGUE: CIRCULATION

Poor circulation may represent an inner fear that you have nothing to give, even that you are unlovable, so better to retreat and not get emotionally entangled at all. Perhaps there is a fear of intimacy, of being touched and caressed, so your emotions contract; you act like a snail, pulling your outer extremities inward.

- Do you feel cold or numb to a relationship?
- Do you feel you have nothing to give, no love to share?
- Do the parts of you that meet the world feel threatened, shy, ugly, or unlovable?

- What do you need to do to feel warm or emotionally expansive?
- What needs to change for you to be able to reach out with love?

Coronary Artery Disease

There are two main causes of thickening or hardening of the arteries, a condition known as **arteriosclerosis**—one is the narrowing of the arteries that takes place as we get older, and the other is the constriction that develops due to fatty deposits. Both lead to a restriction of the blood supply.

BODYMIND DIALOGUE: ARTERIOSCLEROSIS

In bodymind language, the arteries and veins represent the distribution and expression of love throughout your being. A restriction in these vessels implies a restriction in your ability to express yourself, perhaps a withdrawal or repression of feeling, and in particular a narrowing of your emotional perspectives.

- Are you limiting yourself or denying yourself love or support?
- Is this because you are trying to do too much and not recognizing your own needs, not seeing where you need to ask for help?

The blood vessels are containers for your feelings, so you need to see if you are feeling boxed in or constrained by your circumstances. These limitations may be ones you have imposed on yourself so that you can feel safe, emotionless and uninvolved.

- Are you very hard on yourself or hard on others, expecting more from them than they can give?
- Are you holding yourself back from involvement?

Narrow or blocked blood vessels imply a breakdown in the balance of giving and taking.

- Have you become narrow in your outlook?
- Have you become overly critical or prejudiced toward others?

- Are you very rigid or fixed in your attitudes, inflexible with your feelings?

The fatty deposits imply a build-up of toxic feeling, an accumulation of shame, guilt, or unworthiness that is weighing heavily on you, causing a clog or restriction in the flow of your life energy.

- Do you let your feelings build up inside before they finally burst out?

The blood vessels need to soften, ease up, and get flowing again.

- What do you need to do in your life to become gentler, less critical, less restricted, and more in the flow?

Thrombosis

Thrombosis is a blood clot that blocks a vein, usually in the lower legs (**deep vein thrombosis**). Any such clot is dangerous, because it can break away and then move to the heart. The fluidity and vitality of the blood has become congealed and stuck, causing a lack of movement. Movement means change, so being solidified implies a resistance to change, an inability to flow or move.

BODYMIND DIALOGUE: THROMBOSIS

A thrombosis indicates a blocking or solidifying of feelings, so that the flow of energy is inhibited.

- What change are you resisting?
- Are you clinging to a situation for fear of what will happen if you let go?
- Where are your feelings getting stuck or shut off?
- Are you blocking off something within yourself?
- Are you denying your need for help or nurturing?
- Are you trying to do it all on your own?

• Where are you holding back and ignoring deeper issues?

As a thrombosis is more common in the veins than in the arteries, it indicates that the issue is more in receiving, rather than in giving.

• Are you willing to receive nourishment and care from others?
• Or do you push help away and try to do it all by yourself?

A thrombosis is also most common in the legs, implying that there may be a fear of the direction or movement that lies ahead.

• Are you fearful of an impending emotional change?
• Do you feel stuck to the ground you are standing on, as if embedded in concrete?
• What do you need to do to release the blockage and begin moving again?

Stroke

A stroke is caused by a clot blocking the blood supply in the brain, so that the activity of that part of the brain is disrupted or stops functioning altogether. This usually leads to some form of partial paralysis, depending on the severity of the stroke and the side of the brain that is affected. Contributing factors include high blood pressure, diabetes, obesity, stress, and cigarette smoking.

In this situation the blood vessels—the means you have of expressing love and transmitting life-sustaining qualities throughout your being—become constricted, shutting off a part of the brain, the centre of the nervous system. A stroke stops you in your tracks, immediately limiting any further movement forward. Strokes happen mainly in the elderly and usually at a time when movement forward is not a very exciting prospect: into a nursing home, into a wheelchair, or at the least into a growing loss of independence and dignity as age increases. This may be combined with a strongly controlling personality finding it increasingly difficult to accept a loss of power, while also unable to express feelings of need, help-lessness, or love.

Such immobility also creates a limitation in the expression of feelings so that the fear, loss of personal power, frustration, loneliness, or anxiety all become locked inside. There may be financial worries or a fear of being unable to cope alone, especially if a spouse has recently died. The resistance to what lies ahead unconsciously puts the brakes on and stops the body from going any farther.

In younger people, a stroke tends to occur as a result of stress combined with a lifestyle that contains little exercise and lots of high-fat fast food.

BODYMIND DIALOGUE: STROKE

If you think of the word *stroke*, then it is an act of striking you still, stopping you from going any farther in the present direction or manner. Time out is required, along with deep relaxation and a lifestyle overhaul.

- Is there something happening in your life that you want to avoid, stop, or reroute?
- Has your lifestyle been contrary to your inner longings?
- Is your soul or spirit wanting to go one way but you have been heading off in the opposite direction?
- Does the future appear depressing or overwhelming?

Haemorrhage

This is an acute loss of blood, whether external or internal. It is like an outpouring of emotion, a release of deep feelings that have been gathering beneath the surface and now pour forth, as if the heart is overflowing. They are so powerful they have to find an outlet.

BODYMIND DIALOGUE: HAEMORRHAGE

The bleeding due to a haemorrhage is like a pressure valve blowing. It is a blasting out of emotion.

- Have you been keeping your feelings locked inside?
- What do you need to heal this emotional outpouring?
- Are you feeling emotionally out of control?
- Is this a deep cry for help?

Varicose Veins

Varicose veins occur when the valves in the veins fail to do their job, which is to let the blood flow upward without coming back down again. Blood accumulates in the vessels, making them swell. This condition is found in the legs, where the muscles usually help to keep the blood flowing upward. It often happens when someone is standing for long periods or during pregnancy, both activities putting extra pressure on the valves.

The veins carry the blood back to the heart, representing your ability to receive love and be nourished by that love. The failure of the valves indicates difficulty with being able to receive love, leading to an inner longing to collapse.

BODYMIND DIALOGUE: VARICOSE VEINS

When varicosity is due to standing for long periods, it is connected to feeling unsupported—hence the need for "support stockings."

- Are you feeling overwhelmed by having to carry too much emotional weight?
- Are you having to emotionally stand on your own and is it wearing you down?
- Is there a longing to emotionally give way or collapse?
- Are you losing your emotional resilience and need greater support?

If due to pregnancy, varicose veins may be connected to inner fears about having to be responsible for another person. So often all the attention is on the child-to-be, while the mother may be feeling confused and insecure.

- Are you able to express your fears or do you feel ashamed of them?
- Are you receiving the help and support you need?
- Do you fear you will not love the child, or will lose the love of your partner?
- What do you need in order to feel more supported?

Anaemia

Anaemia is a lack of haemoglobin in the blood. Iron-deficient anaemia may be due to poor diet, blood loss as in menstruation, or not meeting the body's demand for iron during pregnancy. Pernicious anaemia is due to a lack of vitamin B12 (folic acid) caused by dietary deficiency, or by a lack of the substance needed in the stomach to absorb B12. In both instances it is important to look at lifestyle and attitude. Lifestyle causes may include an insufficient diet that is not meeting or recognizing your nutritional needs.

BODYMIND DIALOGUE: ANAEMIA

Anaemia indicates an inability to absorb life-sustaining nourishment. When we think of iron, we have images of strength and endurance, of a quality that adds depth and fortitude to the blood. If you are lacking this, you need to ask where in your life you are lacking these qualities. Anaemia is a weakening of the life- and love-giving energy.

- Have you been working too hard and not caring for yourself?
- Do you think your diet is unimportant?
- Is something draining your vital reserves?
- Have you lost the sense of endurance that adds purpose and meaning to life?
- Have you lost the desire to be involved?
- In what way are you feeling under-nourished or under-loved?
- Are you overwhelmed or exhausted by emotional demands?

THIRTEEN
BUDDHA IN THE BELLY
The Digestive System

The digestive system begins in the mouth with your taste buds, the release of saliva, chewing, and swallowing. It continues on through the stomach into the intestines and down into the rectum until it reaches the anus and final elimination. This whole process is vital to your well-being, as your body survives on everything you put in your mouth. For instance, without the right balance of foods you can clog your arteries, strain your heart, decrease your immune functioning, aggravate your nerves, or develop an apathetic or lethargic attitude.

However, eating is not just about getting the right nutrition. It is also about emotional and psychological satisfaction. In the same way, the digestive process is not just about taking in food. It is also about swallowing and assimilating reality. Here you absorb everything that is happening to you along with your feelings, sensations, and experiences, and eliminate that which you do not want. Digestive difficulties may well be connected to having to swallow distasteful emotions, such as someone's anger, or because your own adverse feelings are rotting inside. In fact, the digestive system is a wonderful monitor of your emotional balance. If you are happy with what is happening in your life, then your digestion will probably be reasonably maintenance free. But if you are experiencing conflicts, stress, or difficulties, then these often show up as indigestion or constipation, before they appear anywhere else in the body.

FOOD

Eating is probably our most controversial and emotionally laden activity. We all need to eat, but what we eat and how much we eat will vary with each one of us. Few of us only eat when we are hungry or only what we need rather than what we want. We binge, diet, pig out, indulge, fast; we eat junk food, healthy food, only fruit, high-protein, low-fat, raw food, vegetarian, vegan, macrobiotic. We use food as a substitute for love, as a way to win love, to fulfill desire, as a means of punishment through deprivation, or as a reward through treats. In every women's magazine there are articles on the ultimate diet, recipes for a lover's meal, how to feed hungry teenagers, the contents of a celebrity's refrigerator, and what foods will cure arthritis. In other words, food is an issue.

Perhaps this is not surprising. From the very beginning we are focused on food, crying when our stomachs are empty and being rewarded with warm milk. As infants, our needs are extremely basic. We want food, dry clothes, a warm and safe place to sleep, lots of love, and a few friendly faces to look at. As we grow older these needs do not change much; they just get bigger. We want more food, drawers full of clothes, a whole house with a big bed to sleep in, and some loved ones to have fun with. When we are first born, food is accompanied by either a breast or a bottle and the familiar soothing voice of mother. At this early stage there is little separation between food, mother, and love. They all tend to come at the same time, and they all do much the same thing, which makes us feel good.

It is only as we grow that these three get separated. Then food does not always come from mother, mother does not always love, food is given in place of love, and so on. Whatever the circumstances, food remains an issue. Mother cooks it and makes you feel guilty if you do not like it. You get sent to bed without food if you misbehave. Or parents are absent, and you are placated with special food treats. Even worse is when you are in need of being held or loved and you get candy instead, simply reinforcing the belief that food and love are not only connected but also interchangeable.

Later in life you use food in much the same way, such as giving a box of chocolates as a sign of your affection or to assuage your guilt for not having visited sooner, or bingeing after a relationship upset. Sweet food is a universal replacement for love, but where love is nurturing and makes you feel good, sweet food rots your teeth, makes you fat, and lowers your immunity.

The love and emotional nourishment we try to find through food is the love every human being deserves to receive. It is, therefore, essential that you learn to give this love to yourself. Without self-love you will search endlessly for love from somewhere outside, and when you are disappointed or rejected, food will become the obvious substitute. When you have respect and love for yourself, then you have the Buddha in your belly—you do not need to use food to soothe your inner pain or to gain emotional fulfillment.

BODYMIND DIALOGUE: FOOD

Eating represents the taking in of nourishment. Your eating habits and relationship to food are indicative of your relationship to yourself and to what extent your needs for emotional nourishment are being met.

- Where and how do you obtain nourishment? Through food or through love?
- When you feel emotionally uncared for or rejected, do you turn to food for comfort?
- Do you only eat when you are hungry?
- Does what you eat depend on how you are feeling?
- Do you eat the same food when you are happy as when you are depressed?

- Do you get cravings for certain foods at particularly emotional times or when you are around a certain person?
- Does eating make you feel emotionally satiated?
- Do you use what you can or cannot eat as a way of drawing attention to yourself?
- Do you deny yourself food (and nourishment) in the same way you are denying yourself emotional nourishment?

To become aware of your relationship to food, keep a diary or daily log of a) how you are feeling, and b) what and when you are eating. This will help you see your deep patterns of behaviour.

Food Allergies

Food allergies have increased enormously in recent years. Physically this is attributable to the massive increase of chemicals used in food production and processing. Many people are simply unable to deal with such chemicals. The more we process food the farther we move away from how food was when the human body originally evolved, so perhaps it is not surprising that we are unable to adapt to factory-made foodstuffs. There is also no doubt that certain foods, such as coffee, peanuts, chocolate, shellfish, or wheat, can cause extreme physical reactions, while many adults are allergic to, or unable to digest, dairy products.

However, there are also important, and sometimes very unconscious, psycho/emotional issues that may be involved with food allergies, especially issues of control and power.

BODYMIND DIALOGUE: FOOD ALLERGIES

Foor allergies may well have physical causes, but they may contain many emotional causes as well.

- Does being unable to eat certain foods make you feel special because you cannot eat in certain places or eat the same food as others?

- Does it bring you more attention?
- Does it give you a certain control?
- In rejecting particular foods, are you actually rejecting aspects of yourself?
- Is it easier to blame the food than to look at your own behaviour?
- A food allergy can stop you playing, participating with life and being spontaneous. What would happen if you let go and joined in?
- How much self-centredness is involved with being allergic to food?
- Do you need to let it dominate your life?

EATING DISORDERS

As food and eating occupy such a huge place in our lives, it is not surprising that there are a number of eating disorders. As we have seen, food and emotional nourishment are intimately bound together in the depths of our unconscious, so eating disorders are inevitably connected to issues of love—self-love, self-acceptance, self-dislike, self-denial, rejection, loss, etc. Just as you may try to fill an inner emptiness with food, so you can reject or deny your needs, and therefore reject food, in the misbelief that the smaller the body the less the longing for love. Food is also closely connected to power issues. Digestion is connected to the third chakra and the consciousness of having personal power or a lack of it. Those who are obese often say they feel out of control around food, while people with anorexia exert massive control to the point of eliminating their instinct for survival.

Obesity

Obesity has become a problem. In the United States approximately 127 million people are overweight, sixty million are obese, and nine million are severely obese, and most other Western countries now have similar issues. It seems to have happened in tandem with social pressure to be model-stick thin: two extremes of the same problem. More than nine million children are obese in the U.S., more than four times the number forty years ago. This is a huge concern, as the more fat cells produced when you are a child, the more likely you will become a fat adult, and the more dangerous it is to your overall health, leading to high blood pressure, diabetes, heart disease, and stroke. Food is not the only cause of obesity, as a low metabolic rate can create unnecessary weight gain, but in most cases it is our relationship with food and love that is the originating issue.

Eating has a wonderfully soporific effect. It numbs your feelings and leaves you emotionally satiated. The more you eat, the less you feel, as if the food becomes ballast against the tides of emotion washing your insides. Invariably, therefore, eating beyond your physical needs occurs at times of emotional stress, relationship breakdown, grief, loss, depression, fear, guilt, or shame. Remember, most of these feelings are unconscious.

You may not be aware of what you are feeling or why you are eating, simply that there is a huge hole inside that needs to get filled, and food is the only thing that works. Even when emotional nourishment is on offer, the pain inside can be too deep to accept it—food is safer, there are fewer demands, less danger of rejection. Excessive eating then leads to excessive weight gain, constructing a wall that serves to ward off potential causes of hurt or rejection, but also blocking out your own feelings. The wall may be a layer of protection but inside is someone longing to love and be loved.

Grief or shame is often hidden beneath an obsessive appetite. Many women put on excess weight around their hips and thighs following sexual assault. By covering up the sexual area the feelings are shut away beneath layers of fear and mistrust.

It is fairly easy for most of us to repress our feelings and still appear sorted, confident, in control. A friend of mine who is quite heavy once remarked how most people can hide their neuroses and repressed feelings, whereas she wears them in plain sight for everyone to see. She only has to look in the mirror to know she still has some major emotional issues to work on.

You can help yourself by exploring your relationship to food and how that relationship was defined when you were a child.

- Were you fed treats instead of attention?
- Did you feel guilty or powerless around food?

Rather than focusing on what is wrong with being heavy, start exploring the benefits. Try writing down all the ways that being heavy is OK for you. Explore what was happening emotionally when you began to put on weight and try to connect with the feelings that are locked inside.

- What is the weight hiding?
- What does being heavy enable you to do, or not do?
- Does it make you feel safe?
- Most particularly, imagine how it would feel to be lighter than you are and watch your feelings around this. Does the idea make you feel exposed or insecure?
- Does it feel as if you have nowhere to hide?

Anorexia Nervosa

Anorexia nervosa is a condition of near-starvation in which so little food is consumed that the body begins to fade away. It is intimately bound up with the complexities of receiving nourishment and love. While longing to be nurtured and loved, we reduce our presence so as to reduce our need for that love. Anorexia is primarily a teenage/young adult problem, more often occurring in girls.

Puberty is one of the most excruciating times of our lives and is especially so for girls, when their bodies begin to bleed, grow breasts, and accumulate extra fat. No longer a child and not yet an adult, wanting to stay thin and immature, pressured to look like a model—the conflict is enormous. Combine this with the dilemmas of a lack of self-confidence, a longing to be accepted, acute self-consciousness, a chronic lack of self-worth, and no wonder a girl's self-image becomes distorted.

With anorexia there is a denying of yourself and an unconscious longing to disappear, as if by becoming small your needs and presence also diminish, especially your need to be loved. Such physical denial stops the maturing process, repressing sexual and physical development, so that impending maturity and adulthood get put on hold. It keeps the body like a child's: immature and undeveloped. Growing up may be happening too quickly, or social pressures to look and be a certain way are too strong.

BODYMIND DIALOGUE: ANOREXIA NERVOSA

Anorexia often arises as a result of feeling out of control of what is happening, perhaps due to dominating parents or teachers, or changing life circumstances. One way to have control is through refusing food, which is also a way of refusing feelings. Where there is no expression of emotion, there is complete control. The refusal of physical nourishment indicates a powerful denial of the need to be nurtured.

- Do you feel you are not good enough, that you do not deserve to be nourished or loved?
- Do you believe you have to help others and deny yourself?
- Is it wrong to acknowledge your own needs?

Bulimia

Bulimia is a complex eating disorder consisting of bingeing and vomiting so that no weight is gained, with periods of refusing food followed by secret eating. There is a conflict here between desperately wanting to appear perfect, with the ideal thin body (hence the starvation), combined with a great longing and love for life (hence the desire for food). Caught between the two, there is a space that becomes filled with self-dislike, if not self-loathing, and guilt.

To eat with such desperation, often in the middle of the night when no one can see, or to enjoy a meal only to throw it up later, indicates how much emotion is being repressed by the eating. This is a desperate attempt to maintain control over your feelings.

As the vomiting indicates a fear of accepting nourishment into yourself, or a deep rejection of your own needs, it helps to explore what is being so denied, what feelings are being so violently rejected.

- What feelings are being thrown out (vomited) before they can influence you?
- What part of yourself are you rejecting so violently?
- Are you trying to be someone you are not?

THE DIGESTIVE PROCESS

The Mouth

The mouth has two main functions: to take in and to give out. This is the place where the inner and outer worlds meet, a reception area where reality is vetted to see if it may pass through, and a departure lounge for emotions, thoughts, ideas, and feelings. Here you kiss, smile, pout, snarl, spit, chew, and bite. Here too you speak, sing, whisper, and shout. You take in reality and spit it out again when it doesn't taste so good. Bodymind difficulties, therefore, may be due to either the reality you are taking in or the emotion being expressed.

The mouth is where the digestive system begins with the intake of food and drink, as well as the intake of reality. Biting, chewing, and tasting all stimulate the release of digestive juices, but it is not just food you have to digest. Physical difficulties in the mouth may indicate conflict with accepting your reality—the events or relationships in your life that may not taste so good.

Chewing begins the digestive process. Through the act of chewing you break down incoming food and information into usable parts. How you do this is indicative of your attitude to life: taking small or large bites, chewing quickly or lingering over each mouthful.

- Do you relish biting into life?
- Do you sometimes "bite off more than you can chew"?
- Or do you prefer to go carefully, but perhaps never accepting a challenge or reaching for new heights?
- If you swallow food without really chewing or breaking it down, do you also tend to leap into things without paying attention to the details?
- Are you trying to swallow your reality without tasting it?
- Or are you swallowing a reality you don't like?
- Do you take a long time "chewing things over" and perhaps get so involved with the details that you lose sight of the overall picture?
- Is eating very slowly a way of maintaining control, perhaps by making others wait for you?
- In the meantime, do you miss out on experiencing life, or being spontaneous?

This area is also a major communications centre where you express your feelings through the use of your voice and lips.

- Have you been kissing the person you want to kiss?
- Or do you really want to hiss or shout?

Feelings can get locked in here—just as they can in the throat—if it is inappropriate to express them, as when you have to "hold" or "bite your tongue."

- Are your feelings getting trapped in your mouth?
- Do they come up but you can't let them out?
- The mouth is where you speak your truth. Is that the case?
- Are you able to be truthful, or are you hiding your real feelings?

The word *ulcer* means a corroding or corrupting influence. **Mouth ulcers** imply that something is upsetting or corroding you, making you feel irritated or attacked.

- Are you being affected by unexpressed negative or irritated feelings?
- Are they "eating away at you," giving you a sore mouth?
- What is really making you sore?
- Who or what is having a corrupting influence?
- Is worry or fear eating you up?

Cold Sores

Herpes is a viral infection leading to blisters around the mouth that can also be found in the genitals. The blisters can burst, leaving a sore. Although difficult to eliminate completely, outbreaks are invariably linked to times of emotional stress. As herpes has a direct impact on any intimate relations, you may want to explore how you are feeling about such intimacy, if you are with the right partner, or what is making you feel so sore and withdrawn.

Annie broke out in cold sores on her lips within two days of her honeymoon starting. Shortly after they began clearing up she went into hospital with tonsillitis. The message was simple. The new marriage was bringing up huge issues of intimacy that she did not know how to deal with, so she put up a big "keep away" sign. The appearance of these two conditions gave her the time to adjust. Unexpressed anger is very good at finding expression this way, and it can be anger with yourself as much as with someone else.

See also: Immune System, Herpes, Chapter 10

The Tongue

Your taste buds recognize only four tastes: salt, sour, sweet, and bitter. Yet, from these four you can compile memories of myriad flavours that stay with you for your lifetime.

BODYMIND DIALOGUE: THE TONGUE

Flavour is due to air passing from the mouth to the nose, so if the nose is blocked for any reason, taste is usually lost.

- Does something taste bad?
- Is it making you recoil?
- Is it leaving a bitter taste in your mouth?
- Have you lost your taste for life?

The tongue is also used for clear expression and speech.

- If you "bite your tongue," are you holding back from saying something?
- Are you biting down on your feelings?
- Have you been saying too much?
- Have you been too "sharp-tongued"?

The Teeth

Teeth develop at the same time as you begin to crawl. Their appearance marks the time when you start being weaned from milk and onto solid food. Difficulties can, therefore, be associated with issues to do with dependence and asserting independence, especially from your mother—and this can equally apply to adults as it does to children. The teeth enable you to eat and take in nourishment; they are the first in line to receive love in the form of food. Rotten teeth may be an indication of the food/love syndrome, when too many sweet foods have replaced love, adversely affecting your health.

The teeth are like gates protecting the entrance to your being. This is where you get a "grip on things," or clamp your jaw tight so nothing can get in or out. It is connected to honouring your boundaries, where you discriminate and determine what will be taken in or released. You may feel something has gotten to you, is undermining your defences, leaving you unprotected with a loss of independence. At this first reception point there is a festering and reluctance, a pain in receiving.

Through the teeth you bite down and get serious, so problems may also indicate the need to get more involved, or the need to let go and relax. For example, Mary was having trouble with her teeth. She was also very irritated with her mother, who was trying to dominate her life. Mary wanted to build a barrier between herself and her mother, but it was constantly being undermined. She also needed to actually express her feelings and talk with her mother, rather than clenching her teeth and hoping her mother would just go away.

BODYMIND DIALOGUE: THE TEETH

Teeth also indicate whether the reality you are chewing and assimilating is nourishing or damaging.

- Do you need to discriminate more between what is good for you and what is harmful?

Teeth also clarify communication. You can talk without them but the words will be unclear.

- Are you being clear in your communication?
- Are you saying what you really mean?

A tooth **abscess** indicates that something has affected you and is now creating an infection—perhaps there is grief or guilt connected to the mother-food-love issue.

- Are you feeling rejected or undernourished?

The abscess is an eruption of negative energy at the very gateway of your being. Both rotten teeth and abscesses may show that unexpressed feelings, such as aggression, frustration, or fear, are festering inside.

Tooth grinding is an expression of frustration or anxiety, indicating a build-up of stress, emotional tension, or repressed aggression getting locked into the jaw. With children this may indicate repressed feelings against one or both parents, insecurity, or fear at home or at school. This is an unconscious reaction to stress, so deep relaxation or psychotherapy may help bring that unconscious level to the conscious, where it can be dealt with more easily.

The Gums

The gums hold your teeth in place, providing the strength and security from which you can assert your bite or chew things over.

Receding gums indicate a weakening of resolve, a backing down of confidence, a letting go or loss of power, often happening as you get older or retire.

BODYMIND DIALOGUE: RECEDING GUMS

Receding gums can indicate a lack of strength to "get a grip on reality," as if your inner confidence is weakening. If they are swollen or bleeding, it implies an emotional conflict or upset.

- Do you feel secure in your boundaries and your ability to discriminate between what you want or don't want?
- Are you able to stick to your guns—to stay with your beliefs—or do you usually concede to others?
- The gums are a part of the jaw, and especially the expression of anger or aggression. Are you feeling helpless in the face of adversity?
- Is the act of defining your boundaries too demanding?

The Jaw

When you **clench** your jaw, you are holding tight so as not to lose your cool or express something inappropriate such as anger, but it also closes your mouth so nothing can get in.

BODYMIND DIALOGUE: THE JAW

Your jaw can hold back your feelings as much as it can keep everyone out.

- What would happen if you relaxed your jaw?
- Would there be an outpouring of unacceptable emotions?
- Or would you be letting something in that you are trying to keep out?

A **locked jaw** implies that you are cutting off your feelings such as tears, or stopping tears in mid-flow, or repressing rage.

- Are you trying to stop something from happening?
- Do you feel you have to keep your mouth shut because you always say the wrong thing, or say too much?
- Are you really upset but cannot express it?

The Throat

The throat is a two-way bridge, connecting the head and body, the mind and heart. It has two major roles—to take in air, food, liquid and reality; and to express outwardly your thoughts and feelings. In this chapter we are primarily concerned with the role of the throat in digestion. Refer to Chapter 11 for more on the respiratory and expressive aspects of the throat.

Swallowing is a form of commitment: once something has been swallowed it enters an assimilation process, to be absorbed as nourishment or rejected as unwanted. While food is in the mouth it is under your conscious control—you can choose to spit it out if you want to—but swallowing is where you surrender control. So here are issues to do with willpower and assertiveness. Gagging on food, or feeling as if you are being force-fed, are also conflicts with personal will.

In exactly the same way as you swallow food, you swallow your reality—thoughts, ideas, feelings, event, and experiences. This may also include swallowing your feelings, doubts, fears, or anger.

Swallowing is about allowing change to happen. You can resist change by closing the throat, or you can trust and open to change. To "swallow" something is to accept and believe it—when you swallow your reality you are accepting it into your being. If that reality is unacceptable you may have to swallow hard, or you will, perhaps, get a swollen or sore throat.

BODYMIND DIALOGUE: THE THROAT

If you are experiencing problems in the throat area, ask yourself these questions:

- Are you swallowing your pride?
- Are you swallowing hurt feelings, such as failure, shame, guilt, or disappointment?
- What are you not wanting to swallow?
- What is making you so sore?

You may not want to swallow your reality, or you may want to hold back too many of your feelings, particularly if they are unacceptable or inappropriate. Such repression creates great tension and stress, and can affect the rest of the digestive system, resulting in indigestion, diarrhoea, or constipation.

The Stomach
It continues in the stomach, aided by juices from the liver, pancreas, and gall bladder. Digestion is the ability to absorb what you need and to eliminate what you do not need, both physically and psycho/emotionally. Having a healthy digestion means being able to receive nourishment (from food or from others), and to let yourself be nurtured (to absorb what you need). Without these there can be a constant craving, a longing to fill hidden needs, or a strong denial and rejection of those needs.

This is where your reaction to what you have taken in is either favourable, and therefore you continue the digestive process, or unfavourable, and you reject or vomit it back out.

Indigestion is caused by worry and stress as much as it is by the wrong foods. The stomach is where you harbour worry—the digestive enzymes churning with anxiety—until you can no longer "stomach" what is happening. Invariably, food is used to pacify that anxiety. This can lead to further digestive difficulties, or to eating more to try to appease the upset.

Appetite
The act of eating and swallowing is symbolic of taking in and absorbing reality, as we saw at the beginning of this chapter. An **increased appetite** may be a healthy response to increased

energy consumption, but it may also be a replacement for emotional nourishment, indicating an inner insecurity, fear, guilt, or unexpressed longing, eating in an attempt to fill a bottomless pit inside. A child may eat more in order to get a word of praise from parents because the love that is really needed is not forthcoming. A demanding or devouring appetite indicates a personality that devours information, experiences, or relationships, yet may be missing the insights or wisdom these things offer by consuming them too quickly.

A **lack of appetite** may simply mean that your energy is needed elsewhere in the body, as when you are ill. However, it can also indicate a withdrawal from participation, a retreating inside, as seen in those experiencing a relationship breakdown—they may go for days without food, nurturing the hurt within. In children, this may be due to bullying at school, a lack of confidence, or emotional hurt. Accumulative stress can also adversely affect appetite.

Indigestion and Heartburn

Indigestion and heartburn may be caused by eating bad food, or food that is hard for your system to digest (e.g., dairy foods if you are allergic to them). These conditions can equally be caused when the reality you are digesting is too bitter or sour, or is proving too much to bear, and you literally cannot stomach it any more. Or it can be that worry and anxiety are flooding your stomach with acrid juices.

BODYMIND DIALOGUE: INDIGESTION AND HEARTBURN

If indigestion is an issue, see if you can find out what is making you upset.

- What issues are you swallowing that are so sour?
- What feelings are being swallowed that are so bitter or upsetting?
- Is your heart burning up about something or someone?

Nausea

Nausea indicates that something is churning your feelings in the wrong way, making you want to throw it up and away. This is a physical expression of rejection or even repulsion—there is something you do not want to absorb, integrate, or deal with.

BODYMIND DIALOGUE: NAUSEA

- Is something making you feel emotionally repulsed?
- Is it a part of yourself you are rejecting?
- What does that part need to do to be accepted?

Stomach Ulcer

This is a good example of factors coming together and combining to create a difficulty. Stomach ulcers are often physically due to a specific virus but invariably occur at the same time when you are very stressed and the reality you are dealing with is becoming corrosive, wearing away at your coping mechanism. You may be taking in too much acidity from others, or your feelings are eating away at you.

Aggravated by digestive juices, ulcers usually arise when you are under too much pressure, worried by financial or work situations, relationships, guilt, or shame. Worry is the key word here—it is almost as if the worry itself is eating you. All of this creates the perfect environment for the virus. The ulcer creates a feeling of being raw and exposed, as if there is nowhere to hide. There may also be repressed aggression, a desire to get revenge or to lash out at someone. There is a deep need to be soothed and nurtured, to return to the safety of being cared for—as seen in having to eat baby foods as a form of treatment.

The Intestines

The intestines are not only where you complete digestion, absorption, and assimilation of nutrients and prepare the unwanted for departure. This is also the place where you assimilate and absorb the details of your reality. It is here that you process your "stuff," where you digest what you have taken in and your various responses.

Intestinal difficulties are related either to stress and tension from your daily life, or to deeper layers of fear, guilt, or grief that are holding you back from releasing and letting go. Such holding creates tension and mistrust, or a fear of spontaneity.

The belly is the feeling centre where you have intuitive "gut feelings," or can get emotionally wounded, as when you are "hit in the guts." Feelings can get locked in here, unable to find expression or release. Your belly may be extended with emotion and unexpressed feelings, or sunk in response to a hollow emotional emptiness. If used correctly this is a place of great personal power and potency, but if you cannot connect with your inner strength it becomes a place of need and emptiness.

Most of the digestion and absorption takes place in the **small intestine**, aided by the liver, the pancreas, and the gall bladder. Here, incoming information is broken down into small parts and decisions are made about what to do with each piece. This is a process of analysis, detail, and discrimination. Difficulties in this area suggest an overly analytical or obsessive attitude, or an inability to distinguish between what is really needed and what is not.

In the **large intestine** the matter is finished with, ready to be excreted. This area is about releasing, so difficulties here are connected to clinging to that which has already served its purpose. There may be grief or sadness, a holding on that prolongs the pain; or a fear of letting go, perhaps due to a lack of trust.

Candida

Candida is a yeast-like fungus that can occur in warm, damp areas, such as the mouth, intestines, bladder, or vagina. Normally this fungus lives in balance in the body, but such balance can easily be broken, whether by excessive stress, antibiotics, or birth control pills, that can weaken the immune system. Due to these factors increasing in our lives, so the cases of candida have also increased. Candida has been named the cause of numerous ailments, from depression to behavioural problems, as the fungus is said to be able to move into different organs and systems in the body. Doctors disagree on this, and more medical research is needed. As candida can grow for many years without any obvious effects, it is not always easy to diagnose.

BODYMIND DIALOGUE: CANDIDA

Candida in the digestive system suggests you are being psycho/emotionally invaded by someone or something, and feel out of control. It also implies that your normal living environment has become upset or out of balance, allowing other energies to enter and make themselves at home.

- Are you feeling particularly insecure?
- Is something eating away inside you?
- Are you out of contact with your inner strength and resilience?
- What is needed to regain your stability?

Ulcerative Colitis

Ulcerative colitis is an inflammation in the large intestine, causing a lack of proper absorption, pain, bleeding, ulceration, and elimination difficulties. It is due to allergies or infection but can also be stimulated by stress. It is particularly associated with accumulated tension and irritation, and a holding on to intense feelings such as anger.

This is the area where you have access to resources of personal power, but if you are feeling thwarted or overwhelmed by something or someone, then you may well be feeling powerless and agitated.

BODYMIND DIALOGUE: ULCERATIVE COLITIS

If you can find a way to release the tension, anger, and frustration, then you will find it easier to reconnect with your own inner resources.

- Is rage being internalized rather than expressed?
- If your problem is stress related, then why are you pushing yourself so hard?
- What are you trying to prove?

- If the inflammation is due to infection or allergy, then what or who is getting inside you and affecting you so deeply?

Elimination

Irritable Bowel Syndrome

This creates severe abdominal pain, gas, constipation, and/or diarrhoea. This condition is not so much a problem with the intestines as with the nerves causing the muscles to contract and spasm. Anxiety and emotional stress are undoubtedly a major cause, as are depression and feelings of hopelessness, helplessness, and inadequacy.

As a child you may have learned to clench your abdomen when under stress, and this is still a natural reflex, causing the muscles to spasm. Alternatively, this is where you hold hidden fears and concerns, creating a distortion of the muscles. There may be intense fear, a lack of confidence, or the nervousness that arises when confronting unknown situations. Relationships also affect the colon, especially issues to do with intimacy and security.

BODYMIND DIALOGUE: IRRITABLE BOWEL SYNDROME

IBS is connected with maintaining power and boundaries, or with letting go and releasing control.

- What part of you is getting so twisted—perhaps with fear of anxiety?
- What do you need to do to straighten this part, to unravel the twists or release the tension?
- What stress needs to be released?

Constipation

More laxatives are sold across the counter than any other remedy, as constipation is a common disease—so common that we have come to think of it as being completely normal. There is no doubt that the increased consumption of refined and processed foods is a major cause of constipation, as is a decrease in physical exercise, but they are not the only causes.

Many issues to do with elimination are connected to childhood. As mentioned earlier, a young child has two major ways of controlling his or her parents: through refusing or accepting the food they offer, or by refusing or agreeing to defecate. Battles over the potty are not unusual—some children are made to sit on their potties for hours as parents try to impose their will on them. Having a bowel movement is an act of surrender; constipation is an act of holding on to power.

Lessons learnt at this time will stay with you into adulthood, a parental figure being replaced by a spouse, boss, or other authority figure. Constipation is linked to issues of feeling powerless, fearing authority or lacking control, and exerting control in the only area you can. It is more likely at times of financial problems, relationship conflicts, or when you are traveling, as these are times when you feel more insecure and ungrounded: you want to hold on to everything as it is, as you do not know what will come next. Letting go means trusting that you are safe.

The muscles of the anus get clenched in fear or anger. This is where you can hide those feelings by "sitting" on them. Even as you read this, tighten your gluteal muscles and feel the emotion that goes with doing that. With constipation there is a holding and repression of feeling, compounded by staying busy. The bowels need time to open, but if you are always on the move—having a quick coffee and then out the door—they will simply clamp shut again. Now consciously relax your anal muscles and notice the difference.

A "tight ass" is someone who is mean or unrelenting, but there is no equivalent phrase for a "soft ass": someone who is relaxed, impulsive, and generous!

Learning how to be more playful and spontaneous can go a long way toward relieving the situation. Most important, though, is learning how to express your feelings and, once expressed, to let them go. The deeper issue is trust, trust that everything will be OK, trust in the people around you, trust that events will flow as they are meant to even without your control, trust in the universe to support you.

Constipation is basically an inability or unconscious refusal to let go, "unconscious" being the operative word here. No one wants to be constipated! Constipation represents a muscular holding indicative of a psychological holding.

When you hold on to something it is usually because you fear that if you let go events will happen that are beyond your control. There is a mistrust or fear of the unknown, resulting in a clamping down in order to hold on to the familiar, to what feels safe and secure.

- Where are you holding on, and what would happen if you let go?
- What might happen to your relationships or work if you released control and let things happen spontaneously?
- What is needed for you to develop a greater trust in the unknown?

See also: Rectum

Diarrhoea
Diarrhoea can be due to a bacterial or viral infection, in which case you can ask what it is that is infecting or affecting you so deeply.

Diarrhoea may also be due to feeling emotionally stressed, anxious, upset, or frightened—hence the phrase to be "scared shitless!" Animals empty their bowels when confronted with a fearful situation, and we are no different.

When I first traveled to Cairo, in 1982, the level of poverty and squalour mortified me: twelve million people living in a hot, dry, and dusty city built for three million. They were living in every place imaginable, including the graveyards. I felt literally hit in the guts, and within about thirty minutes I had to find a bathroom. It might have been the food, but it was certainly exacerbated by my emotions.

Diarrhoea is usually caused by food poisoning, fearful or anxious feelings, or excessive stress. It means you are eliminating so quickly that you cannot absorb any nourishment, perhaps because you want to reject what you have taken in, or you are fearful of being close to someone emotionally. It may be that you simply cannot hold on anymore to whatever is happening—it is emotionally too overwhelming. It can occur when you feel emotionally disturbed by what you are experiencing but do not know how to assimilate your feelings, such as panic, anxiety, or grief.

- Are you feeling afraid about something, perhaps your own feelings?
- Do you feel as if you have been emotionally hit in the guts by something?
- If your diarrhoea is due to food poisoning, is something or someone around you very toxic or making you feel poisoned?
- Do you want to run away from someone?
- Is there something you want to get rid of?
- Do you appear strong and stoic, yet feel helpless inside?
- Are you actually feeling scared shitless?

It is important to reconnect with your own inner solidity and strength and to take time to fully experience whatever is happening so you can absorb the full benefits of any experience.

The Rectum

Your relationship with defecation is indicative of how easily you can accept and let go, or if you cling and hold on. The anus is the final exit point from the body. It is intimately connected to the mouth as the first entry point but, whereas the mouth is a conscious area, the activity of the anus is more unconscious. It is a private, hidden part of your being, tucked away out of sight, so here you may find anger, violation, or abuse, perhaps from unwanted penetration.

BODYMIND DIALOGUE: THE RECTUM

Anger in the mouth is felt in the jaw, while anger in the anus is seen in tight muscles, intense irritation, or soreness.

- Is someone being "a pain in the backside"?
- Are they getting too close, and invading your privacy?

This area of the rectum is also used to store feelings when you are confronted with a tense or life-threatening situation. This may be as simple as sitting on your feelings during a job interview or first date—you may have a smile on your lips while the buttock and anal muscles are rigid with tension—or as complex as a more serious continual tensing of the muscles over many years.

- What would happen if you let go?
- Consciously breathe into and release any tension in the rectum and gluteal muscles. How does this feel?

See also: Constipation

Haemorrhoids

Haemorrhoids, also known as piles, are swollen veins that occur when a straining pressure is exerted during defecation, when trying to hurry the process, or because the movement is difficult. Piles can flare up at emotionally tense times, or when you are holding on to issues or feelings that should be released. There is a conflict between pushing out and holding back. This may reflect a conflict between love and loss, surrender and control, or fear and trust.

See also: Constipation

The Liver

The largest organ in the body, the liver has many varied functions. Here fats are converted into energy or prepared for storage, proteins and other nutrients are transformed into usable form, and bile is produced to be stored in the gall bladder, ready to break down fat globules. Any excesses in your diet, such as too much fatty or rich food, refined sugar, or too much alcohol, will be felt in the liver. If you overdo the level of toxins—such as alcohol or drugs—there comes a point when the liver will start complaining that you are taking in more than it can deal with, whether physically or psycho/emotionally. Liver problems are seen in bad digestion, low energy (such as low appetite and/or sexual potency), tiredness, and perhaps headaches and/or eye problems.

The nature of addiction is to continue indulging despite your limitations, the ingested toxins covering up deeper toxic states within. The role of the liver to detoxify is crucial here. It implies that the liver is able to discriminate between a toxin and a harmless substance. However, if you lose that discriminating capacity and start to imbibe large amounts of substances that are actually harmful, then the liver suffers.

BODYMIND DIALOGUE: THE LIVER

If addiction is an issue for you, ask how or why you have lost the ability to evaluate your behaviour.

- Why you have been going too far, taking things to excess?
- Are you hiding from something or someone?
- What deeper issues are being covered up by the addiction?
- What would happen to you if you stopped indulging?

In Chinese medicine the liver is known as a storehouse for anger, particularly repressed anger, which gathers here and may eventually explode outward. Too much anger, especially if it is repressed, is like a toxin in the body, and is often the background to addiction. Unacknowledged or unexpressed anger leads to depression (anger turned inward), shame, jealousy, or irritability, all of which further deplete your energy levels and can damage the immune system. Connected to anger are bitterness and resentment, which are seen in the production of bile, or guilt, hopelessness, frustration, and hatred.

The liver is also connected to deeper issues of meaning and purpose. A sluggish liver leads to depression, which makes life appear meaningless. The liver gives life. Its health therefore reflects how much you embrace life, or how self-destructive you are. A healthy liver encourages enthusiasm, creativity, inner strength, and resilience.

See also: Gall Bladder, Addiction, Depression

Hepatitis

There are different types of hepatitis, some more serious than others. Hepatitis A is caused by unsanitary conditions and food. Hepatitis B is a more serious viral disease and can cause lifelong infection, cirrhosis, and liver failure. Hepatitis C is a liver disease spread by infected blood and is the most prevalent liver disease in the world, with approximately 270 to 300 million infected people worldwide, with many more who do not even realize they are affected. It is often called the "silent" epidemic, as it can lie dormant in an individual for many years before being discovered. The hepatitis C virus began to emerge during the 1960s, related to blood transfusion and injected drug use, but it was not recognized as a specific disease until the 1990s.

BODYMIND DIALOGUE: HEPATITIS

From a bodymind perspective, hepatitis indicates the loss of the ability to discriminate between what is right or wrong. Good and bad distinctions become blurred when toxins or poisons are not recognized as harmful. This applies as much to unsanitary conditions as it does to drug use. With hepatitis there is a feeling of being overwhelmed or of having the life drained out of you.

- What is draining or affecting your deeper sense of purpose or meaning of life?
- If drugs are the cause, what emotions are being repressed or denied through drug use?

The Gall Bladder

The bile produced in the liver is stored in the gall bladder. Bile is a bitter, green liquid that breaks down fats for easier digestion.

A lack of bile means that digestion takes longer and you may feel queasy, indicating an inability to break down or assimilate incoming information, and a feeling of being unable to cope. Gall, as a characteristic, means assertiveness, bitterness, spite, or malice. Bilious attacks imply an attack of bitterness or anger, rising up from inside.

• What is making you feel so bitter and bad-tempered?
• What is so emotionally hard to digest or assimilate?

Gallstones

Gallstones occur when the bile congeals, forming small, hard lumps. Their passage out of the body can be extremely painful. As the stones are made from congealed liquid, they correspond to congealed or unexpressed emotion. The stones take some time to form, so they usually represent resentment that has been building up for a long while. Gallstones indicate the need to soften and ease the bitterness, to realize that it is OK to say no to others and to say yes to your own needs. You do not need to get resentful in order to get what you need.

The Pancreas

The pancreas produces enzymes essential for the breakdown of fats, proteins, and carbohydrates. Enzymes enable change to take place. Without them, you are unable to properly digest incoming nutrients, and so they pass through in an undigested form, causing indigestion, nausea, bloating, even diarrhoea.

BODYMIND DIALOGUE: THE PANCREAS

Problems with the pandreas can represent an inability to "digest" incoming information.

• Are you feeling unable to deal with the situation confronting you?
• Does it appear indigestible or overwhelming?

- What needs to change for you to be able to digest your feelings?
- Are you resisting being nourished?

The pancreas also produces insulin and glycogen, necessary for maintaining the correct level of sugar in the blood. Insulin is released to enable the absorption of glucose and its transformation into energy, while glycogen maintains the balance if there is not enough glucose. This is the balance of sweetness or love in your life. Without the correct balance you swing between being sweet and bitter, between feeling loving and happy and being depressed and sad, between having an upbeat and energetic attitude and lacking energy, purpose, or direction.

Blood-sugar levels are affected by excess adrenaline, particularly when you are confronted with stressful situations. Pancreatic issues are, therefore, connected with maintaining the right balance in your life, a balance of giving and receiving, of working and playing.

Diabetes

Diabetes occurs when there is not enough insulin to cope with the incoming glucose, or if the pancreas fails to produce any insulin. In either case, sugar accumulates in the blood and is released in the urine, rather than being transformed into energy. This can lead to a drop in energy and may be fatal if left unattended. It is the sixth most common cause of death and the second leading cause of blindness. Insulin has to be provided either through a change in diet or through insulin injections, depending on the type of diabetes.

Just as diabetics cannot integrate or use the sugar in food, so it is hard for them to integrate or accept love. Diabetes is particularly related to feeling either a lack of—or an over-abundance of—sweetness in your life. This may be through loss or loneliness. Children can develop diabetes at a time of parental conflict, such as divorce or death, feeling that they are the cause of the loss, or that the parent no longer loves them, or due to a smothering, excessively adoring parent. Adult diabetes can occur during times when you feel under-nourished emotionally. It also occurs in connection with obesity, which is often linked to a loss of love or fear of intimacy, and shows the link between overeating to make up for a lack of love and an inability to receive love. Stress can have an isolating effect, where you feel no one really cares, or you become unable to absorb any love that is available, losing your sense of emotional balance.

It is hard to be independent if there is a constant dependence on insulin. This creates a dependence on the home—diabetic children may live at home longer than others—and a difficulty in making personal relationships last. There is also resentment: a desire to be loved but not to have to love, to be cared for without having to give. When the inner sweetness passes straight through and leaves in the urine, it causes a sadness or sense of loss. People with diabetes often feel emotionally isolated, unable to give of themselves. Learning to love yourself and finding the right balance of give and take is essential.

Hypoglycaemia

Hypoglycaemia can occur when the blood sugar level drops, whether due to excess exercise, a lack of food, or from too much insulin. It may be that you have given out so much to others that there is nothing left for yourself. You need time to replenish, to come back to your own being, to receive some nourishment. This condition also tends to indicate a desire for affection and a constant need for reassurance.

FOURTEEN

KEEPER OF THE BALANCE
The Urinary System

The urinary system consists of the kidneys, bladder, and adrenals. This system has the vital job of keeping the body free of impurities and removing substances with which the body is finished. The fluids in the body correspond to your emotions, so the urinary system is keeping your emotions in balance by extracting those that are negative or no longer needed. If they were not released, you would soon be drowning in your own negativity! Any difficulties will be connected to the release of these feelings. For instance, urinary infections often arise at times of relationship trauma, when there is an overabundance of negative or conflicting feelings that are gathering but are hard to express, or when your independence or individuality is being threatened, such as when you are feeling under pressure to conform.

The Kidneys
You have two kidneys and two adrenal glands that sit on top of them. The job of the kidneys is to maintain a balance of water and

minerals and the acid/alkaline content in the blood, and to act as a filter for unwanted substances by determining what is good and helpful versus what is toxic or damaging.

This is an essential balancing of opposites symbolized by the two kidneys in relation to each other. Issues here are especially connected with relationship, whether imbalances in your relationship with others—particularly with your primary partner—or imbalances of the masculine and feminine energies within yourself.

The kidneys are involved in the production of red blood cells, indicative of their involvement in generating love throughout your being. Yet, they are also about release and letting go, especially of negative feelings, and this is most obvious at times of relationship breakdown. Such a separation causes an imbalance as well as a surplus of negative, confused, and insecure feelings.

At times of kidney difficulties it is essential to find ways to release feelings, even if it means hitting a pillow. By letting the negative go the flow of love can be resumed.

In Chinese medicine the kidneys are known as the seat of fear, mainly because the adrenal glands release adrenaline into the body in response to excitement, anger, panic, and stress. The kidneys respond to fear, to unexpressed grief and loss. Fear motivates action or immobilizes you into inaction. This is seen in the important connection between the kidneys and the joints. Just as the joints give you the ability to express yourself, so the kidneys let go of that which is no longer needed. Uric acid is normally excreted by the kidneys, but if it is not released it can build up in the joints, as is the case with **gout,** which causes painful swelling and immobility. Gout particularly affects the toes, implying deep fears about what lies ahead.

BODYMIND DIALOGUE: THE KIDNEYS

If your kidneys have been bothering you, ask yourself the following questions:

- Do you need to develop more balance in your life?
- Are you able to let go of past difficulties?

- Have you experienced a difficulty in your primary relationship?
- If so, have you released your feelings or are you keeping them bottled up?
- Are you repressing or holding on to negative feelings, such as fear, anger, resentment, or bitterness?
- Is fear a predominant issue in your life?
- Are you worried or anxious about something or someone?
- Do you easily get panicked?

Kidney Stones

Condensed substances such as uric acid and minerals, which are normally passed in the urine, begin to separate and slowly gather more substance, like a snowball, until small stones are formed that are extremely painful to pass. Condensed matter represents condensed thought patterns and emotions, particularly to do with fear and grief: they are like unshed tears that have become solidified. They should be released and let go of, but instead they are held on to, enabling them to grow. This is a blockage of energy, connected to the issues mentioned above—relationships, sadness, loss, negative emotions, and fear.

The Bladder

The bladder is a grapefruit-sized bag, a holding area for waste liquid before it is released. One of its greatest attributes is its ability to adapt—to expand and then shrink, according to the quantity of urine passing through. In this way it indicates your ability to adapt to your circumstances, rather than getting stuck in old psycho/emotional patterns.

BODYMIND DIALOGUE: THE BLADDER

Adaptation implies spontaneity and freedom from past issues.
- Are you getting stuck in old emotional places?
- Are you attached to the past and unable to move into the future?

Frequent Urination

If you are unable to expand within yourself, then you may find you are having problems, such as frequent urination, as the pressure builds in the bladder. In men this may be due to an enlarged prostate gland putting pressure on the bladder. In women it can be caused by the hormones changing in menopause. In both men and women it can be caused by too much coffee or alcohol, stress or fear, or an excess of emotions, causing an emotional overflowing.

It is also indicative of not wanting to deal with deeper feelings. They are being released quickly so that they do not have an undesirable affect.

BODYMIND DIALOGUE: FREQUENT URINATION

Frequent urination implies an inability to adapt to different circumstances or to expand into new experiences. It may also be a way of avoiding interaction, always having an excuse not to participate.

- Are you feeling an urgency or hurry to do things?
- Are you feeling squeezed by circumstances?
- Are you taking on more than you can cope with?
- Are you trying to do things so quickly that nothing gets done properly?
- Is there too much stress or fear in your system that needs to be released?

Incontinence

Because incontinence is the result of a muscular action that has collapsed or weakened, it implies a tendency toward mental feebleness, an inability to focus energy, an attitude of hopelessness or inner collapse. No longer able to psychologically or emotionally adapt to different circumstances—to expand or contract as necessary—there is instead a giving in, especially to grief, loss, or fear.

Incontinence indicates the inability to control your feelings, so there is a continual, unstoppable outpouring. Or there may be a feeling of powerlessness, as if you are a helpless victim and can do nothing for yourself. This can occur when you feel abandoned, isolated, and have lost personal power, as when an elderly person has moved into a nursing home.

Urinary Infections, Cystitis

Different circumstances can add to the causes of urinary infections: tight nylon underwear, vaginal deodorants, intercourse, or excess pressure on the bladder, restricting the flow, as in pregnancy or obesity. An infection makes urination painful and difficult due to the hot, itchy, inflamed tissue. The bodymind connection implies that the emotion is hot too. It indicates a build-up of unreleased negative emotions—you are literally feeling pissed off!

The majority of cases of cystitis occur at times of big emotional change, such as separation or relationship breakdown. At such times there can be numerous conflicting issues going on at once: deep grief; intense rage and anger; feelings of abandonment and loss; a fear of being alone, of becoming single, and of moving from dependency to independency. A urinary infection makes it painful and difficult to pass urine, just as it is painful and difficult to release these feelings.

BODYMIND DIALOGUE: URINARY INFECTIONS, CYSTITIS

It is rarely easy or appropriate to express rage, grief, or fear, and if you have no one to talk to then the emotions get further repressed.

- What feelings are getting repressed inside that are so hot and irritating?
- What is making you so pissed off?
- Can you find a way to release locked-in feelings, such as talking to a good friend or counselor?

Cystitis can occur on a honeymoon, as such an intimate situation can release deeper feelings and fears. Love brings up everything that isn't love, including a fear of intimacy. It is easier to blame or get irritated with your partner, when really it is your own inner fears that need to be dealt with.

- Is there some deep grief or fear arising?
- Are you feeling fearful or overwhelmed by such intimacy?
- What is needed to help you release these feelings?

One way to help heal cystitis is to drink lots of pure water—to flush through with pure emotion—or to do some good emotional releasing, like shouting and pillow bashing.

Bedwetting

Bedwetting indicates an unconscious need to express confused or upset feelings. As it occurs most often in children, it is usually due to emotional pressure from family, friends, or school. Perhaps there has been a divorce, physical or psycho/emotional abuse, constant teasing, bullying, academic failure, or some other trauma. There is an inability to express these feelings, so they build up inside.

Bedwetting is a cry for help. It is a response similar to crying—an outpouring of inner feelings—but far more uncontrollable and unconscious. As it happens at night it is like a hidden secret, a dark pain. There may be a deep grief, guilt, or shame; or an unacceptable need to cry, perhaps due to fear of a reaction from the parents. There is a strong desire for love, reassurance, security, and emotional safety. It may be that the child is unaware of the depth of his or her feelings, or simply that there is nowhere that feels safe to release them. It is very important to help the child to talk through his or her feelings, perhaps with a teacher or child counselor.

The Adrenal Glands

Like the kidneys, there are two adrenal glands, and they have similar connections to their role in maintaining balance. The adrenals are also the place where adrenaline and other hormones are released as a reaction to excitement, passion, or fear, or whenever stress overloads and activates the fight-or-flight response. This may happen when there is a real danger, but it can just as often occur when there is simply a build-up of tension. You feel you cannot cope; the pressure is too great. You fear the responsibilities mounting. And then you lose your sense of inner balance; the adrenals release even more adrenaline, and your whole body goes on red alert.

The stress response tells your body to get ready to fight the situation or to run from it, when in fact neither response is usually appropriate—as when stuck in a traffic jam or trying to deal with an irate customer. If the adrenals are continually activated—due to ongoing stressful situations or fearful feelings—it will cause extra wear and tear on related organs, with a corresponding increase in exhaustion, muscle ache, and immune and digestive problems.

The fact that you have two adrenal glands implies a need for balance. Without this balance you can build up excess fear or irrational anxiety. You can push too much and suffer related disorders. Balance is the key word here, a balance of inner and outer, and an emotional balance within you.

FIFTEEN
HIS AND HERS
Sex and the
Reproductive Organs

The reproductive organs, and problems related to them, invariably have psycho/emotional connections to issues of sexuality, childhood traumas, feelings of worthlessness or repulsion, anxieties or confusion surrounding sexual preferences and gender roles, guilt and shame about previous sexual experiences, or fears concerning conception and parenthood.

As we mature into adulthood we begin to explore and experience issues of intimacy, sexuality, and relationship. Your innermost feelings about your body and your sexuality are influenced by the nature of your early primary relationships, and, hopefully, these relationships are safe and supportive ones. But it is not always so simple. Problems may occur with issues of acceptance or rejection, communication or the lack of it, experiences of misuse and distrust, self-dislike or a lack of confidence. Sexual repression, hurt, or abuse can lead to low self-esteem and to an increase in aggression, a desire to dominate or manipulate, loneliness, marital breakdown, or depression.

Each culture throughout the world has its own stereotype of what a man is meant to think or feel versus that of a woman. In the West, this stereotyping determines that men aren't meant to cry or show emotional weakness, women aren't meant to be aggressive or strong, men don't clean houses, women don't fix cars, and so on. This creates images of men being macho and brave and women being soft and weepy, which also influences our sexual behaviour. Men are meant to be dominant; women to be dominated.

As no one is purely masculine or feminine (we all possess aspects of both), such stereotyping has alienated men from their ability to be caring and sensitive, and women from their assertiveness and personal power. In the Tibetan tradition wisdom is seen as being a feminine characteristic and compassion as a masculine one, yet in the West women are barely able to claim credit for their understanding and insight, while men only tentatively reach out with gentleness and kindness. Until we re-establish a true balance within ourselves, we will have to deal with the effects of such stereotyping and its influence on our health.

HIS

We traditionally think of the male as dominant, not just in sexual relationships but also in worldly and political matters. Religion is extremely patriarchal, as shown by the widespread outrage when The Church of England began to ordain women priests, while the number of female politicians is still extremely low. Women are just beginning to enter the upper echelons of the business world, but the boardroom remains a largely male stronghold, and there are virtually no women in the world of economics and money. Enormous pressure is placed upon men to live up to these images of domination or leadership. They are meant to be intelligent and capable, brave in the face of adversity, never weak, helpless, or demonstrative.

In the light of this, it is not surprising to find men having difficulty sharing inner conflicts about their masculinity—how can doubts or fears be aired in an atmosphere where he is meant to be in control? If he has been taught that "brave boys don't cry," then personal conflicts have no means for expression, no way of being acknowledged, and simply get repressed.

Many men feel unable to live up to the typical male image, but considering oneself a failure in the eyes of society leads to feelings of inadequacy, helplessness, stress, and an inability to cope with social responsibilities. It doesn't take long for these to manifest as difficulties in the sexual organs or sexual functioning, with feelings of confusion or inadequacy regarding sexuality and performance. Unable to embrace the more feminine side of his nature, such as nurturing and loving, a man might condemn or think any such qualities in other men as weak, leading to homophobia and prejudice. Rather than dealing with these feelings in a constructive way, such men get buried by excess alcohol, sporting activity, television, or work, deepening the stereotype, the confusion, the lack of communication, and the separation of feelings from reality.

Throughout history, however, there has been an image of the warrior—the fearless yet tender-hearted male who is in balance with both his masculine and feminine energies, with both strength and tenderness, wisdom and compassion. Here the qualities of masculinity are not dependent on competition, aggression, or exerting power, but on the protection and care for all beings equally. The warrior is fearless, not by pretending he feels no fear but by accepting his fear; through acknowledging his weaknesses he gains his strength. The warrior is one who knows the depths of his own heart and feels the pain of all beings—none are rejected, denied, or abused.

The warrior image can support a man in exploring what it means to be male. Just as the feminist movement created an opportunity for women to question what it means to be a woman, so men need to do the same. For times have changed, roles are not so clearly defined. In most families the man is no longer the sole breadwinner, yet in sharing the money earning, is he also sharing the child rearing, the laundry, or the cleaning? Who cooks dinner? Who stays at home if a child is sick?

A recent documentary celebrating seventy-five years of the feminist movement highlighted a woman who worked in a post office alongside her husband. "We do the same job at work," she said, "but I also get to cook and clean and deal with the children. So where's the equality?"

As there is a strong social pressure to deny or hide his feelings, it is not easy for most men to open up, for if a man does share his inner pain or anxieties he may be called an "old woman." Yet the warrior teaches that when a man acknowledges his feelings he is made stronger, not weaker—that the more he loves, the more fearless he becomes. This image of the warrior can therefore provide an impetus for you to acknowledge your insecurities and fears and to discover your tenderness and love. For the challenge is to open your heart, to make friends with your feelings, to be fearless in your compassion. The actor Richard Gere, recently featured in a woman's magazine, shared how, "Making movies is easy but opening your heart is the real challenge."

Impotence

The size of the penis is invariably compared to a man's capacity and power; a strong and assertive male is presumed to have a large and healthy erection. The inability to get or maintain an erection can, therefore, devastate a man's confidence, undermining his self-esteem, self-acceptance, personal power, and capacity to have relationships. And given the number of erectile-enhancement medications now available, this is a more widespread problem than most men would like to admit.

Although there may be a physical cause for impotence, most cases are due to psycho/emotional issues. The communication between you and your partner is of prime importance. This is especially so if your partner is demanding too much emotionally, subtly undermining your masculinity, or if there are concerns about conception. You may have a fear of your partner—perhaps due to emotional threats—a fear of entering in and being consumed by her, or lost within her power.

You may be playing the submissive role, losing touch with your innate masculine qualities, or have conflicting feelings about your sexual preferences. Impotence is also linked to child abuse. Memory is stored in the soft tissue, so memory of past abuses can be found in the penis. Impotence can occur when there is a build-up of guilt or shame, particularly if that abuse has not been shared.

Impotence can also be caused by stress at work, and by focusing too much energy in mental activity at the expense of physical expression; or if you are being asked to perform beyond your normal capacities, and this is weakening your confidence; or perhaps a critical or aggressive boss is emasculating you at work. It may also be due to a lack of work, as happens with unemployment and retirement, making you feel you are no longer of any use.

Beneath all these possible causes lies fear—fear of losing control or being powerless, fear of sharing real feelings and intimacy, fear of having to stand up for yourself, to achieve or perform. These fears lead to ignoring or repressing feelings, to becoming a perfectionist, denying spontaneity, and keeping a tight hold on sexual expression.

Potency is an expression of masculinity, so to lose it is to feel as if you are losing your manhood. It can lead to marital breakdown, deep depression, even suicide. Finding the inner cause is essential in order to restore self-esteem and self-acceptance. It is also vital to recognize that true masculinity is not dependent on sexual performance, but on a deeper, more meaningful relationship with yourself and your world. Many men choose to be celibate and happily relate to the world in a non-sexual way.

The Testicles
The testicles are the starting point for sperm and, like the ovaries in women, are the source of a man's creativity. Issues of being infertile—of "firing duds"—and therefore issues of being no use and life appearing meaningless, will be found here. Testicle cancer is on the rise in men between twenty and forty years of age, the time when all a man's fears and conflicts to do with sexuality and reproduction are prevalent. Here too, are all your issues of fear of responsibility, fear of fatherhood, repressed sexuality, gender confusion, a lack of

self-esteem and worthiness, or past abuse. Testicle cancer implies a rejection or deep inner conflict with these issues.

The Prostate

The prostate is a small gland situated very close to the top of the urethra. Its job is to produce one of the components that constitute semen, but its health is largely influenced by the health of the urinary tract. Any swelling of the prostate gland directly influences the bladder, making for frequent urination. An **inflammation** of the gland is more common in younger men. This condition is similar to cystitis, caused by urinary tract infections and creating painful and frequent urination. It often occurs at times of relationship crisis or stress.

An **enlargement** of the gland is more likely to occur in older men. It puts pressure on the urethra, causing frequent urination but with a sluggish stream. There may also be a blockage of urination. **Prostate cancer** is also fairly common in older men and is usually slow to progress.

These prostate problems are to men what breast cancer is to women, as there is a strong relationship of the prostate to the flow of semen and therefore to a man's sense of personal power, sexuality, and fertility. All these issues become more pertinent as the body ages. After retirement it is not unusual to find a man feeling worthless and powerless; financial pressures can be worrisome and stressful, and relationships habitual and boring. If you find it hard to connect to your emotions and have used sex as a means to communicate, you may become even more emotionally isolated at this time.

An enlarged prostate or prostate cancer is indicative of these issues of expression and worthiness. The increase in the desire to urinate, even if there is nothing to pass, indicates a difficulty with expressing the inner conflicts and longings.

HERS

The role of women has changed enormously in the past century: from not being able to vote to becoming heads of state, from being homemakers to having both careers and families. With the advent of birth control, women can choose to have sex whenever they want without fear of pregnancy, and to have a greater control over their future. All these factors have radically changed women's relationships with men.

Although many women prefer to be independent and enjoy working, this has created a tremendous shift in feminine values and roles. How is a woman to be assertive at work during the day, a caring mother in the evening, and a seductive lover at night? How does she cope with having a heavy period at the same time as conducting a vital business meeting? Or dealing with menopause while trying to teach a class? Or having a sick child at home and sick patients to be seen at work?

Learning how to balance these opposing forces means facing the challenge of balancing the masculine and the feminine: being assertive without being aggressive, feeling equal to men without losing the ability to mother, being worldly as well as intuitive. Gone are the days of all women being submissive, emotional, and helpless. Increasingly, women are reclaiming their voices and, finally, their wisdom is beginning to be heard.

However, despite breakthroughs in women's equality, it has not come without some cost. At the same time, there is a corresponding increase in female reproductive difficulties such as breast cancer, premenstrual tension, and early menopause. The greater the pressures and demands on a woman, the more likely her body and its needs will be ignored. Conflicts arise to do with having children, feeling guilty for not wanting children, being able to mother adequately when working all day, or not being able to conceive and feeling a failure; as well as sexual problems to do with wanting to dominate or be more assertive, feeling put down by men or treated as inferior, or feeling guilty and shamed by past abuse.

The image of the warrior is equally relevant for women as it is for men. This image reminds us that fulfillment as a woman is not dependent on having an ideal body, bearing children, being a perfect mother, being a passionate sex partner, or even a successful career person. The feminine nature is one of insight and intuition, the "wise woman," combined with the depth of love and compassion of the open heart.

The ability to conceive and create a child is symbolic of a woman's tremendous creativity and ability to change within herself, but it is not necessary in order to feel complete. The feminine nature is one of surrender, not just on the level of surrendering to a man during sex, but in surrendering the ego to higher dimensions of spiritual understanding.

The Breasts

The breasts are the one area of the female body that creates more anguish than all the other parts put together. As the symbol of femininity, sexuality, and desirability, the breasts are constantly stared at, groped, exposed, photographed, talked about, and agonized over. We delight at the sight of a bare breast on the beach but frown at seeing one feeding a baby in a public place. We covet the sexual nature of the breast but want to cover up its nurturing role. There are two very different tasks for the same body part, hence numerous conflicting emotions.

Women rarely like their own breasts, believing they are too small or too large, too high or too droopy. Social conditioning requires them to be a certain size and shape in order to be attractive, yet few women fit this requirement. Hence the enormous number of breast enlargements and reductions that take place, often to the detriment of the woman's health. Breasts create embarrassment, insecurity, shyness, and shame, as well as pride and confidence. They influence a woman's sense of identity, how she feels about herself and her attractiveness. Some women are even unable to touch their own breasts because they are feeling fearful or repulsed or completely unable to accept this part of their being.

The breasts are also a source of nourishment, nurturing, and caring, an expression of the heart, a sacred and tender place. They offer nourishment to a new being, not only providing life-sustaining food but also comfort and security. How often do we see a child snuggle up to the breast despite being long past suckling? This same comforting quality can be present in a sexual relationship, offering a partner a place to feel safe and nurtured. Through the breasts a woman shares her love, giving a part of herself for the benefit of another. But the job of nurturing does not always come easily; it can also cause guilt and feelings of inadequacy and shame.

There may also be a tendency to over-nurture, treating a grown person as a child by keeping them "close to one's breast." Or, equally, there may be a tendency for a woman not to nurture herself, to always put others first, denying any personal need for care and attention. A woman may also feel under-nurtured in her relationships, not honoured or nurtured by her partner or children, leading her to feel rejected or no longer valued as a woman. In an attempt to gain that love she undervalues herself. All these issues can give rise to breast problems.

Breast Cancer

With breast cancer now affecting one in four women it is vital that we understand it more deeply. There is no doubt that the rise in environmental changes is a contributing factor, as more hormones and chemicals are penetrating our water and food, but invariably there are also psycho/emotional issues involved. This is verified by research showing that women who participate in group therapy and have a chance to share their inner anger and fear are less likely to have a recurrence of breast cancer than those who do not. Many studies have shown that women with breast cancer have a developed tendency toward repressed anger often masked by extra niceness and self-sacrifice, while feeling unsupported, inhibited in their sexuality, and unresolved in their conflicts.

Breast cancer is known as the "feminine wound," indicating its relevance to your feelings of being a woman. Emotional conflicts will be related to conflict between being a worker and a lover and a mother, confusion and uncertainty over your femininity, conflicting sexual preferences, a rejection of your breasts or longing for them to be different than they are, rejection or abuse from a lover, rejection or dismissal from a child who you have nurtured at the breast, shame at not being able to breastfeed, a feeling of being a failure as a mother or as a woman, a lack of nourishment and support for yourself, or a deep rage at being unappreciated or uncared for.

As breasts are so integral to feelings of worthiness and attractiveness, it is important to explore these issues openly and honestly.

- Do you enjoy your breasts or do they repulse you?
- Are you ashamed of them?
- Has your femininity been abused or rejected?
- Do you feel you have failed as a woman or mother?
- Are you being nourished and cared for?
- Were your breasts a topic of conversation or a point of ridicule as you grew up?
- Can you hold them and love them, or do you try to avoid touching them?
- Do they make you feel sexually exposed or insecure?

It is vital to remember that your breasts are only a part of you and that having large breasts, small breasts, or having a breast removed does not make you any more or less of a woman.

See also: Cancer

The Vagina and Cervix

The vagina is the hidden entrance to a woman's being, where she can easily feel exploited or violated. The ability to open and surrender is an expression of the feminine nature, but it is a tender and sensitive activity, easily damaged by force or brutality. This is where conflicts with sexuality manifest, such as issues of past sexual abuse, sexual rejection, a fear of being out of control, guilt or shame over past acts, conflict over sexual orientation, or a fear of intimacy.

Vaginal Prolapse

A prolapsed vagina indicates a collapse or loss, a sense of having no control over what is happening, a feeling of hopelessness and helplessness. As a prolapse tends to occur more often either after childbirth or after menopause, it can indicate conflicting feelings that have to do with losing control. It's as if your body is no longer yours, and in the process you fear you have lost your femininity. This is often combined with feeling either sexually unattractive or rejected, or no longer desiring any sexual involvement.

Candida and Thrush

Candida is a yeast-like organism that infects warm, damp areas, such as the mouth or intestines. In the vagina it is known as thrush. It is normally kept in check by the acid/alkaline balance in the vagina, but if this balance is upset, whether due to antibiotics, the contraceptive pill, or to psycho/emotional issues, then the yeast flourishes, causing a heavy, white, foul-smelling discharge along with irritated membranes. This discharge is indicative of discharging feelings.

BODYMIND DIALOGUE: THRUSH

An infection implies that something is affecting you in an irritating or angry way, and these feelings are proliferating inside without being given full and necessary expression. They will invariably be connected to sexual activity or intimacy issues— perhaps a fear of intimacy, sexual abuse or exploitation, repressed anger, or even repulsion.

- Is intimacy giving rise to conflict?
- Are you being intimate with the right person?
- Do you feel sexually abused or exploited?
- Are there hidden feelings of guilt or shame, or repressed sexual longings?
- Is something affecting you so deeply that it is breaking through all your defences?

If thrush recurs, then you need to see what issues are not being dealt with, but are simply repressed each time they arise. It can help to keep a diary of psycho/emotional events, noting diet as well, and correlating these with any outbreaks.

Cervical Cancer

Cancer of the cervix would probably be better classified as a sexually transmitted disease, as more than 95 percent of all cases can be attributed to three types of the Human Papilloma Virus (HPV), although this is not the only contributing cause. Besides HPV, smoking, diet, hormonal factors, and the presence of other sexually transmitted infections such as chlamydia and/or herpes all contribute to the climate that produces cervical cancer cells. The incidence of cervical cancer is second only to breast cancer.

As a virus is the most dominant cause, the bodymind connection is one of feeling violated or penetrated by someone or something that is deeply disturbing you. Look at issues having to do with your vagina, your sexuality, or abuse that you may have been ignoring or denying. These may be experiences of past sexual abuse, issues of shame or guilt, repressed longings that have never been fulfilled, or confusion with your own sexual preferences.

There may be a feeling of being disgusted by sex, alongside a belief that you have to "do your duty" by complying and putting your partner's needs first. It may be due to having been a victim of sexual abuse, leaving you feeling dirty or violated. All the issues to do with the vagina are relevant here, especially ones concerning a rejection of yourself as a woman.

The Womb

The womb is the dark centre of a woman's being, the miraculous place where life begins, the place of nurturing that contains all life's knowledge, otherwise known as the "female heart." Complications or problems that arise here correspond to those deepest feelings within you, the ones that are so often denied or repressed: how it feels to be a woman and whether or not you want to be a mother. There may be layers of doubt or guilt, conflicts from your relationship with your own mother, rage at how you have been treated in the past, fear of conception, fear of failure, feeling uncared for or emotionally undernourished, feelings of shame, resentment, hurt, loneliness, being unable to nourish—all these and more are connected with the womb.

A **hysterectomy** can seem like the ultimate rejection of womanhood, generating feelings of hopelessness, that you are of no more use, that you have lost your creativity, or that you are no longer desirable. It is vital to reconnect with the essence of womanhood, which is not dependent on what organs you may or may not have, but is the light of your wisdom shining from within. **Haemorrhaging** is indicative of deep sadness, a huge outpouring of emotion, a great welling up and release of feeling to do with the issues mentioned above, as well as a loss of emotional control.

Fibroids

Fibroids are benign muscular growths that can cause problems with bleeding and conception. Any form of growth indicates a solidifying of mental thought patterns, perhaps arising from past shame, guilt, loss, grief, or trauma. When fibroids hinder conception, it is important to examine your feelings about motherhood. There may be some serious doubts, some leftover issues from your own childhood, or a deep sense of inadequacy.

The Ovaries

The ovaries represent the source of life or creativity within a woman. This does not just apply to creating new humans but also to creating new life within herself. Difficulties in this area are connected to any conflict you feel about having a child, the pressures you may be experiencing to reproduce when actually you may not want to, or your ability to nurture and create new aspects of yourself. **Ovarian cysts** can cause menstrual problems or hinder pregnancy and are connected to issues of being a woman or becoming a mother. There may also be a hidden hurt, perhaps from past sexual abuse. With **ovarian cancer**, it is important to explore all the issues mentioned in this chapter, as this implies a separation from or ignoring of conflicts in the deepest life-giving part of your feminine being.

Menstruation

A woman's "curse," the monthly period should be a natural and reasonably uneventful experience, yet it is often difficult and painful. There are many variations on the twenty-eight-day cycle, most of which are perfectly normal, but this is an aspect of womanhood where you can easily feel out of control, as if your body has a mind of its own. It is the monthly token of your femininity, and that reminder is not always welcome.

Stress, traveling, illness, poor nourishment, weight gain or loss, and hormone imbalance all affect the menstrual cycle, as can your fears of or longing for pregnancy, past guilt, or a conflict with your femininity. This is seen in the pressure that you may experience juggling the many roles of mother, wife, lover, daughter, and worker. A period only tends to get in the way of all this, such as trying to run a business meeting while enduring bad period pains. Every woman also knows how the hormones released at this time can affect her psychological well-being, moods, and behaviour. However, resistance or unconscious resentment can make this much worse.

Premenstrual Syndrome (PMS)

Premenstrual syndrome (PMS) is period problems at their worst! PMS affects a high proportion of women for anywhere from one day to a week every month. It can be debilitating, affecting your moods, causing headaches, food cravings, fluid retention, a decrease in energy levels and thinking capacity, depression, weepiness, irritability, sudden outbursts and emotional imbalance, puffy hands and feet, weight gain, swollen and/or painful breasts, constipation, and a tendency to be clumsy and accident-prone, or vague and forgetful. Obviously, it is telling you that you need to rest or at least have time out to yourself, and usually this is impossible—demands do not just stop when you need them to.

There are certainly some environmental concerns at stake here, as the influx of hormones into our food and water is bound to have an effect on hormonal balance. But PMS is on the increase as the pressures on women increase. The more women go out to work, the harder it is to surrender to the rhythms of nature. It is not easy to cope with a period if you also have to do a demanding job that requires clear thinking, or want to look your best while feeling bloated and swollen.

Women get caught between the pressure of work and the longing to be quiet or restful. Add a large measure of guilt, a lack of self-love, and certainly some stress, and is it any wonder that you dislike having periods, tense up around them, and then have menstrual problems?

- Do you resent having a period?
- Or are you resenting having to work?
- Do you feel you are struggling to prove yourself as a woman?
- Do you prefer to dominate rather than surrender?
- Does this monthly reminder of your femininity fill you with disgust?
- Do you find it hard to flow with nature, preferring to be in control?

Pregnancy

Obviously pregnancy and childbirth are not illnesses, and ideally there are few complications. However, there are some psycho/emotional issues that can arise and affect your health at a time when you are meant to be your most radiant and happy.

Society places some very high expectations on a pregnant woman: you are supposed to be looking forward to having a child and to be glowing with good health despite the reality that pregnancy can involve a mass of doubts, fears, resentments, and insecurities. Not only are there tremendous and uncontrollable physical and hormonal changes taking place, but the idea of actually having a child to care for can be terrifying. For some women it also marks a farewell to youth and freedom and a sudden thrust into adulthood.

It is totally natural for you to feel anxious and fearful. Some of the difficulties experienced in pregnancy are indicative of these inner concerns. What you most need is strong and unconditional support so that you do not feel so alone.

Childbirth

Childbirth is certainly one of the most powerful moments in a woman's life, and most births are completely normal, with few complications and a quick recovery. However, complications in childbirth do occur no matter how prepared you may be. There are two beings at work here and each has their own agenda. Unconscious fears can unexpectedly arise as you suddenly confront the reality that you have to get the child out—even though it seems impossible—and in so doing there will be a separate person demanding attention. In theory this sounds fine; in practise it can be daunting, so much so that fear can halt the whole process, clamping the muscles down. How will you know what to do? Will you be able to cope as a mother?

Being able to relax, let go, and breathe into the fears will help release the tension, as will being able to express whatever feelings are arising. Most important is accepting whatever happens and not feeling guilty or ashamed if the birth does not go as planned. It doesn't make you any less of a mother.

Postnatal depression is due to the massive change in hormones not coming back into balance after the birth. But it may also be connected to all the issues mentioned above, in particular to the tremendous shift that is needed in order to care for this new person. The responsibility can be overwhelming, frightening, and exhausting, leading to anxiety, guilt, and shame. If your partner is not understanding, it can exacerbate this. The act of childbirth may also trigger past memories of your own birth or childhood, and if these memories are uncomfortable then depression and grief may replace the joy of becoming a mother.

Breastfeeding problems can develop due to inner conflicts about making the change from lover to mother, or a fear of being intimate in this way. There may be feelings of resentment, compounded by guilt, inadequacy, and helplessness. The new responsibility of caring for another life can be daunting; or there may be a tendency to over-mother. You may also feel very unnurtured or unappreciated, as the baby gets all the attention.

Menopause

Menopause is another of those strange times when your body, beyond your control, takes over and does its own thing. Thinking that hot flashes only happen to other people, you suddenly find yourself having a "tropical moment" or being "thermostatically challenged." Suddenly your periods are changing, you are putting on weight, experiencing hot sweats and flushes, feeling overly emotional, bitchy, irrational, and perhaps sad at the end of this cycle of your life. This "change of life" affects not only your body but also your relationships and your feelings about yourself. It is at this time that you come to know yourself more deeply, drop all the labels, and come into your own sense of who you are.

It can also be a time of depression, loss, and insecurity. There is a fear of being unattractive, of losing your sexual appeal and appetite, alongside a loss of purpose. For most women, mothering a child gives their lives meaning and direction. Menopause usually comes at a time when children are leaving home, so it can feel as if your role or reason for being has now gone. Any tension or sadness that you feel will add to the physical difficulties experienced, as stress affects the hormone levels and balance. This is especially so with temperature changes—hot sweats increase with stress and can decrease with deep relaxation.

Many women spend their thirties and forties caring for others and putting their own needs on hold. Now is the time to make friends with yourself, to find out what you want to do, to find your own passion, to respond to your own needs. This does not have to be at the expense of your partner or family; instead, share your changes with them and ask for their support. It is a time for you to emerge! You may want to start dancing or rock climbing, become a poet, write a book, or work for the homeless—whatever it may be, allow yourself the freedom to explore and discover a new way of being.

Frigidity

The sexual act is very different for men and women. Whereas for a man there may be a fear of entering into and being consumed, for a woman there may be a deep fear of being penetrated or invaded by another being. During sex a woman opens and surrenders, an act that can leave her feeling powerless, or without protection; before penetration there is still a measure of safety but after penetration any defences are destroyed. In surrendering there may also be a sense of losing something that, once lost, is irrecoverable. The inability to share sexually often reflects deeply held inhibition or a fear of intimacy, perhaps from childhood, or due to past abuse or sexual trauma.

This particularly applies to **orgasm**. Inherent in orgasm is a quality of uncontrollability, of spontaneous free-falling. For some women this is terrifying, especially to those who cling to order, perfection, or control as a means of security. Any form of emotional expression may be difficult with the feelings locked inside while a smooth veneer is offered to the world.

BODYMIND DIALOGUE: FRIGIDITY

Frigidity implies a tremendous holding on to control by clamping the muscles tight. This may be due to conflicting sexual preferences, or it can arise if you are ashamed by your erotic desires and so block all feelings in your body. You may feel ugly and unattractive and want to hide your body from others. It may be that refusing sexual admittance is the only power you have in your life; or you may believe that sex is dirty, that it makes a woman into a whore. Such feelings often develop in childhood due to your parents' attitudes toward their own sexualities. Sex should be sensual and pleasurable, but will become unbearable if pleasure is seen as an immoral indulgence.

- Was your mother fearful of sex?
- Was she abused by your father?
- Were you abused?

- What were your childhood messages about sex?
- Were you told it was wrong?
- Did someone or something penetrate through your defences?

TOGETHER

In an ideal world we would grow up with a healthy enjoyment of our own body, with no sexual misuse or abuse, an appreciation of and by the opposite sex, an awareness that sex and love are best when they go together and that sexual intimacy with another person is to be respected and valued as well as enjoyed, at ease with our sexual preference, and we would be surrounded by plenty of happy relationships, showing us how marriage or a long-term partnership can and does work.

However, we do not live in an ideal world! You may have grown up feeling uncomfortable in your body and unsure of your sexual attractiveness. You may have been abused. You probably felt misunderstood by the opposite sex. You have had sex with different partners. Intimacy is often scary, as it makes you feel exposed. And you know few happy or healthy long-term relationships to use as a guide for your own partnerships. Problems you may have experienced include issues of abuse, rejection, self-dislike, a lack of confidence, aggression, domination, and sexual confusion. In other words, few issues in your life have as much influence on your emotional health as does your sexuality.

One thing for sure is that sex is the most talked-about, longed-for, misunderstood, misused, fantasized, and joked-about activity. Little else occupies so much of our thinking time. This is partly because being desired sexually is the proof that you are attractive and lovable, that you are not as insecure, unattractive, or incompetent as you think you are.

Feelings of sexual inadequacy are rampant. Peer pressure makes you believe that you should want (and have) sex a minimum of four times a week, so if you are not then there must be something wrong with you. Yet we are all different with differing needs; there is no norm for sexual appetite. Desire can come and go, can be stronger or weaker depending on numerous factors in your life.

The gonads—the endocrine glands associated with the reproductive organs—have an energetic relationship with the pineal gland in the midbrain, which is associated with spiritual awareness. The balance of sexuality and spirituality can, therefore, influence your desire level: you may have less sexual desire when you spend time in meditation or prayer, but more if you are involved in physical activity such as sport or dancing. Honouring your own needs and preferences is far more important than conceding to peer pressure.

Orgasm releases all control, boundaries, and limitations. As a result there can be a tremendous outpouring following orgasm, a release of long-held emotions, a letting-go of fear. But such ecstasy does not always come without difficulties. To release control—to allow your body to express itself—takes courage. Being intimate with another human being is fraught with inhibitions, colored by past experiences of abuse, hurt, and fear. The closer you come to each other, the more these issues arise. If they become overwhelming both of you may pull back into your separate selves, unable to reach out into the shared space.

To be intimate is to allow another being into your inner world, either by sharing your love and friendship, or by sharing your passion and sexuality. Intimacy is seeing another as they are—intimacy: *into me you see*. In the moment of shared ecstasy there is total intimacy, as the individual self no longer remains. The "I" dissolves. One way of maintaining a degree of safety from such closeness is to have a deep friendship or heart connection with one person, while having a physical relationship with someone else. In this way, one part of you is always held back, private, and protected. It is far more challenging to have the two together. When that happens there is nowhere left to hide. The intimacy of both heart and sexuality with the same person demands a profound level of surrender and trust.

The union and partnership of sex when combined with love in a safe and caring environment can bring tremendous healing and fulfillment. Sexual energy is a force so powerful that it forms the basis of certain esoteric spiritual practices, can stimulate higher states of consciousness, unite two people in a bond that is stronger than blood, and dissolve inhibitions that free the spirit. When you honour the power of sexual energy, it can take you beyond your personal limitations and ego-centred concerns. However, if you misuse this energy, whether through abuse, domination, or perversion, it can backfire. You may suffer mentally and emotionally by being filled with shame or guilt, or physically through sexually transmitted diseases. It is important to recognize this, as a healthy or an unhealthy attitude toward sex will influence your entire life.

BODYMIND DIALOGUE: SEXUALITY

Be honest with yourself as you answer these questions:

- Am I at ease with my sexuality and if not, what do I find difficult?
- Do I respect and feel comfortable with my sexual preference?
- Can I let someone get close and be intimate, and if not can I find the source of that fear?
- Do I enjoy myself sexually, and if not, what needs to change to make it more enjoyable?
- Can I voice my needs?

Sexually Transmitted Diseases

A sexually transmitted disease is a transmitted dis-ease or unease, an inner longing or unhappiness trying to find release through physical pleasure.

Such unease may imply guilt or self-dislike, feeling that you are somehow dirty, or perhaps that you are knowingly abusing someone. The feeling of self-dislike can be so great that you continue to abuse, or allow yourself to be abused, almost as a form of punishment.

Chlamydia is probably the most common sexually transmitted disease, although it often goes undiagnosed. If left untreated, chlamydia can lead to a risk of infertility, pelvic adhesions, and chronic pain. It is a bacterial infection and is most common in sexually active young women between the ages of eighteen and thirty-five. There are few immediate symptoms other than increased vaginal discharge, a possible light bleeding after intercourse, burning during urination, and/or pain in the lower abdomen or pelvis.

Sexually transmitted diseases have become progressively harder to cure. From syphilis to gonorrhea to AIDS, they are a warning that you need to pay attention to how you are using your sexual energy, that you need to bring more respect, both to yourself and others. The disease creates a space in which you cannot be intimate or have sex, so you have an opportunity to be with yourself and look at your priorities.

BODYMIND DIALOGUE: SEXUALLY TRANSMITTED DISEASES

Such diseases are a loud cry that all is not well with your sexual energy and your feelings about what you are doing; that deeper issues of resentment, abuse, fear, and self-rejection are being ignored.

- Are you being physically intimate with the wrong person, with someone you do not have real feelings for?
- Or are you being sexually active in a way that, deep inside, you are not actually enjoying, such as with multiple partners?

Infertility

Being able to have a child is normally taken for granted; it is usually a question of *when* rather than *if* you will have one. To discover that this is not going to happen can be devastating. In particular there are feelings of being out of control, that you are a powerless victim, that life has no meaning, leading to depression or deep despair, envy, jealousy, or marital breakdown. And infertility is increasing—one out of every five couples of childbearing age experiences problems with conception.

There are many reasons for infertility: environmental causes, hormonal causes (such as too much oestrogen in the system), genetic causes, stress that can affect sperm production and ovulation, drug usage that can limit sperm mobility, childhood abuse causing deep layers of shame, or unconscious fears of passing on the anger or abuse you witnessed in your parents.

This is a time when it is very important to see things in perspective and develop a greater appreciation for the life you do have, rather than focusing on what you do not have. Count your blessings, and you may find you have more than you realized. You can share those blessings. There are many children in need, many in homes awaiting adoption. Very often adoptive parents feel as if their child was always meant to be with them, and it is completely fulfilling.

There are also many people who choose not to have children, and others who cannot but who do not let it hinder them. In these cases they invariably have a strong relationship with themselves, have made friends with their circumstances and discovered a purpose to life that is deeply enriching and rewarding. Very often they are in the creative or caring professions, using their nurturing energy to the benefit of all. There are many ways you can share your love with other beings, and many beings are in need of the love you have.

SIXTEEN

DEFINING BOUNDARIES
The Skin

Your skin is an amazing feat of nature's technology, being waterproof yet able to release water (sweat), washable, temperature controlling, self-mending, and sensitive to touch. It is vital to your well-being, as it forms a protective shield around your whole body. It reflects your every emotion and is indicative of your state of health, diet, and lifestyle. It reflects what food you eat, how much sleep you have had, and your alcohol consumption. Through the skin you face the world, and the world knows you.

Every feeling has an effect—the feeling passing through into the nerve transmitters—hence you blush with embarrassment, go red with anger, go white or sweat with fear, get goose bumps with excitement or horror. Some people have "thick skin," because they appear less sensitive to feelings or criticism, while others have "thin skin," indicating they are too highly sensitive. And it is yours: you can never change or replace your skin, no matter how often you want to "jump out" of it!

Skin issues are also about touch and feel issues. Touching is the most basic form of communication and is essential to life—without it young babies will mentally and physically deteriorate. Without human contact, adults feel lonely and psychologically deprived and can develop mental illness, as if they are shriveling up inside a shell. We are tactile creatures, so being starved of touch is the ultimate isolation, hence the importance of hugging and holding. Through the skin you communicate your feelings with another person. You give and receive reassurance, love, and caring, and the knowledge that you are safe. A mother animal licks her newborn into life, and a child is soothed of its upset by a tender hug. However, touch associated with trauma or abuse can create long-term conflict, making it difficult to be touched again; past fear can make you withdraw and refuse tactile intimacy. Skin is the primary sex organ, as its sensitivity is so stimulating, but such sensitivity and intimacy can also make you hot with anger, fear, or resentment, if it is abused.

BODYMIND DIALOGUE: THE SKIN

Psycho/emotionally your skin is your boundary, the meeting place between you and the outer world. Therefore, skin issues often arise when someone or something has crossed that boundary and "gets under your skin," or where communication is making your "skin crawl."

- Are you are feeling invaded, trespassed upon, or have you gone beyond your limitations and reached out too far?
- Or perhaps you are limiting yourself too much, holding back inside while putting up a protective cover?
- Are your boundaries being penetrated against your wishes?
- What and who is getting under your skin?
- Are you trying to break free of restrictions being imposed on you?
- Is a fear of intimacy making you resist touching and feeling?

Dermatitis
Dermatitis is an overall term meaning any number of skin irritations,

which may be caused by diet, chemicals, or allergies, by stress or psycho/emotional issues. All skin disorders are two way: you are affected from things outside you as well as from feelings within you.

Skin problems are a way of keeping the world at a distance, so an irritation implies that something is bothering you, causing your boundaries to react. Refer to the Bodymind Dialogue on the previous page.

Very dry skin implies a withdrawal of emotion, a holding back so you do not to have to deal with communication or feeling. **Oily skin** implies an excess of emotions—often passionate or angry ones—that are not finding release.

Acne

Eruptions on the skin represent inner emotional eruptions: all the erupting chaotic, hormonal, sexual, and confused feelings involved in being a teenager, and all the issues of confidence, self-esteem, worthiness, and acceptability in both teenagers and adults. Younger people are more prone to acne. It occurs at the very time you are trying to discover your individuality and seeking peer approval. You are no longer a child yet not fully an adult—this is a time of enormous change and turmoil when everything you do seems inept or stupid, combined with huge sexual surges that you are not yet ready to explore. Life can appear unfair, as if you are always being picked on, when in fact it is your own inner torment that is causing you pain. And anything going on inside shows up on the outside.

Acne isn't helped by the usual junk-food diet of most teenagers, as such food puts extra strain on the liver, which in turn affects the skin. The liver is the seat of anger, indicative of the stored up anger and frustration you are feeling inside. A clean, healthy diet will go a long way to clearing the skin, as will making friends with yourself as you are so that the raging battle within you can stop.

Adult acne is often associated with bad diet or with hormonal changes, such as breaking out at times of a monthly period. But you also need to see where you may be putting more emphasis on how you appear rather than discovering the true beauty within yourself.

Acne is a form of self-protection. It creates a "time out" from social intimacy, so you may want to explore what or who you are hiding from.

- What inner fears, lack of confidence, or self-doubt is erupting?
- Do you feel socially nervous or inept?

Getting more in touch with your inner beauty will help heal the outer pain.

Acne Rosacea

Occurring most often in middle-aged women, acne rosacea leads to a reddening of the cheeks and nose due to dilated blood vessels, followed by pimples. Usually associated with poor diet or smoking, alcohol and cirrhosis of the liver, it also indicates suppressed anger or resentment—issues connected to the liver energy. As acne rosacea affects the face, it has to do with feeling unnoticed or unacknowledged, giving rise to bitterness and frustration.

Itching

When something is causing your skin to itch, then either someone or something is scratching your surface, rubbing you the wrong way, or really getting to you and bugging you; or something inside you is itching to get free, to break out of familiar or restrictive old patterns.

BODYMIND DIALOGUE: ITCHING

Itching is a way of getting your attention. But what is really bugging you?

- Are you trying to scratch someone out?
- Or dig something up and out from under your skin?
- What is needling you so much?
- What are you trying to obliterate or get free of?

- Or is this a distraction from the real feeling of wanting to hit out at someone?

Rashes

A rash is an irritation at the very edge of where you and the world meet, so it is connected to communication issues, times when you feel unprotected or overly sensitive. It can be caused by an allergic reaction to food or a chemical substance, or an overreaction to something or someone; or it implies you are feeling embarrassed or ashamed by something you have done.

BODYMIND DIALOGUE: RASHES

- Is there something inside that is desperate to come out?
- Or are you being too reactive?
- Are you jumping into something too quickly and then regretting it?
- Or are you feeling allergic or very sensitive to someone or something?

Eczema

Eczema indicates an extreme sensitivity to the circumstances and emotions around you. It is certainly linked to allergies, particularly to dairy or sugar in young children, and it is greatly exacerbated by stress. The word "eczema" means to "boil over," indicating the heat, redness, and soreness that it causes. It also creates a situation where you cannot easily be touched, as if your protective boundaries have been raised and you are locked inside, unreachable and unable to reach out.

BODYMIND DIALOGUE: ECZEMA

If you experience eczema, perhaps your boundaries are feeling threatened or imposed upon and you are pulling back. It may also be a way of gaining extra attention, such as where there is sibling rivalry.

- Are there areas of contact and communication that are causing irritation?

If there is **peeling skin**, it implies that your boundaries are thin, weak, and disintegrating. This may be due to other people dominating and overpowering you, showing where you are easily influenced by others and have little sense of your own identity; or because there is a new you inside waiting to emerge once the old patterns of behaviour and ways of thinking have been released.

- Are you like a snake wanting to shed its old skin?
- What new part of you is trying to emerge?

Abscess

Abscesses indicate a gathering and final eruption of angry and inflamed emotions, or of incensed thoughts focused on a partner or parent, or even on yourself.

These feelings may have been fermenting for some time before the abscess appears. Abscesses on the face tend to indicate that you are feeling angry about something you do not want to face up to or deal with. If they are on the back, it is more likely to be an issue that you are trying to hide from or avoid.

BODYMIND DIALOGUE: ABSCESS

- Is someone or something really making you hot, making you boil over and get angry, and this is now coming to a head?
- Who is making you so irritated you are boiling over?
- What is making you want to burst out?

Melanoma

There are obvious environmental causes of melanoma, such as the decrease in the ozone layer and the increase in carcinogens. But melanoma also implies that your self-protection is down, due to someone or something penetrating your boundaries. As with other skin issues, there are two considerations here. Either something is affecting you and causing deep turmoil from the outside; or that turmoil is inside and is trying to make itself known. It may be connected with issues of touch, intimacy, sexuality, self-acceptance, or self-dislike, made worse by stress and emotional upset. The result is that you feel raw, unprotected, and exposed.

Bruises

You do not normally go around purposefully bumping into things, so when you do it implies you are going in the wrong direction or doing the wrong thing. You are, symbolically, hitting a brick wall.

BODYMIND DIALOGUE: BRUISES

When bruising happens easily and often, it implies that you are seeing yourself as powerless, a victim, unable to defend or protect yourself, no matter what you do you keep getting hit down. Bruising implies your boundaries need to be reinforced and your sense of personal power needs strengthening.

- Are you looking too far ahead and missing the details right in front of you?
- Are you wishing you were somewhere else and not where you are now?
- Do you keep bumping into the same issues inside yourself?
- A bruise hurts, it gets angry or livid, it swells: are you hurt inside, livid or angry, or swelling up with unexpressed feelings?

Cuts

A cut is like a mental wound, a psychological hurt due to something outside you—a cut is caused by an external object and not by an internal eruption—or due to your extending and reaching out too far. Cuts affect your powers of protection and weaken your boundaries.

Small cuts may simply be reminders to be aware, to pay attention to detail, to watch how you are psychologically or emotionally affected by your environment. They are small breaks in your defences, moments when something painful or hurtful has penetrated and got inside you, or because you have reached out too far and gone beyond your limits.

Larger cuts imply deeper levels of inner pain, as if you are being cut open or cut to pieces by someone or something. The feeling of hurt is a raw inner wound.

BODYMIND DIALOGUE: CUTS
- Has something or someone broken through your defences?
- Do you feel emotionally open, exposed, raw, or tender?
- What or who is getting to you so deeply that you feel so exposed?

Burns

Small burns indicate the need to slow down and pay attention to the details. They are little reminders that you are trying to do too much or reach out too far without taking due care.

Big burns are a big message that life is precious and not to burn it up. They indicate that some very hot emotions—anger, frustration, or pain—are burning up inside. You may be playing with fire or high emotional stakes and not realizing how dangerous it can be. Such a burn means a loss of your protective cover.

BODYMIND DIALOGUE: BURNS
- Are you feeling particularly vulnerable or defenceless?
- Are you being burned by someone?
- Is something burning you up inside?

Calluses and Hard Skin

Areas of hardened and thickened skin indicate that thought patterns—such as fear or prejudice—have become hardened, unmoving, or stuck. To be callous is to be emotionally cold and unfeeling. A build-up of skin deadens your ability to feel and receive input. It is like a protective wall preventing any trusting or open communication with others. It indicates that you have become insensitive or closed off from others or from your own tenderness.

Verrucas and Warts

Both caused by a virus, **verrucas** appear on the feet while **warts** can appear anywhere. There are two main bodymind connections. One is the feeling of being invaded and having a strong reaction to such an invasion. Verrucas, for example, dig into the feet and can stop you from putting your feet down fully.

Another aspect of this condition is that you can feel so negative about a part of yourself that there is a self-dislike or rejection and that part becomes a separate, ugly thing. Very often the part of the body affected represents strong feelings of shame or guilt that you wish you could hide or cover up. Warts usually appear on the hands, particularly at times of emotional stress. There may be issues of self-dislike or a lack of self-esteem, a belief that you are unattractive, or a deep shame about what you are doing emotionally. They are like an outward manifestation of unhappy or sad thoughts.

BODYMIND DIALOGUE: VERRUCAS AND WARTS

When a virus takes hold it is like something penetrating your outer layer of protection, and this generates feelings of repulsion or disgust. You feel exposed and powerless, as if you are a victim of this other energy.

- Is there a situation that is bugging you but you are not doing anything about?
- Do you need to be firmer or clearer about asserting your needs?
- Is something emotionally eating away at you?
- Has something got past your boundaries and is now making itself at home in you?

Athlete's Foot

Athlete's foot is characterized by itching, cracking, and soreness between the toes. It is caused by a common fungal infection, which is easily spread in damp places such as locker rooms or swimming pools.

BODYMIND DIALOGUE: ATHLETE'S FOOT

From a bodymind perspective the toes represent the details, and in particular the direction you are going in and what lies ahead.

- Do you need to deal with some details that are irritating or annoying?
- Is something affecting you, making you sore, or getting under your skin?
- What is making you crack at the edges?
- Are you walking in the direction in which you want to go?

Sweating

The sweat glands are part of the body's temperature-control system, so when the heat gets turned up you cool your body down with water. Excessive sweating usually occurs when your emotions are getting too hot, and you need a release. You are steaming up inside with embarrassment, shame, anger, or passion. **Cold sweats** are associated with fear, particularly a deep fear of communication or confrontation and with feeling insecure and unprotected. Sweating is also due to exceptional nervousness or shyness, indicating a need to become more relaxed and at ease with yourself.

Hair

Humans used to be covered all over by hair, so hair is connected to that animal/primitive part of our nature. It is interesting to see how the more "civilized" we become, the more we tame, cut, style, and shave our hair and bodies, as if trying to distance ourselves from our more instinctive animal nature.

Hair is made from cells within the skin that harden as they are pushed upward. Each hair follicle actually contains a small muscle, which makes the hair stand upright when you get frightened. Growth is affected by stress, as this can limit the blood flow throughout the muscles and skin. Hair is also affected by severe shock that affects the nerves, as seen in white strands resulting from trauma.

Dandruff

Flaking, dead skin on the head symbolizes an accumulation of old ideas and thought patterns, ways of being that are no longer needed, a layer of dead tissue that you need to let go of. You may think you are not clever enough, or think of yourself as being "flaky." Stress is also a major contributor to dandruff, as it is to all scalp conditions, particularly the stress that arises from big changes such as moving. It can also be that too much energy is in the head, and you need to come into the body through more exercise, which in turn increases the circulation and improves skin condition.

Nails

The nails, like hair, are a reminder of your animal nature, the remnants of claws that can tear flesh and fight. Very long nails are symbolic of the diva of passion and sexuality, yet are also indicative of aggression and self-protection. Nails are associated with the smaller details of your life. Situated at the end of the fingers and toes, they take the brunt of your outward movement. They suffer when you are looking too far ahead but aren't noticing the smaller issues or details going on closer to home.

Nail biting is strongest at times of nervousness, tension, or insecurity. It indicates a deep self-dislike, as you are biting at yourself, gnawing away at your own being as if you are trying to eliminate something. It is often connected with a fear of expressing sexuality or assertiveness, as it is a way of limiting any aggressive or sexually dominating tendencies. There may be a deep fear of what would happen if that energy were released.

In a child, nail biting may indicate that family dynamics are limiting the child's full expression of assertiveness, passion, or creative communication.

BODYMIND DIALOGUE: NAIL BITING

If nail biting is an issue, you need to explore what is affecting you so deeply that you want to eliminate it.

- Is there a part of you that you are trying to sublimate or repress?
- What is really eating away at you?

SEVENTEEN

GETTING FOCUSED
AND TUNING IN
The Eyes and the Ears

The eyes and ears enable you to perceive your world through sight and sound. These sensory impressions can be so affected by trauma that your capacity to see or hear clearly becomes distorted. This is especially so with children. Watching murder, war, or severe accidents, hearing parents fighting, or being verbally rejected or abused can all have a devastating effect, making a child want to stop seeing or hearing, to withdraw their senses, and instead to create a private fantasy world inside. Difficulties to do with sight and sound are, therefore, often linked to repressed emotion, fear, or a rejection of the outside world in preference for a private inner world.

The Eyes

Through the eyes you see your surroundings, you perceive other people's feelings, you know what is taking place. Here also you are seen and known, your feelings are available to be read like a book, for your eyes are the windows of your inner being. This is a two-way communication system with information constantly being fed to and from the brain.

You cannot hide your feelings from another pair of eyes, just as it is hard to lie when faced "eye to eye." Eyes can be empty and lifeless, as if no one is home, or bright and lively. They may be half-closed, the inner person hidden from sight, or wide open with nothing to hide. They can be filled with anger or fear, they may appear hard and calculating, or they can be soft and filled with tenderness.

Sight is more than just seeing. It is also to perceive, to sense, feel, comprehend, and know. Your perception is invariably colored by your own feelings. You see the world according to your upbringing, education, or religious beliefs. It is rare for two people to perceive a situation in the same way. For example, a friend told me how she and her husband had just had a big argument. They were outside in their garden digging weeds, working in silence, as they could barely say a civil word to each other. A neighbour passed by and enthusiastically remarked, "How wonderful to see such a happy couple quietly enjoying each other's presence!"

Sight is also about seeing into ourselves and seeing our true feelings. Sarah had an infection in the optic nerve that had made her temporarily blind in her left eye. She realized at the time this started that she was trying to ignore (or "not see") the reality that her marriage was over. The left side representing more emotional and personal issues, the eye becoming blind on that side was showing her that she was blinding herself to her real feelings, ones of anger and irritation (the infection) with both herself and her marriage.

Seeing Clearly

Images created from the nerve impulses are sent to the brain by the retina, so clear sight does not depend on the eyes as much as on having a functioning nervous system. If you do not feel comfortable with what you see, your vision may become distorted to make it more acceptable. You may deny or close off from the vision, seeing only what is right in front of you and not what lies ahead, or you may only see what lies farther ahead, while being blind to the immediate details. Children with distorted eyesight can wrongly be given glasses to correct it. A recognition of the emotional issues perceived by the child along with good counseling may go a long way to rebalancing the sight, as problems with the eyes are more often connected with what has been perceived than what can be seen.

Glasses provide a place behind which to hide. They not only enable you to hide your feelings, but they also act as a filter to block out the intensity of life. Making the shift to contact lenses can be an enormous emotional challenge as there is no longer a safety barrier between yourself and others.

- Do you use your glasses as a shield?
- Do you feel defenceless or exposed when you take them off?
- What are you seeing or perceiving that is so upsetting?
- What are you ignoring or refusing to see?
- Are you turning a blind eye to your needs?

Nearsightedness: Myopia

Myopia is usually due to contracted eye muscles. Psycho/emotionally, this condition implies a desire to contract or retreat, perhaps through having witnessed a trauma or emotional upset. The eye muscles tense and tighten, and sight is shortened to only that which is directly in front of you, while the far distance is blurred and hazy. Such contraction can imply a self-centreed or subjective attitude. It can also be that the future appears fearful or overwhelming, and it feels safer to stay focused only on the present. Shortsightedness is often accompanied by an introverted or shy personality, quiet and withdrawn, or perhaps obsessed with detail, yet there may be a very rich and imaginative inner life. It is important to explore where there has been emotional trauma or upset, or if there is an emotional desire to hide.

Farsightedness: Hypermetropia

Farsightedness can indicate that the reality around you is not so easy to deal with or accept. It is easier to focus on distant, far-away images—ones that involve imagination and creativity—rather than on the details or facts that make up your immediate world. Far-sightedness is connected with more extroverted, involved, and busy personalities. However, such business may be a way of avoiding the present and related emotional issues. Perhaps what is happening on an immediate level is upsetting or unacceptable. There is a fear of intimacy or closeness, and so the emphasis is on a fantasy world, separate and far away.

It helps to explore what psycho/emotional issues are difficult to deal with and what you may want to avoid. There can also be difficulty in forming close, intimate relationships. It is important to look at any resistance you may have to accepting your immediate and intimate reality. In the elderly farsightedness may be connected to long-term relationships that have become loveless or empty of feeling, with financial fears, or concerns about getting older and feeling useless.

Blindness

There are many different causes for the loss of sight, and it is important to investigate them all. Blindness may be due to genetics, as a symptom of another disease such as diabetes, or because of environmental pollution. From a bodymind perspective blindness is connected to unconsciously wanting to withdraw or retreat from whatever is upsetting, a desire to no longer witness your reality. It can occur following a traumatic incident, or slowly over a period of time due to continued abuse or conflict.

BODYMIND DIALOGUE: BLINDNESS

By shutting out sight you are really longing to shut out everything that is being perceived and felt in yourself. It is important to explore your feelings, to see what you are turning away from so completely, and to connect with the pain, sadness, anger, or fear inside yourself.

• What are you turning a blind eye to, in yourself or others?

- If your sight is getting dimmer, are there issues you are avoiding looking at?
- What needs to be brought out into the light of day rather than shut away in the dark: past memories, accumulated shame, a deep fear?
- Is there something in yourself you do not want to see?
- Are you creating a fantasy world in preference to the real world around you?

Cataracts

Often caused by poverty and malnutrition but also prevalent in the elderly, cataracts develop when the lens of the eye becomes cloudy and progressively blurred. This blurs your vision of reality. It distances you from the details, perhaps because of a disenchantment with seeing a world of poverty, where you have to struggle for the bare necessities, or because the future appears so fearful. This is particularly so in the elderly and indicates a fear of seeing what lies ahead: the dread of impending helplessness, sickness, and loneliness. It can occur when you project a mental image of what will happen in the future, and then live in fear of this occurring. Withdrawing behind the cloudiness creates the illusion that nothing is really changing.

Glaucoma

The eyes need fluid to keep them cleansed and lubricated. In glaucoma the drainage canals become blocked, causing a build-up of pressure that leads to vision becoming more and more restricted, until there is tunnel vision and you can only see what is right in front of you.

Firstly, this condition indicates a build-up of unshed tears, of emotion, a blocking or repressing of feeling until it grows and begins to affect your clarity.

Secondly, tunnel vision implies that the world is narrowing down to only what is right in front of you, while the rest is blurred. Perhaps there is a fear of change, or a fear of what the future looks like. The elderly are particularly prone to glaucoma at a time when changes take place that may appear beyond their control. There can also be great loss at this time, either of your own capabilities or the loss of a loved one that leaves your future looking bleak.

Blurred vision means that you do not have to be concerned with what lies ahead and can ignore the feelings of fear or emptiness.

- Is there some deep grief on hold here?
- Do you feel a need to cry or mourn?

Conjunctivitis

Any infection indicates that something is getting to you, is infecting and affecting your feelings and behaviour. Here the infection is in the eye, so it is connected to what you are seeing or perceiving. It causes watery eyes, swelling, and soreness, indicative of a build-up of conflicting emotions, anger, or irritation. Closing your eyes to relieve the soreness does not shut out the cause of the infection. Cleansing the eyes helps, as this is like a balm of purity calming your frustration.

BODYMIND DIALOGUE: CONJUNCTIVITIS

It is important to find what you are witnessing or perceiving that is affecting you so adversely.
- As there is so much liquid around, is there some crying or grieving you need to do?
- What is it you are witnessing that is making you feel so sore?

Tears

Tears are the most obvious example of the bodymind relationship: you get emotional and the water works flow. They are wonderfully healing and an essential release of repressed energy. If you do not release tears or emotions but keep them bottled up inside, you are more prone to being infected—or affected—in the eyes. The release of tears helps cleanse and protect the eyes, thus ensuring that your vision does not become blurred; in the same way, releasing your emotions ensures that your perceptions are clear.

Crying is not easy for everyone. If children are told not to cry, they learn to suppress their feelings. Boys, in particular, are often told that crying is a sign of weakness, so they grow up being unable to express their real feelings for fear of appearing as sissies. Instead of crying, many will have a runny nose, hay fever, or sinusitis: the emotions have to find a way out.

Seeing someone cry immediately pulls your own heartstrings, so both children and adults will use tears as an emotional bribe. Children cry unnecessarily if they know it gets them attention; adults cry if it makes others feel sorry for them. It is important to be able to discriminate between genuine tears and superficial ones, or where tears are being used to express a deeper need for affection.

The Ears

Able to detect minute vibrations in the air, the ear translates those vibrations into electrical impulses that are sent to the brain. You hear words, music, sounds of pleasure, sounds of pain, sounds that are joyful, sounds that make you cry out or contract. Through the ears you do not just hear sounds but you also listen, which is to take in, interpret, and understand.

Difficulties in the ears are directly connected to your ability to cope with what you are hearing. You cannot close your ears to unpleasant sounds as you can your eyes to unpleasant sights; your only recourse is to become hard of hearing or deaf. The ears also maintain your sense of balance, as through them you are able to be in a state of equilibrium.

To "lend someone an ear" is to listen and really hear what they have to say. That is, to be without judgment or criticism. Being able to listen is quite difficult, as your own pain or discomfort may get in the way and stop you from being able to really hear what someone else is saying; or your thoughts may distract your attention from simply being present with another person. You may hear the words, but real listening is different: it means hearing the intent, the story behind the words. To listen is to hear with awareness and presence. To receive someone else without judgment means putting your own issues on hold and being fully open and receptive.

Hearing is also about listening to your inner voice, your own needs and feelings. As much as you may turn away from listening to someone else, so also do you "turn a deaf ear" to yourself and what is happening on the inner planes. Listening to the voice inside is as vital as listening to voices outside.

BODYMIND DIALOGUE: HEARING

It may be that you have never really been heard or listened to. How often were your parents too distracted or busy to listen to your stories, your conflicts? Do "Never mind, dear" or "Not now, I'm busy" sound familiar? There is a natural longing to be heard, acknowledged, and recognized. The lack of such recognition can lead you to feeling locked inside, unable to share, alienated from communication. When someone else really hears and receives what you are saying there is a tremendous sense of relief, an offloading—hence the proliferation of psychotherapists!

- What am I listening to that is so upsetting me?
- What am I refusing to hear?
- Am I turning a deaf ear to my own needs?
- Am I out of balance with my world?

Deafness

There are both genetic and environmental causes for deafness, but a lessening of the ability to hear—from being hard of hearing through to complete deafness—implies a withdrawal from communicating or participating in what is being heard. You can close your eyes and pretend the world does not exist, but you cannot close your ears. The only way is through going deaf.

One rather grumpy old man, who had lost his hearing as he grew older, told me that it did not surprise him that he had gone deaf, as, "I never thought anyone had anything worth listening to anyway." The elderly often have very selective hearing—they are only able to hear nice things but nothing unpleasant. I had an elderly client who could easily hear me from across the room if I was offering her a chocolate, but I had to shout for her to hear me if it was about her daughter, someone she had no positive feelings for.

Loss of hearing can be due to trauma, but can equally be through having heard enough and simply not wanting to hear anymore. It may occur when a partner or parent is very dominating or loud; if you witness parents shouting or abusing each other; if you are made to feel insecure, unsafe, or fearful; or if you are constantly told you are worthless, ugly, or a hopeless case. Loss of hearing (and earache) can also be from being over-criticized. In the above case, the daughter was all too fond of criticizing her mother, and as a consequence her mother had simply tuned her out.

Difficulties with hearing are a way of cutting yourself off, not just from other people but also from your own feelings. If you cannot hear, you do not have to deal with your response to what you have heard, such as feelings of anger, hurt, rejection, fear, or insecurity. It indicates a lack of participation, a withdrawal, possibly an inability to cope with responsibilities. It creates a barrier behind which you can hide without being bothered. You can be left in peace. You can live in a fantasy world where everything is fine and everyone is happy. (Refer also to the Bodymind Dialogue on the previous page.)

In children a loss of hearing is often associated with emotional and psychological factors, so it is important to make sure that the child has a means to express any hidden feelings and fears, perhaps to someone not involved with the immediate family. The child may develop a fantasy world, a secret and private place where the characters are completely different from the ones in normal life.

Earaches

An earache implies that what you are hearing is hurting or aching. Children seem more prone to them than adults, but children also have fewer ways of being able to express their feelings. Listening to your parents arguing, or hearing abuse taking place, or being shouted at or bullied at school can all create pain in your ears, making you want to close them down to stop the sound coming in. It is very important to create a way for the child to share any bottled up feelings. An ache in the ear is like an ache in the mind or heart—something being heard is causing inner anguish or confusion.

Ear Infections

An infection implies that what you are hearing is infecting or affecting you deeply; it is really getting to you and creating heat and soreness, which suggest anger and rage.

In children it is important to find a way for them to express themselves, perhaps with a teacher or counselor.

BODYMIND DIALOGUE: EAR INFECTIONS

Something is affecting your ability to receive.

- Can you discover what is so upsetting you?
- Is it someone you are listening to, or someone who is not listening to you?
- Or something you are not listening to in yourself?

Tinnitus

Tinnitus is a condition in which the boundaries between the ear and the brain become distorted and there is a constant ringing sound, sometimes quite loud. It often increases with stress, or at times when you are likely to be paying less attention to yourself and your needs, when all your energy is focused outward. The ringing makes you focus inward, forces you to listen to your own voice, to pay attention to feelings, to whatever is going on within you. There is no known cure, but deep relaxation can alleviate much of the intensity.

Loss of Balance

Within the ear is an area called the labyrinth, which consists of three semicircular canals, each at an acute angle to each other. Fluid moving between these three canals indicates to the brain the position of the head and the body and the angle between the two, in this way maintaining a sense of balance. This keeps you upright, centred, and clear in your direction. It is the balance between heaven and earth, between self and other, between inner and outer.

BODYMIND DIALOGUE: LOSS OF BALANCE

Losing your physical balance is synonymous with losing your sense of dignity and inner security. If this happens you need to look at how balanced your life is, if there are areas where you are getting unbalanced or unhinged. A stressful situation or emotional trauma may create a loss of balance and an inner dizziness: you don't know in which direction to turn. Losing the ability to discern makes you feel as if the world has been turned upside down.

- Do you feel unbalanced?
- Do you feel out of order?
- Do you feel as if everything is in the wrong place?

EIGHTEEN

ALL IN THE MIND
Mental Disorders

The medical approach to mental disorder is fraught with confusion over what is a real illness and what is "all in the mind." Doctors tend to view illness as real when there are physical characteristics that can be monitored, labeled, or changed with drugs. Illnesses that do not have obvious physical symptoms are not so easy to diagnose or even to accept as valid. Someone suffering from depression is quite likely to hear a doctor say that there is nothing the matter that a good holiday won't cure. Few doctors are taught how to deal with mental or emotional issues. Most tend to believe that such problems are a sign of weakness and we should just pull ourselves together and get on with life.

From a bodymind perspective every illness has a psycho/emotional connection; some are simply more obvious than others. There is no clear separation between what is happening in the mind and what is happening in the body. Both the physical problems that arise and the mental battles that rage within have the same importance.

Mental and emotional disorders are real, and they are not necessarily cured by medical intervention. Anti-depressants are not a cure. Most of the therapies available aim to normalize according to society's idea of what normal is, although more holistic and sympathetic systems are now emerging that treat the whole person, recognizing that each one of us is a unique individual with specific needs.

Depression

One out of twenty adults suffers from a clinical depression, and according to Dr. Christopher Murray, head epidemiologist of the World Health Organization, major depression will be the second most debilitating disease worldwide by 2020. Fifteen percent of severely depressed patients kill themselves; two-thirds contemplate suicide. Being depressed is the most unsung source of suffering in the world. It is a disease of the soul, and chemicals alone cannot heal it.

There are many environmental and biological causes for depression, and it is important to make sure these are considered. Any imbalance in the hormones can lead to altered mood swings, as in PMS. Side effects from drugs can easily upset the balance in the mind, as can exposure to certain chemicals. The word depression comes from the Latin *deprimo*, meaning "to press down" or "to press under." The inner cause is invariably caused by stress, or from deeply held, unresolved feelings or traumas that get "depressed" or pushed down in an attempt to push them away.

Depression implies a loss of life energy in which both body and mind feel heavy, lethargic, and disinterested. This usually implies that beneath the lethargy there are unacceptable feelings being repressed. These feelings may be connected to a sense of unworthiness, of being unlovable, lonely, or misunderstood. There can also be layers of shame or guilt from the past, perhaps due to sexual abuse, dominating or demanding parents, the loss of a loved one, or a broken relationship with buried hurt, anger, or rage. These feelings may be so powerful that it is too much to acknowledge consciously, and to release any of them would create too much upheaval. So you bury them with layers of dispassion, detachment, and depression. Many elderly people are depressed by the thought of what lies ahead—the loneliness of old age and death: without meaning there is no reason for being. Depression is a way of giving up without actually dying, a desperate and silent cry for help.

Depression is also a hidden longing for attention and love. But you are the one who has to make the effort to come forth. Exercise is a vital component, as the more you move your joints and muscles, the more your feelings will find expression. However, depression does not just depress the mind, it also depresses the body, limiting movement and thereby limiting expression even further. In most cases of depression there is a range of physical symptoms such as exhaustion, insomnia, headaches, reduced or excessive appetite, or constipation.

Anti-depressant drugs can work to help rebalance the brain's chemistry, but if you chose to go that route then do include looking at the underlying causes, possibly with the help of a therapist.

Nervousness and Anxiety

Nervousness implies that you are lacking self-esteem, self-awareness, and connectedness, so that you are not grounded in your own being. This creates a nervous fear of others, a wariness that the world is not a safe place to be, or apprehension that may have no real cause. Extreme nervousness is often connected to severe stress, and anxiety connected to failure or loss. Ongoing nervousness and anxiety create a cycle of tension in the body, so that you are also likely to suffer from muscle tension, stiffness, eating disorders, heart palpitation, rapid breathing patterns, excessive sweating, and headaches. Learning how to relax and breathe more deeply is essential.

Panic Attacks

Panic attacks occur when your strength or ability to cope becomes undermined. Fear overrides all sense of balance or reason, and you can no longer see that the fear is irrational. It simply dominates your entire psyche. Some people who experience panic attacks cannot even leave their homes for fear. This is due to feelings of worthlessness, helplessness, and vulnerability; or to an increase in stress and the inability to cope. Slowly you lose touch with your understanding and perspective, as if you are no longer in your body, creating fertile ground for fear to develop. It is possible to overcome panic through breathing techniques, as the breath grounds you in your body.

Bipolar Disorder (Manic Depression)

We have come to understand this mental disorder far better in recent years. Bipolar disorder, also known as manic-depressive illness, affects approximately 2.5 million people a year. It is a brain disorder that causes a person's mood, energy, and ability to function in such a way that they fluctuate between being manic, high, and hyperactive to depressed, sad, and inactive, with normal mood periods in between. Swings can occur within a few hours, days, weeks, or even months. Different from the normal ups and downs that everyone goes through, the symptoms of bipolar disorder can be severe.

A manic episode usually includes increased energy, activity, restlessness, euphoria, exaggerated optimism and self-confidence, extreme irritability, rapid-fire talking and jumping from one idea to another, decreased sleep with no fatigue, delusions of grandeur and inflated ego, big spending sprees, big eating, drug abuse, and particularly a denial that anything is wrong.

A depressive episode includes sadness, anxiety, feelings of emptiness, hopelessness, pessimism, guilt, worthlessness, or helplessness, loss of interest in physical activities, deep fatigue and need to sleep/rest, difficulty concentrating, remembering, making decisions, change in appetite usually resulting in weight loss, muscle ache or pain, symptoms that do not have a physical cause, and possible thoughts of death or suicide.

Bipolar disorder does have genetic tendencies, so it is quite possible that you were born with the potential and then "something" happens to tip the balance and the illness develops. That "something" may be severe stress that is pushing you to your limits until you feel you cannot cope. It could be a reaction to environmental chemicals, or a lack of lithium. More cases of bipolar have been found where lithium, which is a naturally occurring element, is missing from the earth or water. This is why lithium is one of the main remedies used to balance mood swings. It could also be from drug use, particularly marijuana. As much as I support the use of medical marijuana, as it can be very helpful in certain situations, it can also be detrimental. For some it creates a chemical imbalance in the brain and can flip the user into a manic episode. I have seen this a number of times. The difficulty is that the user then continues to smoke, believing that the dope is actually helping them to calm down.

The most difficult part of this illness is the inability to see that there is anything wrong. Such denial stops you from going for help. As soon as you are aware that there is something out of balance with your behaviour and reactions, then there is a very positive chance for healing.

Nervous Breakdown

Each one of us has a shadow, that part of the psyche that is denied, hidden, repressed, ignored, or pushed away. It contains memories from the past—your innermost feelings that you may not even be aware of—and unfulfilled yearnings. Normally, you go about your life and do not enter into this place too willingly or too often. It may appear in your dreams or in a sudden temper flare up, or in the inability to have a civil relationship with your sibling. But stress, emotional trauma, loss, and grief, or just having too much to cope with, can all pile up until the normal boundaries that keep the shadow in its place start to fall apart.

Communication with yourself begins to break down, taking away your contact with the everyday world. There is a psycho/emotional breaking apart, leading to irrational behaviour or deep depression, sadness, and fragility; you may become irresponsible, withdrawn, or hyperactive. Day-to-day events become blown up out of all proportion. Your behaviour becomes confused and even wild. Your words do not always make sense. Your emotions are flying in all directions, or it feels as if there is no ground beneath you that can contain or hold you. Irrationality takes over from rationality. You lose your grasp on sanity.

The interesting thing about what is called a nervous breakdown is how close it is to a spiritual breakthrough, where all your conditioning comes apart and nothing familiar remains. You can turn a breakdown into a breakthrough by trusting yourself and keeping people close by who can help you. Do not try to go through this "dark night of the soul" on your own, but seek help and support.

Senile Dementia and Alzheimer's Disease

Degeneration of the brain leads to senility, confusion, incoherence, and sometimes abusive or violent behaviour, as well as severe memory loss and delusive imaginings. **Senile dementia** means a general mental degeneration, loss of memory, irritability, and childlike behaviour, occurring predominately in the elderly. **Alzheimer's disease** is the most common cause of dementia among people aged sixty-five and older and affects an estimated four-million adults. The incidences in younger people is growing. It is a form of dementia where nerve cells in the brain are destroyed and nerve fibres get tangled. It affects about 50 percent of those with senility but takes those symptoms further to include incoherence, abusive behaviour, self-centeredness, and slow, progressive deterioration.

There are undoubtedly environmental issues at stake here with the increase of metals such as aluminium and chemicals in our food and water, but from a psycho/emotional perspective both dementia and Alzheimer's are indicative of a loss of ground or belonging. A loss of memory is the same as losing your history, your roots or past, your place of being.

As this condition happens mostly in the aged, we need to examine how we deal with our elders. In the West we treat old people as a nuisance. Aging is not honoured; retirement is not seen as a time to share one's wisdom. The elderly are more often discarded as having long since served their purpose. Whether living at home or in a retirement centre, elderly people have invariably gone from a position of power to a position of helplessness or powerlessness and often extreme loneliness. Unable to look after themselves and not knowing how to cope, once strong and useful people can become weakened and feel worthless or fearful of what lies ahead. Is it surprising that they begin to lose their minds, to become irrational or forgetful?

Senility includes childishness and the need to be looked after like a child. This can indicate a fear of being alone and growing old, a longing to turn back the clock and be cared for again, rather than having to deal with life in its present form. It is a desire to go back to the past, to how things used to be. Alzheimer's can include a total lack of cognizance. This implies an altered state of consciousness, a different perception of reality, perhaps in preparation for transition.

Addiction

Despite living in the most affluent and comfortable times in history we are rarely fulfilled or satisfied. There is a constant striving to find more thrills, more pleasure, more ways to amuse ourselves, more ways to hide from the reality of our unhappiness. Hence addiction. Causes may include external pressures such as financial difficulties, emotional traumas, or growing up in a stressful environment with emotional and/or physical abuse. We can be addicted to almost anything: alcohol, drugs, cigarettes, food, no food, coffee, sugar, shopping, gambling, money, exercising, penance … the list is endless. The object of the addiction is almost irrelevant. Much more important is what lies beneath the addiction, what is being covered over or denied by this behaviour.

Whatever addiction you have serves to distract you from what is really going on. Alcohol makes you feel that everything is fine. Cigarettes enable you to swallow your feelings. Drugs take you into a different world where you don't have to deal with the realities of this one, as well as giving you a false sense of grandeur. Food replaces the love you crave and smoothes over the cracks in your life. All these numb the pain inside, alter consciousness, or fill an inner emptiness. The substance provides a sense of security and enjoyment that is far easier to deal with than the pain. By not feeling the inner discomfort you can maintain an illusion of happiness.

But addiction is not necessarily a numb and happy state. The craving continues, no matter how much you consume. This gives rise to guilt and shame, leads to depression, or is projected outward as anger. There is a deep, rarely acknowledged fear of where you are going to end up, a self-dislike that eats away at your ability to recover. How can you even begin to love yourself when you see such desperation acting itself out each day?

Going sober or straight or clean means being confronted with the deeper issues that the addiction was hiding. You have to face, accept, and bring into your heart all those lost and denied parts of yourself. If you can recognize the craving and its underlying causes, then you have a chance to let go of the addiction. Healing is about your ability to face the reality of your feelings rather than running away from them, and bringing that reality into a place of love.

Insomnia

In an ideal world you would sleep easily and deeply, enjoy plentiful dreams and awaken refreshed and raring to go. In the real world you do not always sleep easily or deeply. You toss and turn. You may have nightmares. And you often awaken groggy and tired, as if you had not rested at all.

There are plenty of reasons for this. On a physical level it may be due to not enough exercise, so your body is not tired. It may be due to too much television or caffeine stimulating the system. It may even be due to having an old or uncomfortable bed that does not support your body properly. It is also invariably due to stress, anxiety, self-doubt, financial concerns, pressure at work, and feeling unable to meet the demands. To peacefully surrender is the exact opposite of what you have been doing during the day when you are faced with competitive work situations, screaming children, or endless traffic. Being able to come back into a sense of yourself in a relaxed and quiet space can be very difficult. Sleep provides you with the means to regenerate and recuperate, but it is also a time when you surrender the ego and have no control, and for some this can be terrifying, particularly the fear of what will happen without their knowledge.

BODYMIND DIALOGUE: INSOMNIA

You cannot control sleep, nor can you make it happen. It has a rhythm of its own that is activated by your letting go. There are important issues of trust here: you need to trust what will happen during the night, that the world will be OK without you, that if you let go nothing will fall apart.

- What has so upset this place of trust?
- What are you holding on to or are so fearful of releasing?

AFTERWORD

If you have now read through this book, you may well be feeling that it seems like an awful lot of work to try to find out what your body is saying, and why not just go to the doctor and get some pills?

And you would be fully justified to feel like this. The journey of getting to know yourself and your body can be an arduous one. It can appear as if nothing is changing no matter how much personal work you do, and at times it can seem pointless, especially if the illness or difficulty you are working with does not improve.

I know this, as I have traveled this journey for many years. And I have heard it over and over from other people.

But I also know that this journey is the most important one you could ever make. You will get to know yourself in a new and intimate way. It will lead you into previously unknown places and into wonderful adventures. It will give you a sense of connectedness and will deepen your insight into human nature. It will fill you with compassion for both yourself and for others. It will show you how we are all a part of each other.

I wish you good luck. May you travel on this journey with equal measures of both courage and laughter. May you be free from suffering. Bon voyage!

BIBLIOGRAPHY

Ball, John. *Understanding Disease*. Essex, United Kingdom: C. W. Daniel, 1990.

Barasch, Marc Ian. *The Healing Path*. New York: Penguin, 1995.

Borysenko, Joan. *Guilt Is the Teacher, Love Is the Lesson*. Boston: Warner Books, 1991.

Borysenko, Joan. *Minding the Body, Mending the Mind*. New York: Bantam Dell, 1998.

Chopra, Deepak. *Ageless Body, Timeless Mind*. New York: Harmony, 1994.

Colligan, Douglas, and Steven Locke. *The Healer Within*. Dutton/ Penguin, 1986.

Connelly, Dianne M. *Traditional Acupuncture: The Law of the Five Elements*. Traditional Acupuncture Institute: Columbia, Maryland, 1994.

Dahlke, Rüdiger, and Thorwald Dethlefsen. *The Healing Power of Illness*. London: Element Books, 1997.

Feild, Reshad. *Here to Heal*. London: Element Books, 1991.

Ferguson, Marilyn. *The Aquarian Conspiracy*. New York: Tarcher/
     Penguin, 1987.

Hanh, Thich Nhat. *The Miracle of Mindfulness*. Boston: Beacon Press, 1999.

Hoberman Levine, Barbara. *Your Body Believes Every Word You Say*.
     Fairfield, Connecticut, 2000.

Johnson, Douglas, Ronald Siegel, and Michael Urdang. *Back Sense*.
     New York: Bantam Dell, 2002.

Kabat-Zinn, Jon. *Full Catastrophe Living*. London: Piatkus, 2004.

Kaptchuk, Ted. *The Web That Has No Weaver*. New York: McGraw-Hill,
     2000.

Levine, Stephen. *Healing into Life and Death*. New York: Anchor, 1989.

Lipton, Bruce. *The Biology of Belief*. Mountain of Love/Elite Books, 2005

Lowen, Alexander. *Bioenergetics*. New York: Penguin, 1994.

Martin, Paul. *The Healing Mind*. New York: St. Martin's Press, 1999.

Montagu, Ashley. *Touching*. New York: HarperCollins, 1986.

Pearsall, Paul. *Super Immunity*. New York: Ballantine, 1988.

Pert, Candace. *Molecules of Emotion*. New York: Touchstone, 1999.

Proto, Louis. *Self-Healing*. London: Piatkus, 1993.

Sarno, John E. *The Mindbody Prescription*. Boston: Warner Books, 1998.

Tillich, Paul. *Meaning of Health*. Berkeley, California: North Atlantic
     Books, 1981.

Wilber, Ken. *Grace and Grit*. Boston: Shambhala, 1993.

Williamson, Marianne. *A Return to Love*. New York: HarperCollins, 1994.

INDEX

abdomen, 126–127
  and solar plexus, 127
abscess, 249, 304
accidents, 64–65
acne, 301–302
acupuncture, 5–6
  See also Eastern medicine
addiction, 329–330
  and stress, 170
  and throat chakra, 62
adenoids, 186
adrenal glands, 272–273
adrenaline, 16, 19, 21
AIDS, 197–200
allergies, 177, 186–187
  and asthmatic reactions,
    214–216

with food, 240–241
hay fever, 207
and headaches, 159
Alzheimer's disease, 328–329
anaemia, 235
anger,
  and inflammation, 142, 183
  and the liver, 262
  and the nervous system, 154
  repression of, 2, 35
  and rheumatoid arthritis, 143
  effect on the muscles,
    146, 147
angina, 223–224
ankles, 133–134
anorexia nervosa, 243–244
antibodies and antigens, 177–178

Buddhism, 6
bunions, 136
burns, 306
bursitis, 144
buttocks, 123–124
    relation to back pain, 123
    and sexuality, 124

calluses, 306
cancer, 188–190
    breast, 283–284
    cervical, 286
    environmental causes of, 31
    melanoma, 304–305
    ovarian, 287
    of prostate, 280
    remission, 92–93
    testicular, 279
candida, 255–256, 285
cardiovascular disease,
    treatment for, 12
cardiovascular system, 219–235
    angina, 223–224
    blood, 226–234
    circulation, 230–233
    heart, 220–226
    heart attack, 224–226
    and haemorrhage, 233–234
    hypertension, 12
    stroke, 232–233
cervix, 284–286
chakras, 56–64
chest, 124–126
    concavity in, 125
    puffed–up, 124

ribcage, 125–126
chicken pox, 194
childbirth. *See* pregnancy
chronic fatigue syndrome,
    5, 195–197
circulation, 230–233
    arteriosclerosis, 230–231
    chilblains, 229
    haemorrhage, 233–234
    Raynaud's disease, 229
    thrombosis, 231–232
    and varicose veins, 234–235
circulatory system. *See*
    cardiovascular system
cold sores, 247
    See also herpes
colitis, 256–257
common cold, 183–185
    and headaches, 158
    treatment for, 12
constipation, 257–259
cough, 210–214
crown chakra, 64
cystitis, 271–272

deafness, 318–319
death,
    of a loved one, 1
dementia, 328–329
depression, 324–325
    ailments resulting from, 12
    anti-depressants, 15
    and candida, 255–256
    and the crown chakra, 64
    and diabetes, 12

fibromyalgia, 163–164, 195–196
fifth chakra,
    and the throat, 208
fight-or-flight response, 18–19
fingers, 115
    See also hands
flu, 185
forgiveness, 93–95, 154

gall bladder, 263–264
    gallstones, 264
gluteal muscles. *See* buttocks
gout, 145, 268
gums, 250
grief,
    connection to sinusitis, 208
    effect on the muscles,
        146, 147
    repression of, 36

hair, 308–309
hands, 113–115
    arthritis in, 114
    cold, 114
    function of, 48
    stiffness in, 114
    sweaty, 114
hay fever, 207
head, 103–104
headaches, 63, 158–161
    migraine, 5, 160–161
    possible causes of, 159
heart, 124, 220–226
    angina, 223–224
    attack, 224–226

disease, 12
    rhythm of, 223
heart attack, 19–20, 224–226
heartburn, 253
heart chakra, 61
haemorrhage, 233–234, 287
haemorrhoids, 261
hepatitis, 263
hernia, 150–151
herpes, 193–194
    and shingles, 194–195
Hinduism, 6
hips, 128–129
    injury to, 1, 128
    pain in, 129
HIV, 197–200
hyperventilation, 217
    See also panic attacks
Hypoglycaemia, 266
hysterectomy, 287

illness,
    benefits of, 39–42
    in children, 65–66
    environmental causes of, 30
    genetic causes of, 31
    predisposal to, 43–44
    psycho/emotional causes
        of, 32–35
    stress's effect on, 168–170
immune system, 177–200
    adenoids, 186
    allergies, 177, 186–187
    antibodies and antigens,
        177–178

broken, 132
bruising of, 131
calves, 131
gait, 130
knees, 132–133
lower legs, 131
muscular vs. weak, 130
and sexuality, 130–131
thighs, 130–131
liver, 124, 261–263, 301
hepatitis, 263
love, 97
See also heart, heart chakra,
sexuality
lungs, 124, 213–218
bronchitis in, 213–214
and shallow breathing, 126
lymph glands, 181

manic depression. *See*
bipolar disorder
meditation,
benefits of, 2, 3
blood pressure, influence
on, 228
for dealing with anger, 2
for healing, 84–85
pranayama breathing for, 205
men's health,
impotence, 278–279
prostate, 280
testicles, 279–280
men, stereotypes of, 276–277
menopause, 138–139, 291
and headaches, 158

menstruation, 279–289
and Anaemia, 235
and headaches, 158
meridians, 5
See also Eastern medicine

metamorphosis therapy, 3, 50
migraine headaches, 5, 160–161
mindfulness, 71–72
multiple sclerosis, 155, 191–193
and Vitamin D, 191
muscles, 145–151
and anger, 146, 147
cramping of, 148–149
and fear, 146, 147
pain in, 147–148
and sprains and strains, 149
stiffness in, 146–147
and stress, 5
torn, 149–150
myalgic encephalomyelitis.
See chronic fatigue syndrome

nails, 309
natural painkillers, 15
nausea, 254
neck, 106
function of, 47–48
and migraine headaches, 160
posture of, 48, 107
stiff, 48, 107–108
nervous breakdown, 327–328
See also anxiety, stress
nervous system, 153–165
and anger, 154

and the back, 117

and the feet, 136

sore throat. *See* common cold, throat, tonsillitis

spine. *See* back, neck

spleen, 181

sprains, 149

of ankle ligaments, 134

stomach, 124, 252–254

heartburn, 253

indigestion, 252, 253

nausea, 254

ulcer, 254

strains, 149

stress, 167–176

causes of, 170–172

connection to root chakra, 58

coping with, 23

and the common cold, 184

and digestive problems, 259

effects of, 22, 168–170

emotional causes of, 21

and fight-or-flight response, 18–19

and headaches, 158

maladies caused by, 5

physical symptoms of, 19

physiological changes with, 18

post-traumatic stress disorder, 175–176

stress response, 168–169

trauma, 175–176

stroke, 232–233

swelling. *See* inflammation

symptoms, 43

before onset of, 46–47

benefits of, 44–45

dialoguing with, 72–80

T-cells, 178, 180

and HIV, 197

teeth, 248–249

abscess, 249

grinding of, 249

tendons, 149–150

tension myositis syndrome, 120

and cramps, 148

and fibromyalgia, 163

and sciatica, 162

See also back, back pain

testicles, 279–280

third chakra,

and the back, 117

third eye chakra, 63–64

throat, 62, 208–210, 251–252

cough in, 210–214

larynx, 208, 210–212

sore, 209

throat chakra, 62–63

thrombosis, 231–232

thrush, 285

thymus gland, 180–181

thyroid gland, 212–213

hypothyroidism of, 212–213

and throat chakra, 62

toes, 136

See also feet

tonsillitis, 21, 185–186

trauma, 175–176

ABOUT THE AUTHOR

Deb Shapiro has trained extensively in various schools of body-work, Buddhist meditation, and Jungian psychology in both England and America. She has been teaching both bodymind therapy and meditation with her husband, Ed Shapiro, for the past 20 years. Their books include *The Bodymind Workbook, Meditation: Four Steps to Calmness and Clarity, Voices From the Heart,* and *Unconditional Love.*